# A WILD IDEA

To Liz,
Thanks for reading!
— Brad

# A WILD IDEA

## *How the Environmental Movement Tamed the Adirondacks*

BRAD EDMONDSON

THREE HILLS
AN IMPRINT OF CORNELL UNIVERSITY PRESS
ITHACA AND LONDON

This publication has been aided by a generous subvention from Furthermore, a program of the J. M. Kaplan Fund.

Furthermore:
a program of the J.M.Kaplan Fund

First published 2021 by Cornell University Press

Printed in the United States of America

Library of Congress Cataloging-in-Publication Data

Names: Edmondson, Brad, author.
Title: A wild idea: how the environmental movement tamed the
    Adirondacks / Brad Edmondson.
Description: Ithaca [New York]: Cornell University Press, 2021. |
    Includes bibliographical references and index.
Identifiers: LCCN 2020050823 (print) | LCCN 2020050824 (ebook) |
    ISBN 9781501759017 (hardcover) | ISBN 9781501759024 (pdf) |
    ISBN 9781501759031 (epub)
Subjects: LCSH: Adirondack Park Agency (N.Y.)—History. |
    Land use—New York (State)—Adirondack Park—History—20th
    century. | Adirondack Park (N.Y.)—History.
Classification: LCC HD211.N7 E47 2021 (print) | LCC HD211.N7
    (ebook) | DDC 333.78/30974750904—dc23
LC record available at https://lccn.loc.gov/2020050823
LC ebook record available at https://lccn.loc.gov/2020050824

# CONTENTS

# A WILD IDEA

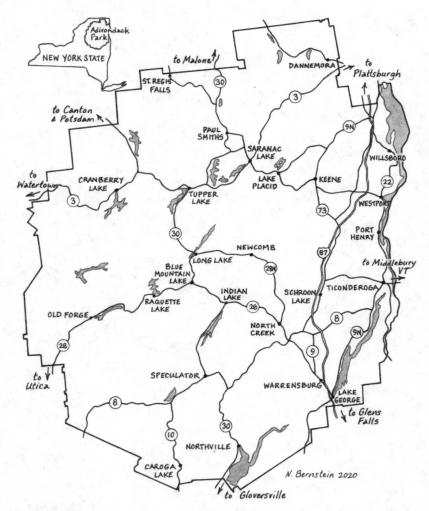

Map 1. New York's Adirondack Park is as large as Vermont. In this map, one inch equals thirty miles. (Map by Nancy Bernstein.)

# INTRODUCTION

## *Two Views of the Landscape*

"The Adirondack Park Agency has taken the theory that Hitler practiced," said Frank Casier. "If you tell a lie often enough it will soon be believed and will become a fact."

It was 2004, and we were sitting in Casier's spotless living room in a large house in the Village of Saranac Lake, New York. The lie, he explained, is the statement that the Adirondacks is a state park. "Sixty percent of the land inside the Blue Line is privately owned, and private land is not part of a state park," he said. "But through generations of people, each being converted a bit more, they have convinced almost everyone that all of this land is a park. There are only a few people left, like me, old enough to point out the difference."

Casier was a poor boy who pulled himself up. Born in a mining town on the northern edge of the Adirondack Park, he contracted tuberculosis while serving in World War II and was sent to a Saranac Lake hospital to recuperate. He regained his strength and began working like a man who had been given a reprieve. He started a furniture and appliance business, expanded into rental properties and local homes, and achieved success as a land developer in the Adirondacks and Florida. He was married for sixty-five years to a woman he adored, and every winter they escaped to their home in Fort Lauderdale. He had a large circle of friends and was generous to his community. He died in 2016, at age ninety-seven. But when talk turned to the Adirondacks he became bitter, like a defeated soldier from the Great Lost Cause.

The law was not on Casier's side, but that hardly mattered to him. The Adirondack Park was established in 1892 by an act of the New York State Legislature. Its boundary is known as the Blue Line because the first state map that showed it used blue ink. Another state law, passed in 1912, clarifies that the park includes the privately owned land within the Blue Line. In 2021, about 3.4 million acres of the 6-million-acre park is privately owned. The other 2.6 million acres comprises the Adirondack Forest Preserve, owned by the state. The forest preserve is freely accessible to the public, but there's a catch.

In 1894, New York's voters added a section to the state constitution that put severe restrictions on how the forest preserve could be used. That amendment, Article 14, included the words that came to be known as the "Forever Wild" clause: "The lands of the state, now owned or hereafter acquired, constituting the forest preserve as now fixed by law, shall be forever kept as wild forest lands. They shall not be leased, sold or exchanged, or be taken by any corporation, public or private, nor shall the timber thereon be sold, removed or destroyed."

Frank Casier didn't have serious problems with the Forever Wild clause or other regulations on state-owned land. He also tolerated several other laws that had been passed to establish parkwide standards for signs and other improvements. But he was infuriated by the Adirondack Park Agency Act, which gave a state agency the authority to regulate privately owned land inside the Blue Line. He was one of many who unsuccessfully challenged that law and its executor, the Adirondack Park Agency (APA). He tried to overturn the law by organizing protests and filing lawsuits, but was unsuccessful. In 2004, Casier continued to believe that the law was illegitimate and unjust. When he referred to it, his face twisted into an expression of disgust. "Private property is private," he said.

The truth is that the park's privately owned lands are like precious metal that forms the setting for an elaborate collection of jewels. The jewels are state-designated wilderness areas and wide-open spaces in the forest preserve, ranging in size from the 7,951-acre Jay Mountain Wilderness to the 19,000-acre

Saint Regis Canoe Area and the 275,460-acre High Peaks Wilderness. They add up to about a million acres of designated wilderness and another 1.6 million acres also protected under the Forever Wild clause. It is America's largest undeveloped area east of the Rocky Mountains.

The federal government defines a wilderness as "an area where the earth and its community of life are untrammeled by man, where man himself is a visitor who does not remain." The 1973 law places significant limits on the density and uses of most of the private land in the park in order to protect the "primeval character and influence" of the entire park. The wild lands are jewels that make the park glitter.

The 1973 law passed with the support of millions of visitors who love the feeling they get from wide-open spaces. A park resident who favored a strong APA captured these feelings in an article directed at visitors. "It is a landscape of infinite variety," wrote Courtney Jones. "It has millions of acres of forests, thousands of acres of wetlands. It has high waterfalls, deep gorges, rolling countryside, alpine summits. It houses both endangered and abundant species of plants and wildlife. It has names that linger in the ear, names like Noonmark, Boreas Pond, Tahawus, Lake Tear-Of-The-Clouds. Its images linger in the mind. It is, in short, a natural pageant of unusual richness, a feast for the eye and spirit in a time of unusual need."

The expansive feeling is hard to capture in words. Another writer, Lincoln Barnett, counted "no less than 20 Long Ponds, 10 East Ponds, 16 Clear Ponds, 20 Mud Ponds, 10 Round Ponds, 10 Duck Ponds, and 12 Otter Ponds" in the Adirondacks, "and no one can define the difference between a pond and a lake." Each of these ponds, lakes, campsites, and cottages is also someone's cherished memory. When regular visitors of the park daydream, those places are often what they see.

Frank Casier said that he loved scenery as much as the next person. But in his opinion, which is still shared by many in the North Country, preserving unspoiled nature is less important than serving people's needs. The state already gives tree-huggers millions of acres to roam around in, he said. He spread his hands out wide as he asked, "Isn't that enough?"

Casier was a developer who sold land in the same way he sold washing machines and living-room furniture. Land, to him, was a commodity. He had built his business on the assumption that he was free to develop the land he owned without concern for the wishes of neighbors or tourists. Residents of most small towns and rural areas in the United States still held to this view in the early 1970s. Those in a few big cities did, too. And when the APA changed the rules and restricted what a developer could do with private land in the park, Casier was fifty-four.

The law that infuriated Frank Casier had a long incubation. Its principles emerged in the 1950s, when a few experts and activists began arguing that open space is more than just a commodity. They said that natural areas are also resources that should be regulated to protect the public interest. This view gained broad support when the public's concern about pollution exploded between 1965 and 1970. Voters demanded laws that protected the purity of air and water. And with a little bit of prompting, they also demanded legal protection for the natural integrity of ecosystems.

A small group of hikers, hunters, and naturalists spent decades pushing for the protection of open space in the Adirondacks. They played an important role in a seven-year national campaign that succeeded in 1964, when Congress set aside millions of acres to be managed according to the official definition of wilderness cited previously. The activists became far more numerous, well organized, and well funded in the mid-1960s. They began promoting the idea that open space protection should extend to private as well as public land. The idea caught the attention of a powerful state politician who loved to take cutting-edge ideas and turn them into law.

Governor Nelson Rockefeller appointed a study commission and asked its members to recommend ways to preserve the essential wild qualities of the Adirondack Park while also allowing many other uses, including continued residential construction, forestry, and mining. The commission recommended the most ambitious land use plans ever attempted. The APA would write and enforce these plans.

The goal of the Temporary Study Commission on the Future of the Adirondacks was to protect entire landscapes by balancing human activity with the needs of healthy ecosystems. Today that idea is called sustainable development, and regional land use plans are common in the United States and other developed countries. But even fifty years later, few other places on earth have tried to do land use planning on such a large scale.

Sustainable development plans depend on the belief that government programs can ameliorate complex social problems. Their supporters struggle to overcome opponents who say that government programs are the problem. Politicians drive the divide further by pandering to their core supporters and demonizing their opponents. As opportunities for compromise become harder to find and the public's trust erodes, government becomes less effective. The birth of the APA shows how that polarization began.

This book is based on more than five dozen lengthy interviews with people who played primary roles in the APA's founding. The group includes Harold Jerry, Arthur Crocker, and others in the elite group of activists and policy-makers who were early champions for the idea of regional land use planning. It includes George Davis, Clarence Petty, and other planners, lawyers, and naturalists who implemented the Land Use and Development Plan. It includes Frank Casier and other activists who fought to abolish or weaken the plan, as well as David Newhouse and others who fought just as hard to defend it. And it includes Richard Wiebe, Henry Diamond, and other public officials who had to find ways to turn it into a workable law.

New York State spent twenty years struggling to write a master plan for the Adirondack Park before the APA was established. Activists had been calling for a master plan for twenty years before the state even started trying. Chapters 1 through 4 describe the controversies and projects that culminated in 1967, when the completion of an interstate highway and a proposal to turn the core of the Adirondacks into a national park forced Governor Nelson Rockefeller to act.

Chapters 5 through 7 describe the Temporary Study Commission on the Future of the Adirondacks (TSC): how it formed, how hard-core environmental activists wrested control of it from the State Division of Parks, how it conceived of two complementary plans, both of them audacious, and how a singular combination of political power and good timing persuaded the legislature to set up a new agency. The agency's job was to complete the two plans and turn them into law.

The state legislature gave the APA an extremely ambitious to-do list and a ridiculously small budget. Chapters 8 through 11 tell the story of how the early APA struggled to meet the state's assignments. Much of the work depended on three men who had also worked for the Temporary Study Commission. The APA chairman, Richard Lawrence, overcame opposition on several fronts as he struggled to maintain a working majority of board members. Peter Paine, a well-connected lawyer, worked tirelessly and argued stridently for the two plans. And the story's fulcrum is George Davis, who turned the idea for his doctoral dissertation into a big map that transformed life in the North Country.

Davis led a motley crew of talented and mostly unsupervised staffers, many of whom were just out of college. They produced two plans, each of them organized around a big map. One plan zoned the state land into progressively stricter classifications, culminating with wilderness. That plan was the product of twenty years of study, including a three-year ramble through the forest preserve by Davis's friend and mentor Clarence Petty. The other map rated each acre of the 3.6 million privately owned acres in terms of its suitability for development.

The APA completed both regional maps in about eighteen months, because Governor Rockefeller insisted that all the work had to be put before the state legislature in 1973. Life at the APA became a series of long drives, tough meetings, and all-nighters. The stress of it put severe strains on staffers' health and families. An office refrigerator Davis kept stocked with free beer helped make it possible. The beer cooler was flagrantly illegal, but the office was so far from Albany that no one noticed.

The maps the team produced are amazing and imperfect. Public reaction to the state land map was fairly quiet, but the release of the Land Use and Development Plan at the end of 1972 was the political equivalent of throwing a lit match into a large puddle of gasoline. Most Adirondack landowners had never been subjected to zoning before, and the rules the APA proposed were strict and complicated. Public hearings on the land use plan were so hostile that APA staffers occasionally had to be guarded by state police.

In March 1973, the state legislature passed a bill to delay consideration of the land use plan by one year. That bill was vetoed by Governor Rockefeller, who used his immense influence to force the legislature to pass an amended law in May. In the aftermath, some environmental activists celebrated the plan's passage, while others said it didn't go nearly far enough. Some full-time residents of the park shrugged and went back to their business. A few of them seethed and vowed resistance.

This book was written to mark the fiftieth anniversary of the law that created the APA in June 1971. It's an unfinished story. In 2021, partisans on both sides continue to argue that the APA has either saved or ruined the ecological and economic health of the park. Others say that it has become irrelevant. Usually the different sides talk past each other, as they always have. But most of them will now grudgingly admit that the agency is trying, however imperfectly, to balance economic activity with the preservation of biodiversity and scenery.

The story is different outside the Blue Line. Over the last half-century, the governance of the Adirondack Park has been praised, studied, and emulated by elected officials, planners, and conservationists around the world. The Adirondacks represent "a hope that damage caused by human beings is not irreversible," according to author Bill McKibben, who has written movingly about his cabin near the foot of Crane Mountain. McKibben wrote that the Adirondacks are "a metaphor as much as a place." His only child's middle name is Crane.

It's often said that a successful negotiation ends when both sides are dissatisfied. By that measure, the APA is a runaway success. Environmentalists still complain that the agency isn't tough enough on developers, and businesspeople remain eager to share their frustrations with rules they say are too strict or nonsensical. But almost everyone now admits that some kind of regulatory authority is needed for the entire Adirondack Park, and that the park would do a far worse job of serving the public if the 1973 law had been repealed.

In fact, it almost was. But that's another story.

# Chapter 1

# WHOSE WOODS THESE ARE

George Davis was twelve the first time he saw the Adirondack Park. It happened in 1954, when the family drove George's half-brother Ed to college. George spent most of the day watching scenes scroll by his window—a huge tree, water splashing over rocks, marshes edging into lakes, breaks in the woods revealing hills beyond hills, buildings few and far between—and despite his carsick stomach, he was fascinated. "It grabbed me," he remembered. "The nothingness of it, which, of course, was everything."

George's father had not graduated from high school, but Ed had done well enough to enroll at Vermont's Middlebury College so he could pursue his passion: political science. "He was the bookworm," George said. "I wasn't that focused. I just knew I wanted to be out in the woods."

The family drove east from their home near the Village of Camden, thirty miles north of the geographic center of New York State. They went fifteen miles through woodlots and small farms that looked much like their own, passed the industrial city of Rome, and then sped through another twenty miles of houses and fields until they passed a small metal sign that marked the boundary of the Adirondack Park. That's when everything started to change.

At the end of that day, when the car finally left the park, George was hooked. "It took me in," he said. "I wanted to see more. I wanted to learn more about it."

In 1954, a man who ran a machine at a furniture factory in New York's North Country could support a family and also enroll his stepson in college. Today the factories are mostly gone, and it isn't easy to find a job that pays a living wage in rural New York. Some towns that were once self-sufficient are dying. Others are bedroom communities, or they have found another source of income: tourists. In 1954, 1 million visitors used public campsites and picnic areas inside the Adirondack Park's boundary, known locally as the Blue Line. In 2018, 12.4 million people visited the park.

Some things haven't changed much, though. The nothing-which-is-everything that grabbed George Davis is still there, and that is a remarkable thing.

The population of the United States more than doubled between 1950 and 2020. Eighty-four million people now live within 350 miles of the Blue Line. Most of the land inside the boundary is privately owned and can easily be sold. If one-half of 1 percent of the nearby population bought property and built houses, the park's population would quadruple. Yet thousands of beautiful lakes and ponds, vast tracts of forest, and whole mountain ranges have somehow been preserved less than a day's drive from the most heavily populated region of the United States. It's amazing. What keeps people from moving in?

The Adirondack Park is deceptive. It still beckons to adventurous souls, and the people who live there cherish the feeling they get from its natural beauty. But it has never been an easy place to live, or to earn a living.

The Adirondacks also might be the best-protected wilderness in the world, and George Davis had a lot to do with protecting it. George worked on plans to preserve the Adirondacks for seven years, then spent another fifteen years fighting to protect those plans. He was rewarded with international acclaim and a MacArthur Fellowship "genius grant." He also received death threats and had a nervous breakdown.

New York's North Country consists of three large regions. The first is the Adirondack Park, which covers 6 million acres, more than 17 percent of the state's land mass. The second is Tug Hill, a 1.3-million-acre plateau located west of the park that takes up another 4 percent. Tug Hill has few roads,

and parts of it feel as remote as any Adirondack wilderness. The third region is an apron of flat, fertile land that runs west from Tug Hill to Lake
Ontario and north from the park to the Saint Lawrence River.

In 2020, the park had about 130,000 permanent and 200,000 seasonal res-
idents. Another 100,000 live in Tug Hill, and 400,000 live on the plains.
Most North Country residents outside the park live in the cities of Oswego,
Watertown, or Plattsburgh, and in smaller places like Ogdensburg, Potsdam,
Canton, and Malone.

It might be surprising to learn that one-quarter of New York's land mass is
so sparsely populated. After all, 19.5 million people live in New York State. But
most of them are packed into New York City and its adjacent counties, a pattern that has not changed since George Davis was a boy. In 1950, a majority of
New Yorkers lived inside the city's five boroughs and one-half of 1 percent lived
inside the Adirondack Park. In 2020, the share who lived inside the Blue Line
was seven-tenths of 1 percent. The Adirondack Park is a different world. Its
geographic center is 270 miles from midtown Manhattan.

There are several reasons so few people live in northern New York, and the
reason that everyone mentions first is the weather. From November to May,
Arctic winds pick up moisture from the surface of Lake Ontario, loft it into the
air, and dump precipitation, usually frozen, on the land to the east. You can see
a lake effect squall coming. It's a line on the western horizon—huge, cold,
dark, and wet—and the leading edge of it churns as it approaches you.

Camden is on the southern edge of Tug Hill, and George Davis grew up
roaming around in those deep woods. He learned to scan the western horizon whenever he was out hunting or checking his traplines. If he saw a lake
effect line, he headed for shelter immediately. Lake effect bands are narrow,
but they can be intense. They can drop three inches of snow per hour, with
high winds that reduce visibility to a few feet. Any tracks that you've made
will quickly be erased. The air temperature can drop to well below freezing, and it all happens very quickly.

Storms like these bring about 140 inches (11.5 feet) of snow to Camden
during a typical season. That is more than twice the snow Denver receives,
and four times what falls on New York City. The higher elevations of Tug
Hill, just a few miles north of Camden, routinely get twice as much snow as
the village does. A few of the older hunting camps up there have doorway
entrances on the second floor.

The critical variables in a lake effect storm are wind direction and "fetch," or how far the water vapor travels before it falls back to earth. When the winds and fetch are right, intense bands of snow can set up anywhere in the Adirondacks, and temperatures below 0 degrees Fahrenheit are routine. From November to May, North Country people steadily battle snow, ice, and mud. The mud deepens when the snow starts melting, and billions of biting bugs emerge as soon as night temperatures stay above freezing. Conditions in the deep woods between Mother's Day and Father's Day range from difficult to unbearable.

Weather is the main reason 70 percent of visitors to the Adirondacks arrive between mid-May and mid-October, and why the peak tourist season lasts less than three months, from the end of June to Labor Day. In some places, visitors vastly outnumber locals during the summer. For example, Lake Placid has just 2,750 permanent residents, but in 2015, local hotels and inns there provided 3.3 million overnight stays.

The park that twelve-year-old George Davis saw looked inviting, but most of it was off-limits to him. In the mid-1950s, just 39 percent of the park, or 2.2 million acres, was owned by New York State and managed for free public access. The other 3.5 million acres was privately owned. The public land is called the Adirondack Forest Preserve and is protected by Article 14 of the state constitution, the "Forever Wild" clause, which states, "The lands of the state, now owned or hereafter acquired, constituting the forest preserve as now fixed by law, shall be forever kept as wild forest lands. They shall not be leased, sold or exchanged, or be taken by any corporation, public or private, nor shall the timber thereon be sold, removed or destroyed."

George worked for a commission that analyzed the park's privately owned land in 1970. He found that most of this land was owned by just 626 families, each of which had more than five hundred acres. The commission also listed a superclass of 32 investment firms and lumber companies that each owned more than ten thousand acres. Less than one-quarter of the private land in the park was owned by full-time park residents.

There are also thousands of seasonal homes in the park, including elaborate compounds their owners coyly refer to as "camps" because of their rustic style. But when the leaves fade, the floating docks are pulled onto the lakeshores, and the water supplies to the summer houses are drained, things get very quiet. After a while, full-time residents of the park say they sometimes feel that all of that empty land should be available to them—because, after all, nobody is using it.

About an hour into their car trip, just east of Prospect Lake, the Davis family crossed the New York Central Railroad line. The tracks cut a north-south transect through the park, from Utica to Tupper Lake. Branch lines continued north to Malone and Ottawa, and east to Saranac Lake, Lake Placid, and Plattsburgh. The line opened in 1892, and the last train to Lake Placid ran in 1965.

The New York Central carried supplies and tourists into the park. In early summer, the trains also carried private cars containing members of America's wealthiest families—Vanderbilts, Morgans, Roosevelts, Rockefellers, and Whitneys—on their way to opulent summer compounds known as "Great Camps." Southbound trains carried millions of board feet of lumber cut from the privately owned land.

In 1901, Great Camp owners organized to protect their shared desire to keep the land surrounding their estates undisturbed. The Association for the Protection of the Adirondacks (AfPA) never had a large membership, but its members regularly dined with the governor and state legislators. They also retained extremely clever lawyers who pushed back whenever anyone challenged their strict interpretation of the Forever Wild clause.

George Davis followed the New York Central line for miles on foot while doing fieldwork as a state employee in the 1970s. But in 1954, he had only a second to look down the tracks and wonder where they went.

Just before they passed the Blue Line, the Davises saw an eighty-foot-high apron of concrete on the right, in the center of an earthen embankment three-quarters of a mile long. The Hinckley Dam was built in 1915 to supply drinking water to Utica. Behind the dam is a reservoir that floods thirteen square miles of river valleys inside the park.

In the 1940s, a state agency made a plan to build several more dams inside the Blue Line to provide flood control and hydroelectric power. A coalition of conservation organizations fought the plan, claiming that it violated the Forever Wild clause. The campaign seemed unlikely to succeed because so many industrial and municipal leaders wanted the dams built, but the activists pursued their cause with creativity and passion, and the AfPA quietly provided them with funds and lawyers.

An amendment to the state constitution banning the dams passed in 1953, just a few months before George's first car trip. George would later become friends with the coalition's leader, Paul Schaefer, and his allies. But on that day in 1954, the twelve-year-old had no idea who Schaefer was, or that it had taken a ten-year fight to ensure that the rivers he saw would continue to run free.

The Davis family drove east on State Route 8, which follows West Canada Creek up to a low divide. West Canada Creek flows southwest toward the Mohawk River. East of that low divide is the vast watershed of the Sacandaga River, which contains Piseco Lake, Lake Pleasant, and two long branches that join before flowing into another huge reservoir. The Sacandaga flows into the Hudson just inside the southern boundary of the park, about twenty miles west of Glens Falls. Sacandaga is an Iroquois word meaning "overflowed land," and much of the land around the river is marshy and inaccessible.

Route 8 was a carriage road in the 1880s, when boardinghouses began catering to hunters and anglers. Middle-class tourists were driven to hotels along the corridor between Piseco Lake and the village of Speculator starting in the 1890s. Loggers were also having an impact. They did not often clear-cut in those days, but they did cut pretty much anything they could sell, often with little regard for whether or not they owned the tree. Their abuse of state land was the main reason the Forever Wild clause passed in 1892.

After two hours of driving, the Davises reached Speculator. They probably stopped at Charlie John's Store. Since 1939, people passing through the village have visited Charlie John's to buy a sandwich and pick up groceries. Speculator is surrounded by huge swaths of state land, and it has the only restrooms for miles around.

Speculator had only 370 full-time residents in 1950 (and about 300 in 2020). The area's lumber boom ended around 1910. Thin soils and a short growing season discouraged farming. Hunting, fishing, and summer tourists were about the only things going in 1954. But by the time George's brother graduated from Middlebury, the first gasoline powered "snow sleds" had shown up. Locals welcomed the business the sled owners brought to town during the coldest months. There weren't any rules about where the sleds could or couldn't go, either.

By the mid-1960s, thousands of snowmobiles were breaking the silence in woods all over the Adirondacks. This bothered Almy Coggeshall, a chemical engineer at General Electric who lived in nearby Schenectady. It also irked his friend David Newhouse, chair of the Conservation Committee of the Adirondack Mountain Club, which promoted hiking, recreational snowshoeing, and cross-country skiing.

"I had a very strong reaction to the snow machines," Coggeshall said. "When my neighbor bought one and ran it behind my house, I ran over there and said, 'What the hell are you doing here? What is this goddamned thing?' I really let go." A snowmobile owner once asked Coggeshall, "Do you ever mention the word 'snowmobile' without saying 'goddamned' first?"

"The snowmobile fight was a turning point in my life," said Coggeshall. "I was so threatened by these new machines that I could not be rational on the matter. I acted like a fool. It made me wonder why they had such a profound emotional impact on me and others I knew.

"I realized that the defenders of wild forest land needed a better vocabulary with which to express our feelings. We also needed a strategy to restrict the use of these machines. I concluded that the key was to show that for a lot of people, part of the recreational experience involved feelings of religious intensity." His strong emotional reaction happened because the snow machines were challenging his strongly held "intangible and aesthetic values."

In 1954, Coggeshall and Newhouse were in the early stages of a campaign to convince state legislators that loud, smoke-belching vehicles should not be permitted to go anywhere they wanted and break the deep Adrondack silence. The two men were also irritated by World War II surplus jeeps and other four-wheel-drive vehicles that ignored their interpretation of the rules, and they railed against the generally lax attitude of the New York State Conservation Department toward the protection of natural areas. Something had to be done, they said.

After the Davis family pulled out of Speculator, George watched how the water in the main branch of the Sacandaga reflects light in different ways. It's white when it flows over rocks, sparkling in the shallows, and a cold bluish-green when it forms pools. He saw huge stands of spruce, hemlock, and pine rising on the far shore, with no sign of human habitation. George's queasiness mixed with excitement as he watched the mountains grow closer.

The trees seemed to get bigger as the car moved farther into the woods, crossing the main branch of the Sacandaga and heading up the east branch. George gazed wide-eyed at Eleventh Mountain, which, at 3,291 feet, seemed massive to a boy from a flatland town with an elevation of 500. It is one of many such peaks in a 112,000-acre region now known as the Siamese Ponds Wilderness, and is one of the least-visited parts of the forest preserve.

In 1954, George wanted nothing more than to stop the car and walk into the nothing-which-is-everything of Siamese Ponds. But the car sped on. It left the Sacandaga watershed just east of Bakers Mills, a forlorn collection of overgrazed pastures and clapboard houses in need of paint. White settlers had arrived here after the Civil War. They cleared and drained the meadows and tried to farm, but found subsistence hard to achieve. A tannery operated until all the hemlock trees, which provided tannin, were exhausted. A rich man built an elaborate Great Camp nearby and filled it with expensive antiques; when he died, his wife gave the mansion to a charity that abandoned it around the same time the Davises passed by, unknowing. The state eventually burned down all the gaudy buildings, and by 2020 the site was overgrown.

George looked beyond the pastures of Bakers Mills to hills that were green and full of tall trees. He couldn't see the boundary markers, so he didn't know that some of the trees were on 180,000 acres owned by the lumber company Finch Pruyn, and that others belonged to New York State and could never be cut. He was also unaware that, in 1954, the market was glutted with salvage lumber because of a catastrophic storm that had ravaged the Adirondacks. He didn't know that thousands of acres of forest preserve, including some in the Siamese Ponds area, were still impassable because of downed trees.

High winds are not unusual in the Adirondacks, but they almost always blow from west to east, and tree roots have adapted accordingly. In late November 1950, the last week of hunting season, a large cyclone, or "nor'easter," started moving up the Atlantic coast. On Saturday, November 25, after several days of heavy rains, the storm turned inland and tore through the park with one-hundred-mile-per-hour winds from the southeast. The winds hit the weaker sides of the trees, and the trees fell over.

Paul Schaefer owned a cabin a few miles from Bakers Mills, and he had been out hunting that day. Eyewitnesses say that it was actually a good day for hunting, because the wind made so much noise that the deer could not hear hunters sneak up on them. But "when the top forty feet of a great spruce suddenly cracked and blew almost over our heads," Schaefer remembered, "we knew it was high time to get home."

The storm known as the Big Blowdown damaged more than 800,000 acres of timber. Roads and trails were buried under huge jumbles of branches and tree trunks. Clearing them would be an immense task. The State Conservation Department quickly got permission to allow loggers into the forest preserve to salvage the lumber, a policy that outraged Schaefer and his allies. The ensuing debate became known as the Big Blowup. State officials struggled with the question of how to manage the forest preserve. They formed several commissions and asked them to come up with plans, but it took nineteen years for the legislature to act.

George would hear lots of Big Blowdown stories when he was working for the last of those commissions in the late 1960s. But in 1954, he sped past the damage unknowing. The car left the Sacandaga watershed and headed down a steep grade to the Hudson River. The Hudson is wide but shallow and rocky when Route 8 crosses it in Riparius. George tried to mentally pick a canoe route through the rocks as the car crossed an old steel truss bridge over the river, but he could not do it.

The next stop would have been the remote hamlet of Chestertown. Today this place is known mostly as Exit 25 on Interstate 87, the Northway, which is the main route from New York City to Montreal. You can hear the constant whine of trucks and cars for a mile or more on either side of the road. But the Northway had not yet been proposed in 1954. The drive from New York, Philadelphia, or Boston to Lake Placid at that time entailed a much longer, more arduous trip up twisting, two-lane Route 9. The road goes up the valley of the Schroon River, one of the most majestic places in the Adirondacks, with hills and peaks rising on either side of a free-flowing stream. When George saw it that day, it was quiet.

The Davises continued past Brant Lake and turned onto Route 9N near Lake George, one of the oldest and best-known tourist destinations in the park. They went past the lake's northern tip at Ticonderoga and immediately saw the ribbon of water that is the southern end of Lake Champlain, the thirteenth-largest lake in the United States. Champlain is deep and 125 miles long, but it's narrow; it marks the park's eastern border, as well as the state line with Vermont. When the Davises crossed it on the bridge at Crown Point, they only had sixteen miles to go to Middlebury.

The day was soon over, but George couldn't sleep that night. All of the things he had seen kept rushing through his head. George's parents would make the trip to Middlebury two or three times a year for the next several years, and whenever he could, he went with them.

George was hooked, as so many others have been, by a simple question: *What's out there?* To a first-time visitor, the Adirondacks appear to be untouched territory. But the park is anything but untouched. It is an enormous, unique public resource, and ever since it was established in 1885, competing interests have battled to gain the upper hand in determining how it is used. It is "contested terrain," according to historian Phillip Terrie.

Another remarkable thing about the Adirondack Park is that it is still being contested. Loggers and leather-tanners cleared huge swaths of forest during the nineteenth and early twentieth centuries. Hoteliers built edifices that were, briefly, profitable. Hunters stripped the woods of deer, beaver, and other species to sell to market. The private sector has been harvesting the park's resources for nearly two hundred years. But businesses have never gained complete control over it.

The park has always been guarded by a relatively small number of people who are motivated by a passionate belief in the intrinsic value of wild land. Paul Schaefer, Almy Coggeshall, and generations of activists after them defended wilderness with direct appeals to New York State voters. In the 1960s, this group joined forces with a powerful governor to gain the upper hand. Business executives and local officials in the Adirondacks fought the activists, labeling them "extreme conservationists" and "forever wilders." But the activists knew that most New York State voters agreed with them. They organized to turn their wild idea into law. The rules they wrote would tame the North Country.

George Davis's family lived a mile outside of Camden, population 2,400, a tidy, self-contained world whose residents worked at nearby factories, shopped almost exclusively in local stores, and rooted for the high school's Blue Devils. The Davises had a small house and enough land for a large garden and a few animals. The animals allowed George, later, to refer to himself as "a goat farmer from Tug Hill"—and it's true, he is a North Country guy with blue-collar roots. When George wants to draw something to a close, he might say, "We have to sugar off." He's referring to the last stage of making maple syrup, when the farmer boils the sap down to concentrate the sugar.

But George also admits that he avoided farm chores. He's anything but a farmer. "I went out and explored," he said. He fished in Emmons Brook, which flowed through the family's property, and ran traplines there in the winter to catch muskrat. His father took him deer hunting in the complex of state forests called 46 Corners, where the state bought up failing farms during the Great Depression and replanted them with trees. "The Tug Hill plateau opens up five miles north of town," he said. "You can park there and walk twenty miles north before you come to the next road. I did plenty of that."

George's parents expected him to follow Ed to college. Only about 6 percent of Americans aged twenty-five and older had a four-year college degree in 1960, compared with more than one-quarter in 2020. But North Country parents were just as likely as anyone else to believe in the value of higher education, and the incomes of blue-collar families rose quickly in the 1950s, allowing more of them to afford tuition.

George did well enough in school to get into the honor society; Boys' State, a civic education program sponsored by the American Legion; and the State College of Forestry at Syracuse University. He said that he was resigned to attending college, but that his only strong desire was to stay in the woods. "Looking around for a college, I saw the word 'forestry' and thought, 'that means I can be out in the forest,'" he said. "I was totally naive."

It was rare in 1960 for a North Country native to leave, get professional training, and then return for his career, but George managed to do it. Another who did was John Collins, who grew up in Blue Mountain Lake, a hamlet about ninety miles northeast of Camden in the Central Adirondacks. Collins would become a strong supporter of George Davis's agenda in the 1970s, even as most of Collins' neighbors opposed the Adirondack Park Agency. He said that education made the difference.

Blue Mountain Lake was "a thriving place" in the 1950s, according to Collins. "There was a general store. There was a little snack bar. There was a bar and restaurant. There was a motor car salesroom and a gas station. There were five or six major hotels. The stores stayed open all winter, and the general store was truly a general store. Upstairs was hardware, and downstairs was animal feed. We bought hay there. We bought food for farm animals there. You could buy clothing. You could buy all your hardware stuff, as well as your food. I walked to a two-room schoolhouse for my first four years. There were two rooms, but we only had one teacher."

Collins's parents owned a local lodge called The Hedges. "I had a privileged childhood," he said. "We lived in a beautiful place, and we had educated parents. We had books. We were read to, and we read a lot. We were exposed to the summer people, who were doctors, lawyers, and bankers. So we had a viewpoint that was different than had we just been tannery workers' children. I think that that made a difference in all our lives.

"My parents assumed that we would do well in school and continue our education. It was not really a 'would you?,' but 'where would you?' kind of question. In that sense, we were very privileged. Most of the boys and girls that I went to school with did not expect to go to college and did not go to college . . . but college does two very important things. One, of course, is that it opens your mind. The other thing is, it gets you out of the woods. It gives you something to compare to where you've been."

The State College of Forestry in Syracuse gave George exactly what he wanted, although he went in a direction that was unusual for his time. Forestry schools teach students how to keep trees healthy, cut them safely, and get the highest sustainable yield from a woodlot. Many of their classes are held outdoors, and for over a hundred years, Syracuse's forestry students have spent their summers at a camp on Cranberry Lake that is accessible only by boat. That camp is where George found his calling. It teaches forest biology, and it is surrounded by the state forest preserve, where (according to the state constitution) "the timber thereon" cannot be "sold, removed or destroyed."

Many of George's schoolmates were irritated by the state constitution's Forever Wild clause. Roger Thompson, who taught surveying at Cranberry Lake but was only a few years older than George, loved to attack it. "Roger and I, over many a beer, argued wilderness philosophy as opposed to natural resource use for utilitarian purposes," George said. "Roger argued against wilderness. He is a sophisticated guy, though. I think he was being a devil's advocate, trying to get me to put my thoughts on the table."

George Davis and Roger Thompson were exploring a philosophical debate that had emerged decades earlier. Gifford Pinchot, the father of American forestry, created the idea of multi-use resource management and conservation when he was the first director of the US Forest Service, under President Theodore Roosevelt. Pinchot stated the utilitarian position in his autobiography, published in 1947: "Conservation is the foresighted utilization, preservation, and/or renewal of forest, waters, lands and minerals, for the greatest good of the greatest number for the longest time." His phrase "the greatest number" referred, of course, to only one species. He was saying that nature exists to serve people.

Pinchot's foil was John Muir, founder of the Sierra Club, who wrote eloquently about the beauty and spiritual power of wild landscapes and the importance of leaving them undisturbed. George was partial to Muir's position, although he preferred the way it had been argued by a fellow forester. Aldo Leopold advanced the argument for wilderness preservation in *A Sand County Almanac*, which was published in 1949: "A thing is right when it tends to preserve the integrity, stability and beauty of the biotic community. It is wrong when it tends otherwise." He was saying that nature has intrinsic value.

Every forestry student had to choose a position on the continuum between profit maximization and strict protection. Most of George's classmates needed jobs, so they chose the industry's point of view. Back then, Forestry School students proudly called themselves "stumpies."

George needed a job, too. But as he moved through the Syracuse program, he spent more time studying ecology, the branch of biology that deals with the relations of organisms to one another and to their physical surroundings. He grew particularly close to Ed Ketchledge, a wartime veteran of the Army's Tenth Mountain Division who was then doing research for his book, *Forests and Trees of the Adirondack High Peaks*. "The outwardly stable forests we see in our human lifetime are more correctly understood as dynamic populations of competing species, adjusting as necessary over centuries," Ketchledge wrote. "The so-called 'balance' [of nature] is more truthfully an episodic teeter-totter!"

"I go back to the professors who taught me that there is a system to the woods," said George. In the early 1960s, he said, he and others were realizing that "the whole earth is really one system. Everything is tied together. And if part of it is sick, that affects all of us."

George got in his own car in the summer of 1964 and drove cross-country to his first job at the US Forest Service's office in Steamboat Springs, Colorado. "I wore a cowboy hat, but at first I didn't get cowboy boots because I thought it was affected to come out from New York and immediately start wearing cowboy boots," he said. "But then I got on a horse wearing my logging boots. The horse threw me off, and I almost didn't get the boots clear of the stirrups in time. That's when I got cowboy boots."

George was a skinny twenty-two-year-old with a high forehead and large green eyes. He was bright and intense. He figured things out fast, and once he became interested in a job, his capacity for work was nearly unlimited. So was his capacity for argument. "He had the ability to dominate any room that he was in," said Richard Booth, a lawyer who worked with George at the Adirondack Park Agency. "If he joined a group, he ended up being in charge of it."

Steamboat Springs had just opened its first small ski area when George arrived. Working out of a two-person office, in a town that was far more interested in cattle than skiers, George learned by doing. "It was one of the most influential times in my life," he said. "Even though I had been to college, nobody had taught me about all the different kinds of trees, or how to tell whether or not land is undergrazed or overgrazed, or how you manage land to get a bigger or smaller population of elk, or how you manage wilderness recreation and do the science. I had to learn all of that."

After a couple of years, though, George was ready to move on. He missed the North Country, and he suspected that he would find a better job if he got an advanced degree. He was also still thinking about those arguments with Roger Thompson. When they had talked in the early 1960s, Thompson was completing his doctoral dissertation and George was an undergraduate, so he had mostly listened. Six years later, George was still thinking about Thompson's questions. How do you preserve the natural integrity of nearly pristine ecosystems while also letting people who live nearby build homes, take vacations, cut down trees, and dig minerals out of the ground?

Thompson didn't have much patience with the idea of "wilderness." "The Forest Preserve was the product of an extreme reaction to extreme conditions in an age in which one heard much more of the freedoms of democracy than its obligations," he wrote in 1962. The debate between Pinchot and Muir was a "schism" between "rationalists" and "romantics" within the conservation movement, he said, and it had produced a stalemate in the Adirondacks. Wealthy Great Camp owners appealed to romantics by claiming to defend the sanctity of untouched nature, although, Thompson argued, they were really advancing their own self-interest. Over eight decades, the no-compromise stance had produced "a lack of clarity as to who had the power to do what."

The state and the camp owners tolerated this lack of clarity for decades because so few people visited the Adirondacks. But a rapid increase in the number of visitors after World War II was straining the system. Thompson

said that the Forever Wild clause was hobbling the State Conservation Department's ability to serve visitors. He was irritated that complex issues were
being decided not by experts, but by voters in state referenda that proposed
changes to the constitution. What was needed, he said, was a new government agency that would use forestry and other disciplines to make rational,
science-based decisions about the forest preserve.

"To suppose that an aggressive agency responsive to a concerned public
could not administer a wilderness park is to deny the possibility of effective
government," he concluded. "This is a possibility too expensive for a democratic society to entertain. The fact that the agency might compromise special interests in this process is a corollary of good government. There is
strength in compromise."

Roger Thompson had identified the problem George Davis wanted to
solve. The problem was creating a land use plan for a park of nearly six million acres that was famous for being a "wilderness," even though most of it
was privately owned and managed for many different purposes. It wasn't a
forestry problem. It was a land use problem and solving it would rely on experts in many fields in addition to forestry.

George decided to apply to the graduate program at Cornell University's
Department of Natural Resources in 1968. The department was part of the
State Agricultural College, so tuition for New York residents was affordable.
It was close to the woods George longed for. And he also chose Cornell
because several faculty members were pushing for a broader view of land use.

George's faculty advisor, Larry Hamilton, had been a pilot for the British
Royal Navy in World War II before studying forestry in Canada. Hamilton
had come to Cornell in 1951. He helped recruit scholars from several different fields to the department, including Richard Baer, who taught the popular Religion, Ethics, and the Environment course; David Pimentel, who
produced global models predicting the effect of population growth on food
supply; and Richard McNeil, a wildlife biologist who focused on international
conservation.

Hamilton assigned writing by Luna Leopold, son of Aldo, a hydrologist
who argued that water management plans should include geologic, geographic, and climatic information. Leopold wrote that public officials who
thought only in economic and political terms when managing water resources
were doomed to fail. Hamilton also taught Ian McHarg, a landscape architect whose 1969 book *Design with Nature* outlined a way to use ecological

principles to determine appropriate uses for parcels of land. The first step in McHarg's method is gathering information on soil, climate, hydrology, topography, and other factors.

George Davis was enrolled at Cornell just long enough to make friends with Larry Hamilton and learn about Leopold, McHarg, and their ilk. He read *Design with Nature* as soon as it was released, but he had neither the time nor the inclination to stay in a classroom. A few weeks into George's first semester, Larry Hamilton introduced him to Harold Jerry, a state official who was recruiting staff for a new state commission on the future of the Adirondack Park.

George Davis and Harold Jerry hit it off immediately. Both were smart North Country natives who were eager to put new ideas into practice, and both of them loved the woods—the wilder, the better. For George, the state job was a chance to get paid four times as much as a teaching assistant was paid, while doing work that seemed more interesting and meaningful.

Back in 1962, Roger Thompson had concluded that the stalemate in the Adirondacks was more or less permanent. It was "unlikely that a change proportional to the needs would occur within the next twenty years," he wrote. Thompson got a lot of things right, but he got that wrong.

# Chapter 2

# "A Three-Year Vacation"

Clarence Petty went into the forest preserve on November 26, 1950, to clear a trail and take a firsthand look at the Big Blowdown. "I took a hand ax and a bow saw with me, and the first thing I ran into was a bunch of small tamaracks lying across the trail," he said. "I had a jacket, and after I got warmed up, I hung it over the top of one of these trees I was cutting. It was hard going. It took me two or three hours to get into Five Ponds. When I came back, I couldn't find my flight jacket. I thought, well, where the heck has that jacket gone to? Eventually I realized that the trees whose tops I had cut had sprung back upright. My jacket was hanging thirty feet in the air."

Clarence shook the jacket loose from the tree. It was still a healthy tree, so it was against the rules to cut it down if it wasn't blocking the trail. Then he went back home, and the next morning he got into his plane. The only way to grasp what had happened was to take to the air.

Clarence was a pilot as well as a New York State Forest Ranger, and occasionally his higher-ups at the State Conservation Department asked him to go up and look at something. He spent several days in the air in late

November 1950, charting more than one thousand square miles of damaged timber. Clarence reported what he had seen to the decision makers, including his older brother Bill, a ranger who reported to the Commissioner's staff in Albany. Bill's opinion would carry a lot of weight there. Clarence knew that Bill would want to cut and haul the damaged timber to sawmills. Clarence didn't like that idea.

Much of the damage happened in the Adirondack Forest Preserve, which was protected by the Forever Wild clause of the New York State Constitution. Clarence believed in a strict interpretation of that law. He believed that no tree in the forest preserve should ever be cut except with hand tools, and then only to clear roads and trails.

The Forever Wild clause was the law, but telling a forester that he can't cut a damaged tree is like telling a surgeon that she can't cut a tumor. And so, just as Clarence suspected, the foresters who ran the State Conservation Department appealed to the state legislature and got permission to start a salvage logging program in the forest preserve in January 1951. Their goal was to remove the blown-over trees quickly, before they rotted, so they could be sold.

Salvage logging is a judgment call. The legislature granted permission on the grounds that the downed trees were a public health hazard. The Conservation Department claimed that they could become fuel for massive forest fires. But experience had also shown that removing too many trees from an area that had a dense, mature forest canopy can dry out the thick layer of leaves and humus on the ground, increasing the risk of fires. Clarence knew a lot of state forest rangers, and he suspected that the higher-ups were not being honest about their motives.

He did what he was assigned to do, but he wasn't happy about it. "The rule they set was that they were only supposed to cut down trees that had been so badly damaged that they wouldn't grow any longer," he said. "But that isn't how it happened.

"I went out one day to supervise a crew of French-Canadian loggers who could hardly speak English. This one guy went up to a big, beautiful white pine that had one limb knocked off. He put his hand on it and said, 'the dam-AUGE, the dam-AUGE.' I finally made him understand that the tree wasn't mortally wounded, so he couldn't cut it." But if there were no rangers around, the loggers on blowdown contracts were liable to cut anything that looked like money.

Clarence came to believe—quietly, as long as he was on the payroll—
that state officials couldn't be trusted to do the right thing in the forest
preserve. His beliefs were confirmed in December 1951, when the Conservation Department published articles in its house magazine arguing
that, Big Blowdown or not, scientific management of forest land was in
the state's best interest. By "scientific management," they meant "selective
logging." Worse for Clarence was the fact that his beloved brother was solidly behind the idea.

Clarence and Bill Petty were born in a squatter's cabin on state land at the
north end of Indian Carry, an important land bridge used by early travelers
to get their boats from Upper Saranac Lake to the Raquette River. "The cabin
was originally a tent," Clarence said. "My dad cut down some trees on the
forest preserve to make the lumber for it. That was how it was back then.
Can you imagine?"

Clarence was born in 1905. Bill was sixteen months older. A few weeks
after his ninety-eighth birthday, Clarence walked out to the beach at Indian
Carry. He said that Upper Saranac Lake didn't look all that different from
his earliest memories. He pointed to Deer Island with his cane and said he
remembered seeing his father rowing back from his job as a guide and care-
taker there. He remembered smoke making his eyes burn during the big forest fire of September 29, 1908.

"My father was hauling people from the Wawbeek Hotel to the Saranac
Inn that day to catch the train that ran to Malone," he said. "It was six miles,
and he rowed at least two trips with the people and their trunks. They figured the whole place was going to burn up, the smoke was so bad. The sad,
funny part of it was that the train couldn't get through, because the fire had
burned up the trestles between Tupper Lake and Saranac. The hotel guests
walked into the water and stood there with just their heads sticking up until
the smoke cleared."

It was a cool, sunny October day. Saplings that had sprouted after the fire,
ninety-five years earlier, now towered overhead. The only sounds were the
quiet lapping of water and an occasional car on State Route 3.

Something about the shore of an Adirondack lake takes a person away
from the troubles of the world, and people travel great distances for views
like these. William Chapman White described the feeling.

Everything is as it was last year, the year before that, as it was a century ago. The sense of timelessness is real. That timelessness is also in a museum, in inanimate objects that time cannot change. The lake and the woods are alive and full of life, yet they too are beyond time.

They do change, but only with the seasons. Nothing in or around them tells one year from another. One summer on the lake is like any other, like summers long past and summers still to be. By the lake, apart for a few moments from a worrisome world, a man shares in that timelessness just by noting it. For those few moments he can know and be a part of it.

In the lake, a fish jumped. "Mother sat on the rocks here to fish," Clarence said, "and it wasn't unusual in those days to catch a lake trout that weighed fifteen pounds or more. Once she wanted to spend some time in New York City, where her parents lived. I was three and one-half years old, and Bill was five. She left us with our father, who was working up the lake. He'd leave about four in the morning and get back after dark. We had to prepare our own meals, collect the maple sap that was running, and keep the stove hot.

"I look back at that now and marvel. They would probably be arrested for negligence today. But we were told what we could do and what we could not do, and we believed it, so we did it."

Clarence was a skilled storyteller who told set pieces to his visitors. Many of them were moral lessons about hard work and radical self-reliance. After Bill reached the fifth grade, the brothers walked sixteen miles to and from school in Saranac Lake, often wearing snowshoes. Eight-year-old Clarence left home on Sunday, returned on Friday, and boarded in town during the week. When the boys came home on the weekends, they walked another twelve miles to check their traplines. Their chores were constant.

"When I was five, my father told me that I could either get to work or sit and starve in the woods," Clarence said. "It was just that clear." His first job, at age six, was delivering mail to a neighbor. He walked three miles, six days a week, for $1. He remembered the day he lost his pay on the way home. He ran back and combed the path in the gathering darkness until he found the dollar. Clarence's stories illuminated a world where everyone had an intimate personal relationship with nature, and if you screwed up, nobody else was around to fix it.

He loved to tell stories about Noah John Rondeau, a family friend who became a famous Adirondack hermit. Rondeau lived the dream of escape. When Clarence was eight, he showed up at the Petty homestead pushing a baby carriage filled with steel traps, guns, and an ax. He pushed the carriage eighteen miles into the wildest part of the High Peaks and lived there alone for the next thirty-seven years. Rondeau was intelligent, inquisitive, and funny, and the fishing at Cold River Camp was unequalled, so Clarence was a regular visitor. "I think he was the first hippie," Clarence said. "He hated the government. He loved to say that he was not a slave to industry."

Clarence once asked Rondeau if he was ever scared to be alone and so far from help. "What would happen if you cut yourself with an ax?" he asked. "You got no business cutting yourself with an ax," Rondeau replied.

But it was an unusual kind of frontier. The Petty family shared Saranac Lake with the summer homes of some of the richest people in the world. Clarence's father worked at mansions visited by Rockefellers, governors, and presidents. He earned $2 a day, a high wage for a local man. When their father had a guide job, Clarence and Bill sometimes earned a dollar just to chase deer toward the guns of the wealthy men.

The smoke Clarence remembered was from forest fires that burned 575 square miles of cut-over timberland in summer 1908. There were several reasons for the fires. The land had been logged the previous winter, the spring and summer had been dry, and the leftover tree branches and tops were like tinder. Sparks from coal-burning locomotives set this "slash" ablaze. That was the main reason. But many of the fires were also of suspicious origin. They had likely been set for revenge.

A lot of the burned-over territory belonged to owners of large private estates, the original members of the Association for the Protection of the Adirondacks. The AfPA hired the nation's best lawyers to enforce a strict interpretation of the Forever Wild clause, mostly in order to protect their privacy. Many estate owners took an extra step and hired private game wardens to patrol their properties. One of the strictest of these was William Avery Rockefeller II, the brother of John D. Rockefeller Sr., who acquired more than eighty-one square miles in the northeastern part of Adirondack Park starting in 1897. Rockefeller had zero tolerance for trespassers. Locals who tried to sneak onto his property to hunt and fish were regularly arrested. This came as a shock to them.

The problem was that the land had not always been patrolled, and its streams and deer herds were important sources of food. Despite the fact that many area residents had access to public lands nearby where they still could hunt and fish legally, what Rockefeller did seemed wrong. Public and private lands had both been treated as community resources that were policed informally by local residents. Rockefeller had violated the frontier code.

A group of Tupper Lake residents formed in 1903 to "fight Rockefeller's men." They didn't have the law on their side, but that hardly mattered. Fires consumed 725 square miles that summer, and a territory four-fifths that size burned five years later. In both years, a suspiciously large number of those fires started on Rockefeller's land. Other private estates were also devastated. A total of 1,875 square miles burned between 1891 and 1911, and historian Karl Jacoby estimates that up to one-quarter of the fires were intentionally set.

In small Adirondack towns, where life moves slowly and people have known each other's families for generations, stories like these become parables. It can seem like things that happened a century ago are still happening, because, in some ways, they still are.

Dick Persico, who was executive director of the Adirondack Park Agency in the mid-1970s, learned about the practice after a Tupper Lake man was caught trying to burn down the agency's offices. "George Farrell, one of the local men who worked for us, explained it to me," Persico said. "I was very upset about what had happened. He said, 'You know Dick, in rural areas, this is called "redball." When somebody pisses you off or does something bad to you, you burn their fricking house down, or at least you burn their barn.' He said that revenge burning is part of Adirondack culture."

Clarence and Bill's coworkers used to kid them about their old-fashioned ways. "A guy I worked with at the department used to refer to Bill as Father Time," said Pete Lanahan, who was deputy commissioner at the New York State Department of Environmental Conservation in the 1970s. "Bill would show up in the commissioner's office in Albany looking like an old-time forest ranger. The shirt, the pants, everything."

Bill might have looked like a straight arrow, but Clarence really was one. He was married fifty-six years to the same woman, and, like his father, he provided for the family while his wife, Ferne, raised their three boys. He never smoked, never cursed, and never drank anything stronger than spring water. Bill retired with his state pension in 1977 and died of a heart attack six years later. Clarence retired in 1975 and began another career that lasted thirty-two years. He became an internationally known advocate for the preservation of wild land.

Clarence had bright blue eyes and an easy smile. As he neared his hundredth birthday, he was still able to rely on the muscles he had built from a life of hiking and keeping house in the woods. His energy was legendary. Men and women decades younger than Clarence said they were exhausted by jobs that he insisted they finish before going home. His posture remained straight long after his brush cut went gray. When he wasn't flying, he favored old-school wool hiking gear: heavy pants and a shirt that was olive drab or red-and-white checked, and a watch cap or, in colder weather, an insulated hunter's cap with ear flaps. He rarely wore his full ranger uniform, though.

Clarence didn't think like a typical ranger, either. Bill and his colleagues spent a lot of time maintaining roads that ran deep into the forest preserve. The state constitution made it illegal for the public to drive on those roads, but the rangers exploited all kinds of exceptions. The official purpose of the roads was fire control, but hunters and fishermen who knew how to get around the gates used them freely—and if they also knew the rangers, their trespasses were likely to be forgiven. Rangers also allowed lots of uses that were legal but wrong, in Clarence's opinion. They issued permits to float planes that landed on pristine lakes, and they maintained comfortable cabins scattered throughout land that was legally Forever Wild.

The rangers cut trees to improve winter deer yards that increased the yield for hunters. They stocked lakes with fish, and they released farm-raised pheasants into fields. They built lakeshore campgrounds that had showers, streetlights, and snack bars. They let families rent tent sites in choice backcountry locations, giving the same site to the same family every year, and they looked the other way when the sites sprouted informal cabins.

The district offices of the Conservation Department operated like fiefdoms, with little supervision from Albany. Their rules and standards were often informal. The rangers said that it was all part of their job. They served people who came to hunt and fish on state land. How else were they going to do that?

The rangers also served car campers and downhill skiers, reluctantly. They let hikers and backpackers take care of themselves. The idea of biodiversity—Aldo Leopold's idea, that "a thing is right when it tends to preserve the integrity, stability and beauty of the biotic community"—was not well known or respected in the offices of the Conservation Department in the 1950s and 60s. In fact, many rangers were hostile to the notion that natural areas were best left alone.

The department had a utilitarian attitude toward violations, too. If you went into the forest preserve in those days to cut a tree or shoot a deer out of season, there probably wouldn't be any witnesses. And if a ranger somehow found out about it, he would probably let you off with a warning the first time. "People were considered clever if they outwitted the game protector," said Clarence. "You'd get points for doing that."

When he was a ranger, Clarence had to back off sometimes just to keep things working. "We had to use volunteers to fight fires," he said, "and some of our best firefighters were among the worst game violators. I told my rangers to keep on good terms with them. We kept out of the game law business then, because we needed these guys."

The two brothers also differed in their attitudes toward violators. "Bill was more liberal with people, and they knew it," Clarence said. "He was everybody's friend, and he leaned in their direction. I was more outspoken."

Bill maintained his good-neighbor policy for good reasons, according to Norman Van Valkenburgh, who started working for the Conservation Department in 1955. "Back near the beginning of my career, I worked with another guy to plow the fire lines around the tree plantations," Van Valkenburgh said "We had a bulldozer and plows and everything, and we were way out in the bush. The district forester came up to us and said, 'A guy down the road needs his garden plowed.' That was all he said. So we went down the road and plowed his garden. We did a lot of things like that back in those days.

"I realized why as I got further up the ladder. If some timber thief came along and started cutting on state land, the guy whose garden we plowed would call us up right away. It worked both ways.

"Before 1970, the old Conservation Department, and especially the forest rangers, were there to interact with people and help get things done. Now the forest rangers are law enforcement. The good-neighbor spirit is all gone. And that was the major problem with the Adirondack Park Agency. They had no sense of public relations. They were enforcers. They forgot or didn't know how to deal with the people."

Bill Petty rose through the ranks of the Conservation Department until he was appointed regional director in 1971. He spent his time shuttling between the regional office in Ray Brook and the state capital in Albany. A big part of his job was to curry favor with important people from downstate, just as his father had done.

Pete Lanahan of the Department of Environmental Conservation remembered one occasion when Bill took the state budget people on an outing. The Albany officials rode horses a couple of miles on a dirt road that led to Marcy Dam, where there was a pond with an expansive view of the High Peaks. Petty had submitted a budget proposal to rebuild the dam. Vic Glider, the department's director of field services, arranged to have fresh lobsters and clams flown in from Long Island. "They had a big cookout at Marcy Dam before they held a briefing on their budget proposal," said Lanahan. Needless to say, the request was approved.

Clarence went in a different direction. His biographer, Christopher Angus, describes how Clarence flew tanker planes in the Pacific during World War II. He kept his pilot's license handy after he became a park ranger. Aviation gave him a second source of income, and he also loved the feeling of being alone in a vast sky. In 1957, he switched to flying full time. He spent the next two years dousing forest fires from the air, or flying the governor and other important people from point A to point B. He said that all that time looking down at the earth gave him a different point of view.

Seen from above, the Adirondack region reveals itself as a forested dome of ancient rock. It rises gradually in the west and drops off steeply to the Champlain Valley in the east. The rock is more than a billion years old. It is the southernmost outcrop of the Laurentian Shield, an expanse of Precambrian and metamorphic rock that forms the core of North America. The rock's fractures have eroded into valleys that have a northeast-to-southwest orientation. Eons of uplift, erosion, and glaciation have deposited soil layers at different elevations. The soils support various kinds of trees, and in a few hours of flying Clarence could see them all.

The trees from above look like a patchwork in shades of green. The wetlands and sandy soils of lower elevations support fir, tamarack, balsam, and spruce whose needles are so dark that in low light they appear black. The southern and central hills have the richest soils, so they show much brighter hues of maple, yellow birch, and beech. Dark stands of hemlock cluster on lakeshores and in ravines. The highest peaks have very little soil and a much shorter growing season, so they support only lichen and alpine plants. The view from the air reveals entire biomes and shows how they interact with and depend on each other.

"If you want to see an example of the best kind of waste disposal, go to a wilderness area," Clarence said. "It's beautiful, and absolutely everything is recycled. Nature has a way of balancing things that we don't fully understand."

In Clarence's later years, door-to-door Christian evangelists visited his homestead fairly regularly. "I enjoy talking to them," Clarence said. "I tell them, 'You're talking to probably the worst atheist you'll ever meet. But what you call Jehovah, I call the force of nature, and I won't disagree with you because it's all a mystery to me. The Holy Spirit you talk about is what I see when I'm in a wilderness area. When I need to regain my balance, the best place for me is the most remote place I can find.'"

During the last fifteen years of his state career, Clarence became the undisputed authority on the forest preserve. He combined his years of aerial observation with three major surveying assignments that took him to every acre of state-owned land in the Adirondacks. He called his first assignment "a three-year vacation," and he got it because of the fierce debate that erupted after the Big Blowdown.

A journalist labeled the conflict the Big Blowup. It was really a statewide version of the disagreement between the Petty brothers. Clarence and other Forever Wild advocates were horrified by salvage logging in the forest preserve. They pressured legislators to revoke the state contracts and pledge that no further cutting would be permitted there. Bill and other scientific foresters replied that the friends of the Forever Wild clause were silly and sentimental. Foresters had always considered the clause an aberration and a nuisance.

In March 1951, the state assembly and senate created the Joint Legislative Committee on Natural Resources to moderate the debate and find solutions. Its first chair was Wheeler Milmoe, a moderate Republican assemblyman from a rural upstate county. Milmoe quickly formed an Advisory Council on the Forest Preserve. Most of the advisory council's members came from commercial interests, but Milmoe also appointed Paul Schaefer, who belonged to multiple groups. Schaefer was active in the State Conservation Council, which represented hunters and anglers, and he was also a trustee of the Association for the Protection of the Adirondacks. He was well known for waging the successful campaign against dams in the forest preserve in the 1940s.

Schaefer's seat on the advisory council gave him access to the Conservation Department, whose commissioner, Sharon Mauhs, had become his ally during the antidam campaign. Mauhs was a lawyer and gentleman farmer from Cobleskill who had served two terms in the assembly, and he was also a reliable supporter of the preservationist point of view. In 1957, Mauhs announced a plan to survey the undeveloped areas of the forest preserve in order to protect their wild character and improve public access. There was only one problem. Mauhs's budget couldn't pay for it.

Schaefer volunteered to write a report on the vast Siamese Ponds region, where he had owned a cabin since the 1930s. A year later, he turned in a one-thousand-word sketch that was short on data and long on poetry. "Throughout the region is a lushness of mosses and ferns," he wrote. "In mid-May one can walk all day through heavy hardwoods under which are countless acres of mayflowers. The trails are lined with white, yellow, and blue violets; red, white, and painted trillium; and Dutchman's breeches and Indian pipes."

Schaefer guessed that there might be two hundred miles of informal trails in the Siamese Ponds, and that perhaps thirty hunters parked at one popular trailhead at the peak of deer season, but he freely admitted that he didn't know the actual figures. Near the end of his comments, he could no longer contain his enthusiasm for launching a full-scale adventure. "This is the problem," he wrote: "to *understand* the physical aspects of the region and to understand the present human use of it. Too long we have been generalizing about what ought and ought not to be done. It is time now to become specific, and to come up with recommendations" (italics in the original).

One summer day in the early 1910s, eight- or nine-year-old Clarence Petty was on the grounds of a Great Camp on Upper Saranac Lake, probably helping his father on a guiding job. He was approached by a boy who looked to be about five or six. The boy was wearing fine clothes, and a governess walked a step or two behind him. He was holding a model of a birch-bark canoe about eight inches long and as he came closer, Clarence realized that he meant it as a gift.

"I had been told not to take gifts from strangers, so at first I didn't want it," he said. "But the governess convinced me. She said, 'Nelson wants you to have this.'"

Clarence thanked the little boy, and he never spoke to Nelson Rockefeller again. But almost half a century later, Rockefeller gave him a much nicer gift when he became governor of New York on January 1, 1959. As one of the world's wealthiest men, Rockefeller preferred to conduct state business using a private plane piloted by a trusted employee. Clarence wouldn't need to fly the governor around anymore.

Rockefeller was a Republican and his predecessor had been a Democrat, so he made a lot of personnel changes. Paul Schaefer's friend Sharon Mauhs was out at the Conservation Department, and Harold G. Wilm, an academic forester with few political connections, was in.

Wheeler Milmoe, the chair of the Joint Legislative Committee on Natural Resources, also retired in 1958. The new chair was Watson Pomeroy, a World War II Army captain from a wealthy Buffalo family who had represented Poughkeepsie in the State Assembly since 1948. Pomeroy had been a member of the Joint Legislative Committee since 1952.

Pomeroy had supported the lumbering of damaged timber after the Big Blowdown of 1950, and there was little in his background to indicate that he would support wilderness preservationists. "We were skeptical about Pomeroy at first," said David Newhouse, who, as chair of the Conservation Committee of the Adirondack Mountain Club (ADK), led the group of activists that came to be known as the "Schenectady Mafia." But Pomeroy turned out to be enthusiastic about taking field trips into the woods. As he saw more of the territory, his positions changed. "He ended up being even stricter about wilderness than the ADK was," said Newhouse.

Pomeroy's change "showed me that you can't take anything for granted when you're dealing with state government," Newhouse said. "You have to assume that they're all good people, and that they are educable."

As incoming chair, Pomeroy was inspired by recent events in Washington, DC. The National Wilderness Preservation Act had been introduced in Congress every year beginning in 1956, and was steadily gaining support. The act relied on the definition of wilderness that had been devised by Robert Marshall when he was an official of the US Forest Service in the 1930s. The gist of it was that wilderness areas should have no roads, no motorized vehicles, no buildings, no timber-cutting or other commercial uses, and a minimum size of five thousand acres.

The forest preserve was owned by New York State, so it was not directly affected by federal rules. One of Watson Pomeroy's priorities for the Joint

Legislative Committee on Natural Resources was to bring the management of the forest preserve up to federal standards. Before he could do that, the committee first had to figure out how the word "wilderness" would be defined in New York.

Pomeroy hired Neil Stout, a Syracuse-educated forester seventeen years younger than Clarence and twelve years older than George Davis, to be the joint legislative committee's executive director. Stout's previous assignment had used aerial photographs to investigate forest and farm conditions in rural New York. The joint legislative committee also planned to use aerial observation to begin its survey of the forest preserve, and it wanted to follow up with on-the-ground observations. It needed an experienced bush pilot who also liked to go for long walks.

Neil Stout was "overjoyed" that Commissioner Wilm assigned Clarence to the joint legislative committee. "Clarence came to our initial planning meeting in Albany, and it was clear that his experience and knowledge was perfect for the fieldwork we had to do," Stout said. "That first meeting was when we began our comradeship, which continued all our lives."

Pomeroy assigned Neil Stout and Clarence Petty to do exactly what Sharon Mauhs and Paul Schaefer had called for. They were to make detailed maps and gather as much useful data as possible on the large roadless areas in the forest preserve. At their initial planning meeting, the group decided that they would define wilderness areas as parcels that were at least twice as large as the Forest Service's minimum size, which meant that they had to be ten thousand acres or bigger. "This cut down the work considerably," Clarence said. The parcels could not contain any legal public or private roads, although roads used exclusively for firefighting could be included. They also could not include any inhabited buildings, and their boundaries had to be at least one-half mile away from any road unless slopes were very steep, in which case the distance could be one-quarter of a mile.

Neil Stout and Clarence Petty began their work in summer 1959. By comparing existing maps and other data with eyewitness views from the air, they were able to identify eleven potential wilderness areas in the Adirondacks and four more in the Catskill Forest Preserve, which encompasses 268,000 acres in Delaware, Greene, Sullivan, and Ulster Counties. They presented that list in September and started three years of grueling fieldwork. "We looked at the conditions of trails that were in use," Stout said. "We looked for signs of activity, and things that might be detrimental to wilderness conditions there. And yes, we did some bushwhacking, because we had to see what was over the next ridge."

The surveyors didn't take soil or water samples, because their main purpose was to document evidence of human activity. They didn't climb with ropes or camp in the snow, either, but they did spend many nights outdoors and many days in the rain. Mostly, they walked. Clarence remembered places where a nearby ridge was too steep to climb, which meant hiking a circuitous route five or seven miles out of the way to see a view that was only one-quarter mile away.

Even though Clarence described his time on the Pomeroy Commission as "a three-year vacation," he also said that it got tedious. "We had to walk through every damn one of those areas, back and forth, because we had to make sure they did not recommend something as wilderness and then find out that it contained private land," he said. "We practically went over every inch, walking and flying." By the end of the third summer, even he had had his fill of exploring for a while.

The largest roadless area in the Adirondacks is the High Peaks region. It is the highest-altitude land in the state, containing thirty-four of the forty-six peaks higher than four thousand feet in elevation. It also has the headwaters of the Hudson River; several large, famous lakes; and, in 1960, it had only 480 acres of privately owned land. In 1961, Clarence Petty and Neil Stout estimated its size at 181,000 acres, which is 94 percent as large as the five boroughs of New York City. "You could put a pack of wolves in there, and it's so big that they could roam freely and never bother anybody," Clarence said. "There are also three other places in the Adirondacks big enough to do that."

By the end of summer 1960, "The team of Stout and Petty," as they called themselves, submitted detailed reports on twelve potential Adirondack wilderness areas, totaling 824,000 acres. The twelfth area, Giant Mountain, forms a corridor with the Hurricane Mountain area to the north and Dix Mountain to the south. The corridor includes another eleven peaks higher than four thousand feet. Neil Stout and his assistants also found four more potential areas in the Catskills, totaling 91,000 acres.

Stout and Petty also told the committee that much of the land that met the criteria for wilderness was far from pristine. Stout remembered one area near a Boy Scout camp in the Catskills where several acres of trees were scored with ax marks. They found large piles of garbage left by hunters who had camped in the same spot for decades. Illegal cabins were common, and one day they came upon a shack whose outhouse straddled a creek that drained into a village's water supply.

Perhaps worst of all, Clarence Petty and Neil Stout documented more than a hundred miles of illegal roads that had been cut by four-wheel-drive vehicles and the customized tractors locals called "doodlebugs." "We met one man whose jeep had winches on both the front and the back," Clarence said. "He told us he could go anywhere in that thing."

The two men formed a close friendship in the years they depended on each other. Their bond was further strengthened by a sense they shared that their work was important. These beautiful woods, the places Clarence Petty loved the most, were being desecrated. It had to stop.

Chairman Pomeroy found Neil Stout, Clarence Petty, and their adventures irresistible. Pomeroy was an enthusiastic skier who had also been on the swim team at Yale University. He had a passion for lake swimming. "He loved to come out and see what we were doing," said Clarence. "Quite often he would call on Thursday and one or both of us would go out with him over the weekend. He swam in dozens of ponds. I told him once that in my opinion, he held the record for swimming in the greatest number of ponds in the Adirondacks."

Clarence remembered one weekend when he and Neil Stout took Pomeroy to the forty-three-thousand-acre Pharaoh Lakes Wilderness, east of the Schroon River. Its central feature, Pharaoh Lake, is 441 acres. It is one of the largest lakes that is completely surrounded by the forest preserve and getting to it requires a 3.3-mile hike. "Watson swam it," said Clarence. "He also wanted to hike to a pond even further out called Grizzle Ocean and swim that too, just because he liked the sound of it. He'd just strip off his clothes and jump in and go. He would swim out and back when we stopped for lunch, or I would carry his clothes and meet him on the other side."

Grizzle Ocean is only a few acres in size, but its shoreline is pristine. The surveying crew stopped to rest and talk in a three-sided "lean-to" shelter in a quiet stand of mature hemlocks. "Watson was a wonderful person to have in the legislature, because he had really gotten out and seen what was going on," said Clarence. "A lot of legislators thought he was too extreme in emphasizing environmental matters. We thought he was the one man who was getting the necessary information."

In summer 1961, with work on the wilderness areas winding down, the joint legislative committee directed the team of Stout and Petty to focus on smaller roadless areas of 1,000 acres minimum. They found sixty-seven additional tracts, totaling 1.1 million acres, which included more than three hundred lakes and ponds. These smaller tracts were undeveloped and often had many of the qualities of a wilderness, but they were far more accessible than the 824,500 official wilderness acres.

Well before the survey was completed, Pomeroy started the process of turning its findings into law. He introduced a bill in 1961 that would give the Conservation Department the authority to prohibit motorized traffic in certain areas, among other things. The joint legislative committee held more than a dozen public hearings on the bill, which seemed to be headed for a vote. Then, on December 5, 1961, Attorney General Louis Lefkowitz ruled that the conservation commissioner already had the powers the bill would have given him.

That was a problem. Conservation Commissioner Wilm had a doctorate degree in forestry and had spent five years as dean of the state forestry school in Syracuse. He didn't see the point of leaving land completely undisturbed, especially if a small alteration could improve its productivity. Wilm proposed to insert exceptions in Pomeroy's bill. He wanted to allow tree cutting in wilderness areas to promote the growth of deer herds. But Pomeroy had been tutored by Clarence Petty and Paul Schaefer. He held to a strict interpretation of Forever Wild. He refused, and the bill died.

It was a bitter defeat for Pomeroy, but the wilderness protection movement had gained a foothold and a powerful ally. It was also greatly strengthened by the rich and varied information that Neil Stout and Clarence Petty had spent years compiling in the woods. The Pomeroy Commission's work was foundational.

In addition to giving state officials detailed field data on wilderness and smaller roadless areas for the first time, the commission also identified additional areas that could qualify as wilderness if the state acquired just one or two parcels of land. "Eventually we got three more wilderness areas that way," Clarence said. Their baseline information had a long-lasting impact. In 1960, Clarence Petty and Neil Stout identified a large tract in the central Adirondacks that almost qualified as wilderness. The 41,177-acre Blue Ridge Wilderness was formally designated more than forty years later.

During his visits to the High Peaks in summer 1960, Clarence visited the Cold River camp that Noah Rondeau had abandoned. Rondeau was sixty-seven when the Big Blowdown happened, and in its aftermath, he found it too hard to get around in the woods. "He had moved to town," Clarence said. "He had left a couple of his things out there which I collected and brought to the little room he was renting. The poor guy was completely lost."

The professed hater of government was living on welfare. Even in the Adirondacks, it was no longer possible to escape from the world and its rules.

Chapter 3

# Quickening

Paul Schaefer made his living as a builder in the suburbs of post-World War II Schenectady. The best way to study his work is to visit his own house, which is maintained by Union College. Schaefer's buildings are distinctive and highly sought after. His house is solid and traditional, with stone walls, a slate roof, and small-paned wooden sash windows that recall New England Colonial design.

The college built an addition to Schaefer's house to store the archives of the Association for the Protection of the Adirondacks (AfPA) and other early conservation organizations. It preserved the "Adirondack room," where Schaefer held many meetings in the early years of the environmental movement. This room is dominated by two features: a large, hand-laid stone fireplace and a hand-built, eight-by-twelve-foot raised relief map of the Adirondack Park.

The map required several years of focused effort by Schaefer, his family, and about fifty friends. Each contour of every mountain and valley got loving attention. "We had to trace each elevation level from the topographic maps one at a time with tracing paper," said his daughter, Evelyn Greene. "Then we followed those lines with carbon paper over thin sheets of cardboard, cut each elevation with a razor, and glued it into place by eyeballing it." They fit each raised relief map together and finished the whole thing off with plaster and paint. The map is a fitting memorial to a man who spent his life organizing people to tackle big, audacious goals.

"He always worked in the same way, no matter what it was that needed to be done," said Norm Van Valkenburgh. "Paul always stood up and said, 'Come on, Norm, why don't you help me?' He was forever enlisting people's help without ever asking them first. You'd find out that you had been appointed to work on something. You hadn't even heard of it before." And according to Evelyn, if people didn't say "yes" the first time, Paul would keep calling them back until they changed their minds.

Schaefer was tall, slender, and handsome, with blue eyes and a full head of black hair that remained bushy long after it turned gray. He was Roman Catholic and inclined to study spirituality and literature, but his family's financial troubles forced him to quit school and go to work in 1924, when he was fifteen. The Adirondacks were his escape. He wrote dramatic essays about his experiences there, although he never granted formal interviews because he hated to speak on tape. He always organized his thoughts before he spoke. It was his intense desire to "save" the Adirondacks that drew people in.

Schaefer's charisma also emanated from his strong spiritual connection to nature. He loved to read and write rhapsodic descriptions of it. At the top of his map is a hand-painted passage originally written in 1880 by his hero, Verplanck Colvin, the first surveyor of the Adirondacks.

> Carved by the glaciers or the icebergs of the drift period from the most ancient granite of the world's formation; washed and eroded by the storms of a thousand centuries, the Adirondack ranges rise in dark and gloomy billows, stretching from the hills that skirt the Mohawk away northward to the shores of the river, from which this most ancient rock takes the term Laurentian.
>
> Elsewhere the mountains are more stupendous, more icy and more drear, but none look down upon a grander landscape, in rich autumn time; more brightly gemmed or jeweled with innumerable lakes, or crystal pools, or wild and savage chasms, or dread passes; none show a denser or more vast appearance of primeval forest stretched over range on range to the far horizon, where the sea of mountains fades away into a dim, vaporous uncertainty.

A region of mystery, over which none can gaze without a strange thrill of
interest and of wonder at what may be hidden in that vast area of forest, covering all things with its deep repose.

Schaefer worked for four decades to build a diverse coalition aimed at protecting pristine Adirondack landscapes. He didn't know that his life's work
would culminate in the creation of the Adirondack Park Agency. But it all
pointed toward that goal.

Activism for wilderness protection in the United States came of age in the
1950s, but it began several decades earlier, and one of the places where its
quickening took place was Schenectady, New York. A group of scientists and
engineers who worked in the research labs of General Electric (GE), the city's
largest employer, also shared a passion for camping and skiing at Adirondack sites that were just a few hours away by car. As they became more aware
of threats to their beloved wilderness, their passion drew them toward political action.

"The people who got attracted to environmentalism were often in advanced engineering or discovery," said Almy Coggeshall, who was a chemical engineer for GE when he wasn't trying to stop snowmobiles. "In those
jobs you have to have a lot of imagination, a lot of creativity, in order to puz-
zle your way through something that had never been done before. There is
a mystery in what makes natural systems work."

Coggeshall was a short, jolly man who could trace his English ancestry
back to the early seventeenth century without consulting notes. He was
eighty-six years old in 2003, but he turned back into a young man as he play-
acted one of his favorite experiments. He described how the engineers heated
a glob of glass, attached one end of it to an arrow, and then shot the arrow
down a hallway to create the first fiber-optic cable.

The GE conservationists included innovators like Vincent Schaefer, Paul's
older brother, who developed cloud seeding technology with the help of Ir-
ving Langmuir, who had won the Nobel Prize for Chemistry in 1932. Langmuir was a polymath who held more than five dozen patents in several
different fields. One of them was for a new kind of ski binding that allowed
him to make the first ski descent of several Adirondack peaks. Langmuir
was one of the first visitors to the ski trails at Gore Mountain in the 1930s,

and he almost certainly used the "tow rope," an early version of a ski lift, that was operated by Paul Schaefer's younger brother Carl.

Langmuir's close friend John Apperson, an administrator in GE's patent department, may have been the first Schenectadian to plunge into environmental activism. Apperson was also a genius, but his talents were not in science. He was a political strategist, and a very sneaky one. "He worked by indirection," said Coggeshall. "If he had wanted to be a criminal, he would have been very good at it."

A lifelong bachelor, "Appie" cleaned out his personal savings account in 1939 to buy Dome Island, a sixteen-acre plot of virgin timber in the middle of Lake George. He was occasionally bothered by powerboats that got too close. So he kept logs and plywood scraps in his boat and threw them into the water at strategic moments to force the speeding boats to slow down. He also wanted to discourage trespassers, but he knew that traditional "Posted: No Trespassing" signs were ineffective. So he erected signs that said "First Aid For Rattlesnake Bite" and attached a leather strap for use as a tourniquet.

Apperson became politically active in 1923, when he successfully lobbied Governor Al Smith to stop a proposed parkway near Lake George. Eight years later, he recruited Schaefer, Langmuir, and a few others from the Mohawk Valley Hiking Club to help him fight two proposed amendments to the state constitution: one that would allow tree cutting and tree planting in the forest preserve, and another that would allow the construction of cabins and other recreational facilities. The amendments were defeated in 1932, and in their wake, the Schenectady activists formed the Forest Preserve Association to lobby for strict enforcement of the Forever Wild clause.

The members of the Forest Preserve Association multiplied their impact by encouraging established groups to join their cause. Their main prospects were the Adirondack Mountain Club (founded in 1922), which represented hikers; the New York State Conservation Council (founded in 1933), which represented hunters; and dozens of local outing groups like the Mohawk Valley Hiking Club. They practiced a new kind of lobbying for wilderness protection that emphasized grassroots organizing instead of buying influence. They became such effective advocates that an admirer, William Verner, dubbed them "the Schenectady Mafia."

They were scrappy. Coggeshall remembered the night Apperson's colleague and friend Phil Ham borrowed mimeograph machines from the GE lab to print and distribute materials. They had learned that Harold Wilm, Rockefeller's conservation commissioner, was developing a plan to zone the forest preserve in a way that would allow tree cutting on 70 percent of it. "Phil got a copy of the commissioner's draft proposal and stayed up all night to make a bunch of copies," Coggeshall said. "The next day he distributed the proposal to all the delegates of the Conservation Council, who had gathered for their annual legislative meeting in Albany, with a statement about why it was a bad idea.

"The Conservation Council had a lot of influence with the department, because the fees from their hunting licenses paid the department's bills. Appie and Ham lobbied the right people at the right time. They stopped the plan cold."

Apperson's guerilla tactics inspired many people, including Coggeshall, whom he hired as a seventeen-year-old in 1935 to spy on a backcountry lumbering operation. "I would go to their meetings and listen to these men talking," Coggeshall said. "I began to realize that this obscure group was, in fact, a power in New York State. And I told myself, well, if these guys can do it, I can do it too."

In 1946, Paul Schaefer and John Apperson attended the North American Wildlife Conference in New York City to make a presentation on a threat they had learned about one year earlier. A state agency had proposed dams that would flood large sections of the Adirondacks. One of the dams had already been approved by the governor. Schaefer and Apperson were determined to stop both dams, although they didn't know how. They needed help.

The state's Black River Regulating District had proposed sites for several dams that would flood thousands of acres in the park. Schaefer and Apperson ended their presentation by projecting beautiful color images of the plains of the Moose River, an important wintering ground for deer. The plains would become "mud flats and tree stumps" if the dams were built, they said. After they finished, a balding man with a roundish face and wire-rimmed glasses introduced himself and offered his support. He was Howard Zahniser, executive director of the Wilderness Society in Washington, DC.

The Schenectady activists were delighted to gain the support of the only national organization devoted to wilderness protection, small though it was. Schaefer was even more excited when Zahniser told him he had never been to the Adirondacks and was eager to visit. Schaefer invited Zahniser to visit his family's cabin near Bakers Mills, "Cragorehol," which was named for the three mountains it overlooked: Crane, Gore, and Height of Land.

When Zahniser drove up with his wife and children that summer, Schaefer greeted him with typical enthusiasm. He took his new friend on an overnight trip to Hanging Spear Falls, a narrow seventy-five-foot blade of water that plunges into a pool deep in the High Peaks Wilderness. As they sat around the campfire, Schaefer told Zahniser about his friend and mentor, the late Robert Marshall, cofounder of the Wilderness Society. Marshall's family owned a camp on Lower Saranac Lake, and Schaefer met him on top of nearby Mount Marcy in 1932. "We simply must band together—all of us who love the wilderness," Marshall had said (in Schaefer's retelling). "We must fight together—whenever and wherever wilderness is attacked. We must mobilize all of our resources, all of our energies, all of our devotion to the wilderness."

Two years later, Schaefer found a camp for sale that was a hundred yards away from his own. Zahniser bought it and named it "Mateskared" after his children (Mathias, Esther, Karen, and Edward). It became the family's retreat, and Zahniser cherished it as a place to rest, write, and have leisurely talks with his friend. The friendship deepened as Schaefer's campaign against the dams continued. He came to rely on Zahniser for tactical advice and connections, and also for support and inspiration.

In addition to being the Wilderness Society's executive director, Zahniser was also editor of its magazine, *Living Wilderness*. He was a gifted writer with a broad humanistic philosophy. He argued that it was essential to preserve natural ecosystems for their scientific value, but also because of the awe and humility they inspired in the people who experienced them. He was articulating feelings that were stirring in the hearts of millions of Americans.

"The need is for areas of the earth within which we stand without our mechanisms that make us immediate masters over our environment," he wrote in 1956, "areas of wild nature in which we sense ourselves to be, what in fact I believe we are, dependent members of an interdependent community of living creatures that together derive their existence from the sun."

Schaefer and Apperson were outnumbered when they started fighting for the Moose River Plains in the 1940s, but they weren't alone. Schaefer joined the Association for the Protection of the Adirondacks during those years, was named a trustee in 1949, and served as a vice president for many years. The

AfPA connection gave him funds and regular opportunities to talk with like-minded people about nature and spirituality while sitting on some of the world's nicest porches.

One of the very nicest porches was the summer home of Arthur Masten Crocker, the great-grandnephew of President Chester Alan Arthur. Crocker was the same age as Schaefer, but he came from the world of old money. He managed his family's fortune while spending every summer at his family's home at the Tahawus Club, a private preserve on the southern edge of the High Peaks Wilderness.

George Crocker, Arthur's father, was a trustee of the AfPA and an admirer of Paul Schaefer's. The elder Crocker made sure the organization followed Schaefer's advice. When George Crocker left the board, he got Schaefer's blessing before nominating Arthur to take his place. Within a year, Arthur Crocker had become president of the AfPA.

Arthur Crocker was given the top job because of his enthusiasm, and also because he had time to devote to it. He had retired from business around the age of forty, after a divorce and a nervous breakdown left him debilitated. He recuperated in the family's Adirondack compound, where many of his formative experiences had taken place.

In his later years, Arthur lived in a Florida condominium with his second wife, Barbara. There was a bit of the nineteenth century in him. He had a deep, booming voice, and his stories often did not make their points directly—he would leave it for you to figure it out, ending with a stare or a raised eyebrow.

Crocker remembered one afternoon in the early 1950s when a friend and fellow Tahawus Club member, Samuel Ordway Jr., invited him over after lunch to meet an important visitor. Henry Fairfield Osborn Jr. was president of the New York Zoological Society and had recently founded the Conservation Foundation, which eventually became the World Wildlife Fund. He had also published a bestselling book called *Our Plundered Planet* (1948). All three men were members of the AfPA.

"Osborn had a little hawk sitting on his shoulder," said Crocker. "So we went up to Ordway's cottage, the hawk came too, and Osborn left him out on the porch. Sam had asked the man who ran the club to catch him a mouse. So Osborn sat near an open window and held up this dead mouse. The hawk flew in and grabbed it and flew back out. As we were talking, I could hear the 'crunch, crunch, crunch' sound of the hawk eating the mouse. Anyway, it was about that time that Sam and I began talking more seriously about environmental questions."

*Our Plundered Planet* is a warning that uses florid language and biblical imagery to defend untouched ecosystems. "The tide of the earth's population is rising," Osborn wrote, "[and] the reservoir of the earth's resources is falling." He argued that the earth's resources are finite, and therefore they impose absolute limits on the scale and scope of human development. Huge land development projects and energy-intensive technologies are part of the "avoidance of the day of atonement that is drawing nearer as each year passes," he wrote. "[We have] now arrived at the day when the books should be balanced."

Osborn was updating the arguments of Thomas Malthus, an English cleric who wrote in 1798 that uncontrolled population growth would inevitably exhaust natural resources and cause famine. The answer was to limit population growth, Osborn told Crocker and Ordway as his hawk sat outside, happily consuming its prey.

Osborn was preaching to the choir. Ordway would write in 1955 that "what is needed is a cheap, harmless, edible compound which will prevent conception for a period of one, two, or even three weeks after it is eaten by either man or woman." Barbara Crocker was a major donor to Planned Parenthood.

Population growth certainly contributes to the degradation of natural environments. But by 2020, with the world's population approaching eight billion, the issue had become far more complex than Osborn could ever have imagined. Others have argued with equal passion that human ingenuity is not finite, and that people can be trusted to find efficient, renewable ways to accommodate everyone. Still, the straightforward logic of Malthus and Osborn is hard to resist. It's tempting to believe that the best way to preserve beautiful natural areas like the Adirondacks is to keep people out. And that argument is even harder to resist if you already own a house there.

Arthur Crocker's work was instrumental to the creation of the Adirondack Park Agency, but he preferred to work behind the scenes. He described himself as an administrator and said, "I was just listening, you see." The trustees of the AfPA made the policy decisions, although some trustees had more influence than others. So how, exactly, did the association decide on its priorities? "I did what Paul Schaefer told me to do," Crocker said.

The Schenectady branch of the environmental movement grew stronger in 1955 when another research chemist from GE, Arthur Newkirk, became president of the Adirondack Mountain Club (ADK). "He was my mentor—highly committed and skilled," said David Newhouse, a GE engineer who had been active in the Mohawk Valley Hiking Club. "He accepted the ADK presidency on the condition that the club had to go in the direction of wilderness protection." The ADK had almost two thousand members in 1955. Within a few years, Newkirk and Newhouse, who became chair of the ADK's Conservation Committee, pointed the group toward the goal of wilderness protection.

Newkirk, Schaefer, Apperson, Newhouse, and other activists won their eleven-year fight against Adirondack dams in 1956, but their celebrations were brief. Congress passed the Federal Aid Highway Act that year, which authorized the use of federal funds for the construction of forty-one thousand miles of interstate highways. Governor Averill Harriman announced that he wanted that money to pay for an interstate highway that would connect Albany to the Canadian border. In 1957, work began in Albany.

Everyone, even the most radical wilderness advocates, assumed that some kind of road was going to happen. In 1958, with the support of gubernatorial candidate Nelson Rockefeller, the Albany-Canada connector was included in the national highway system. This meant that Washington would pay 90 percent of its $208 million price tag. Arthur Benson, the owner of the Wild West–themed amusement park on Route 9 named Frontier Town, suggested naming the route "The Adirondack Northway." Rockefeller liked the name and added that, if elected, he would ensure that the road opened in time for the 1967 World's Fair in Montreal. Public support for the project was overwhelming. So the question was not whether a road would be built, but where.

The activists had one card to play. If the route of the Northway cut through any part of the forest preserve, it would require an amendment to the state constitution. To make that happen, the state legislature would need to pass a resolution two years in a row before submitting the question to a statewide public referendum. That gave the activists two years to lobby and organize before a route through the forest preserve could be approved.

The New York State Department of Public Works (DPW) mapped out five options for the route. One of them swung east from Glens Falls and passed through Fort Ann, Whitehall, and Ticonderoga, completely bypassing the forest preserve while hugging the west shore of Lake Champlain. This route was several miles longer than other alternatives, and it had several big elevation changes. The DPW's preliminary report labeled the Champlain route "X" and discarded it as "impractical."

The other four routes all stayed near Route 9 to Warrensburg, and they all followed the same route near Route 9 north of North Hudson. The differences between them lay in the thirty-seven-mile stretch that included the valley of the Schroon River. The DPW's preferred route followed the Schroon River closely and continued along the eastern shore of Schroon Lake. It cut through the Pharaoh Lake region of the forest preserve, one of twelve parcels the Pomeroy Commission had nominated as wilderness areas.

Paul Schaefer was chair of the State Conservation Council's Northway Committee. After meeting with officials from the State Department of Transportation and the State Conservation Department at the end of 1957, Schaefer wrote that the Conservation Council would accept a "practical" route if it kept the number of acres of forest preserve affected to an absolute minimum. He also told the officials that many of his activist friends had already decided that the easternmost Champlain route was the only acceptable choice.

In a January 14 letter to the president of the Conservation Council, Schaefer added that he had also visited both the Schroon and Champlain routes. He wrote that both of them had significant engineering challenges, and that it wasn't clear yet which route the governor would ultimately choose. Schaefer recommended that the council wait for more data before taking a stand. "Questions of this nature are potentially very explosive," he wrote.

In February, the DPW's chief engineer wrote to the commissioner with more information, reemphasizing the fact that the "Adirondack" route was superior to the Champlain route. The route through the forest preserve had fewer curves, fewer steep grades, and required fewer bridges and overpasses, he said. He described its impact on the preserve as minimal, and he estimated that it would cost $33 million less than the Champlain route.

The DPW's arguments didn't make any difference to the Schenectady Mafia, however. They were already committed. Over the next year, an informal group calling themselves the Citizens' Northway Committee tried to discredit the DPW while promoting the benefits of the Champlain route. Yet Schaefer did not join their crusade. He had a close relationship with Conservation Commissioner Sharon Mahus and other officials, and they had convinced him that an Adirondack route was inevitable.

Schaefer privately lobbied state officials to change the route so it would follow the west bank of Schroon Lake, thereby avoiding the Pharaoh Lake area. That worked. In March 1959, Rockefeller chose the route that followed the Schroon River but went up the west side of the lake. The Pharaoh Lake Wilderness was spared, and the route also skirted the eastern edge of the Hoffman Notch and Dix Mountain Wilderness Areas. Rockefeller's choice disturbed slightly less than three hundred acres of forest preserve in scattered parcels over the 180 miles between Albany and the Canadian border. Several of those parcels were small and surrounded by private land. The others were undistinguished. The legislature passed its resolution for the second time, sending the question on to voters in November as Resolution 2.

The Citizens' Northway Committee members and their allies went to the battlements, doing their best to organize statewide to defeat Resolution 2 and protect the absolute sanctity of the forest preserve. But Paul Schaefer belonged to dozens of organizations, and many of them supported the Adirondack route. He remained silent.

The strategic use of media and advertising to sway public opinion on political issues was a relatively new field in 1950. It leapt forward when activists for wilderness preservation began using it. Early that year, Howard Zahniser and others learned about a new phase in the Federal Bureau of Reclamation's Colorado River Storage Project. The bureau was proposing several new dams, including one in Echo Park, Colorado, that would flood the canyons of the Green and Yampa Rivers in Dinosaur National Monument.

In July 1950, the popular writer Bernard DeVoto published a widely reprinted article in the *Saturday Evening Post* under the headline "Shall We Let Them Ruin Our National Parks?" Other editors piled on, which encouraged legislators and federal officials who had private misgivings about the plan to make their concerns public.

The most effective publicist in the antidam coalition was David Brower, who had been an editor at the University of California Press before becoming the first paid executive director of the Sierra Club in 1952. Brower orchestrated a campaign that included well-publicized float trips on the Green River, congressional testimony that was linked to advertising and direct mail, and a lavishly illustrated book with essays edited by the novelist Wallace Stegner that was published just as the campaign peaked, with a copy given to each member of Congress. With public opinion strongly against the plan, the secretary of the interior withdrew the department's support for the Echo Park Dam in 1955.

The Sierra Club had previously restricted its focus to outings and environmental issues in California. It was emboldened by the success of the Echo Park campaign. Its national membership hit ten thousand in 1956 and kept growing, with new members signing up across the country. It was becoming a national force. Under Brower's leadership, the club was also gaining a national reputation for its uncompromising pro-wilderness stance. It wanted as many members as possible, as fast as possible, and after Echo Park, it knew how to make that happen.

In 1957, the Atlantic Chapter of the Sierra Club included all the territory in the United States east of the Mississippi River. The chapter had fewer than a hundred members, many of whom held jobs in media, advertising, and law in New York City. The chapter's informal leader and newsletter editor was Stewart Ogilvy, an editor at *Fortune* magazine.

The impending Northway referendum gave the Sierra Club a cause that was within driving distance of the great cities of the East Coast. Ogilvy built the chapter's membership while lobbying against Resolution 2 by combining the club's traditional emphasis on outings with activism.

In summer 1959, Ogilvy and other club members organized hikes that went along the proposed route of the Northway, covering the 160 miles from Albany to Plattsburgh. "During these hikes, someone would be delegated to talk to the group about a conservation problem during the lunch stop," said Ogilvy. "Very often, after such a talk, as we resumed the hike, someone would come over and say, 'That sounded pretty interesting. Is there anything I can do about it?' And pretty soon they would be chairman of a committee."

David Sive, a young Rockland County lawyer, and his wife Mary went on an Ogilvy-led tour to a spot near Elizabethtown. "That was my introduction to environmental politics," Sive said.

Sive was born in 1922 and raised in Brooklyn, the son of a traveling salesman. "When I was a kid, I defined the wilderness as whatever happened after the sidewalk ended," he said. Sive's hiking days were over by 2003, but his memory remained sharp, and he grew lively as he remembered the beginning of his love affair with the Great Wide Open. He said that he was inspired by reading about the polar expeditions of the 1920s and 30s. The exploits of Admiral Byrd fueled youthful dreams about traveling in wild, frozen lands. "I became passionately interested in snow," he said. "I wanted to become a meteorologist, and whenever it snowed in Brooklyn, I always wanted it to be deeper. I suppose I liked it because snow makes everything in the city white and clean looking, like the country."

Sive attended James Madison High School, a few blocks away from the expansive estuaries of Jamaica Bay. He discovered nineteenth-century nature poetry and memorized works by a fellow Brooklynite, Walt Whitman, as well as by Samuel Coleridge and William Wordsworth. In 2003, he paused to recite a favorite poem from memory. Wordsworth wrote "Suggested by the Proposed Kendal and Windermere Railway" (1844) as a protest against a proposal to extend a rail line through England's Lake District, and enclosed the poem in a letter to the British prime minister.

> And is *no* nook of English ground secure
> From rash assault? Schemes of retirement sown
> In youth, and 'mid the busy world kept pure
> As when their earliest flowers of hope were blown,
> Must perish;—how can they this blight endure?
> And must he too his old delights disown
> Who scorns a false utilitarian lure
> 'Mid his paternal fields, at random thrown?
> Baffle the threat, bright Scene, from Orrest head
> Given to the pausing traveller's rapturous glance;
> Plead for thy peace thou beautiful romance
> Of nature; and, if human hearts be dead,
> Speak, passing winds; ye torrents, with your strong
> And constant voice, protest against the wrong!

After returning from their weekend in Elizabethtown, the Sives joined the Sierra Club and immediately began working with the Citizens' Northway Committee. Within a few years, David Sive was chair of the Atlantic Chapter.

In 1959, the battle over the Northway moved toward its climax at the polls. The Citizens' Northway Committee's position that the road should not touch the forest preserve was endorsed by at least thirty state and local organizations, including the Sierra Club, the Adirondack Mountain Club, the Izaak Walton League, and a new group called The Nature Conservancy.

The New York State Conservation Council represents the interests of hunters and anglers. The AfPA (which merged with another organization and changed its name to "Protect the Adirondacks!" in 2009) represents the interests of people who own houses in the park, especially vacation camps. By 1959, both groups had earned seats at the tables where state conservation policy decisions were made, and both used Paul Schaefer as their representative. Neither group took a public position as the Northway fight heated up, and neither did Schaefer. They saw the Northway fight as a distraction from more important issues, such as the continuing pressure to impose zoning on the forest preserve that would allow tree cutting and construction.

In January 1958, Father Peter Ward, a Catholic priest in Malone who was active in the Conservation Council, wrote to Schaefer. "I have written long lectures tonight to Art Newkirk and John Jamison (chairman of the ADK Conservation Committee, you must know him) in which I try to caution them not to fight losing battles, but to save their energies for the big battles. Jamison in particular, who is the main instigator of the ADK going on record, has completely made up his mind and is convincing himself with more and more fallacious arguments that he is absolutely right."

On July 1, 1959, the state superintendent of the Department of Public Works made a direct appeal to voters to support Resolution 2, proposing the Adirondack route for the Northway. That same day, several prominent conservationists bought a full-page ad in the *New York Times* to endorse Resolution 2. The signers included Horace Albright, former director of the National Park Service and a consultant to the Rockefeller Brothers Fund; Karl Frederick and Fred Smith, board members of the Conservation Council; publisher Alfred A. Knopf; and AfPA trustees Fairfield Osborn and Lithgow Osborne (no relation).

A schism between environmentalists deepened as the vote approached. On October 19, ADK member Eleanor Roosevelt endorsed the "No on 2" position in her nationally syndicated newspaper column, "My Day." And on October 26, the editorial board of the *New York Times* endorsed a "no" vote to prevent "nibbling away at the Forest Preserve."

Some who opposed the Schroon route also voiced an objection to interstate highways in general. "The tyranny of the gasoline motor, mustering its full horsepower, has launched a revolution of road-building," wrote Robert and Leona Rienow in the national magazine *Harper's*. "The gasoline motor is making America a fit place for wheels to roll around in. Whether America will also be a satisfying place for human beings to live in, seems neither here nor there."

The Rienows, who were active in The Nature Conservancy, wrote that the Northway wasn't just a road. "We are opening a land rush," they said. The three hundred acres of forest preserve sacrificed by Resolution 2 "are only the ante. After the draw, the table stakes are going to be high." They opposed the amendment because it was not attached to a plan that would preserve the Adirondacks from overdevelopment. State highway officials don't care about "the social impact of their roads," they concluded. "Only a wide-awake, crusading, and determined public can bring them to heel."

Rhetoric like that might seem prescient now, but in 1959, it did not do much to persuade millions of middle-class Americans who depended on their cars. To them, it might have sounded like the complaint of someone who already had a place in the country and wanted to keep things quiet. Critics said that the real reason for the "No on 2" movement was that the privileged few who already owned retreats in the country didn't want the roads to get better. They wanted to keep the masses away.

Resolution 2 passed with 56 percent of the vote in 1959. John Apperson, who died four years later, never spoke to his old friend Paul Schaefer again. Still, the hard-liners found reasons for optimism when they analyzed the 4.81 million ballots that had been cast. The biggest number of voters (40 percent) had left the line blank on Resolution 2. One-third (1.62 million) had voted for the Schroon route. That meant that about one-quarter of all state voters (1.26 million) had sided with them, refusing to give up a single acre of forest preserve. And the "no" votes in New York City had outperformed the state average.

In their postmortem, the Citizens' Northway Committee's leaders concluded that the main reason they lost was because they did not have a strong statewide presence. They had won decisively in Schenectady County and had come close to winning in Rochester (Monroe County), where they had many active members. Their recommendation was to work harder. Within a year, the group had renamed itself the Citizens' Forest Preserve Council and had found a new cause: stopping ski trails from being cut on Hunter Mountain, in the Catskill Forest Preserve.

Paul Schaefer usually drove an old pickup truck that had bald tires and bad brakes. The trip from his home in Niskayuna to his cabin in Bakers Mills was seventy-five or eighty miles, depending on the route he took. When the weather was wet or icy, the Northway was safer and faster. The section that bypassed Glens Falls opened in 1961, removing a major bottleneck for him.

Fellow camp owners who lived in Plattsburgh got their reward when the thirty-eight-mile stretch between the Canadian border and Keeseville opened in 1963. So Schaefer probably did not spend much time mourning the three hundred acres of forest preserve that had been lost to the new road. He had his sights set on a much larger goal.

During the campaign against Echo Park Dam, Howard Zahniser had met several members of Congress who supported a national system of wilderness areas. Zahniser drafted a bill, and on June 7, 1956, Congressman John Saylor and Senator Hubert Humphrey introduced the Wilderness Act. In his original draft, Zahniser defined a wilderness as "an area where the earth and its community of life are untrammeled by man, where man is a visitor who does not remain." He fought to retain the unusual word "untrammeled," rather than "undisturbed," because he wanted wilderness areas to include places like the Adirondacks, where much of the land had been cut, grazed, or mined, but would return to a natural state if left undisturbed.

Zahniser revised the Wilderness Act more than five dozen times over the next eight years. He overcame many obstacles, including the opposition of National Park Superintendent Conrad "Connie" Wirth. But his side kept inching the bill closer to passage. By 1964, it looked like the act might finally go through.

The problem was that Zahniser's heart was giving out. He had survived a serious heart attack in 1951, at the age of forty-five, and ever since then he had struggled in a weakened condition. At the end of April 1964, after testifying for the nineteenth time in favor of the Wilderness Act, he wrote to Paul Schaefer that he had "survived the questioning but was soaked and breathless." He said that he looked forward to seeing Schaefer again at their Adirondack cabins "in lilac time," but added that "the prospects for a post-Wilderness Bill controversy period of book writing doesn't seem too good."

A few days after he sent that letter, Zahniser died in his sleep. Four months after his death, President Lyndon Johnson signed the Wilderness Act into law, creating a national system of nine million acres. By 2019, the National Wilderness System had expanded to more than 111 million acres, or 4.5 percent of the land area of the United States.

The campaign for the Wilderness Act was a boon to environmental organizations like the Sierra Club, whose national membership increased from sixteen thousand in 1960 to thirty-three thousand in 1965. But the club's breakout moment happened because of another dam. In summer 1966, the club mobilized to stop a congressional proposal to build two dams in the Grand Canyon. As part of their campaign, they bought full-page newspaper ads designed by San Francisco advertising executive Jerry Mander. One of these, in the August 23, 1966, *Wall Street Journal*, responded to claims that the two gigantic concrete plugs would make the canyon's scenic wonders more accessible to boaters. The ad's headline famously replied, "Should we also flood the Sistine Chapel so tourists can get nearer the ceiling?"

The ad created a huge stir. The dams were ultimately removed from the Basin Project bill for multiple reasons, including the Sierra Club's campaign. And the battle secured the club's national reputation as a go-for-broke fighter for wilderness. Its membership more than tripled between 1965 and 1970, to reach 114,000.

Summer 1967 was when it all came together. New York's coalition of environmental groups had become a powerful, well-coordinated political force. John Apperson was dead, but most of the original activists of the 1940s and 1950s were still engaged in politics. The rifts caused by the Northway battle were papered over as the general public's concern about air pollution, water pollution, solid waste, and suburban sprawl grew ever more acute. It was time to focus on a new threat to the Adirondacks.

The threat came in the form of a state constitutional convention that opened on April 4, 1967. A convention bypasses the rule that makes changing the state constitution a difficult, multiyear process. Convention delegates can propose changes to the state constitution and if those proposals pass in September, they will go directly to voters in November. Although no one suggested that the Forever Wild clause should be repealed, it could happen quickly if convention delegates decided to recommend it.

The New York State Assembly voted to call a constitutional convention in fall 1966. "The same evening that vote was held, David Newhouse and several other environmental leaders and I got on the phone, like minutemen rallying the troops," said David Sive. They organized the Constitutional Council for the Forest Preserve to guide the convention at each stage of the process, beginning with the selection of delegates.

"I suggested that we contact every person who might be seeking nomination by either party," Sive said. "I developed a postcard which we mailed to about eight hundred people. The postcard had just a simple legend on the back, with two boxes, and we asked them to check one: 'I will, or will not, protect the Forest Preserve.' Most of the people who replied checked the box that said, 'I will.'"

Sive got himself appointed to the staff of the convention's Committee on Natural Resources and Agriculture. "I then spent the summer of 1967 mainly in Albany, educating delegates about the forest preserve, particularly the Democrats who were mainly from New York City and did not know much about the Adirondacks."

After the convention convened, Sive and his allies—who were labeled "forever wilders" and "extreme conservationists" by their opponents—focused on stopping an amendment that had been proposed by Charles Froessel, a delegate who was also a well-regarded retired judge. Froessel pointed out that state campgrounds in the forest preserve existed in legal limbo. The campgrounds had been built in the 1930s, when enforcement rules were looser. They were within the forest preserve and therefore should be subject to the Forever Wild clause, but they had electric lights, flush toilets, and other amenities that clearly violated the constitution. Froessel, who cared more for the law than for the campgrounds, wanted to clear things up by inserting language that legalized their status.

The constitutional council opposed Froessel's amendment because its wording might allow additional construction in the forest preserve. Sive found an ally in Dollie Robinson, a Black delegate from Brooklyn who was a graduate of New York University's Law School and a representative of labor unions. Robinson took the floor on July 31 and read the following words:

I speak for myself and some who have not yet heard a loon, or seen the morning mist rise from Spruce Lake, or intimately known the forest that has escaped from highways, smog and overpowering noise. Perhaps some of us in many corners of this state and of many different heritages are still overwhelmed by the struggle to leave some rural or urban ghetto, and we have not yet had the time to feel as personally and as deeply as those of you who have picked the blueberries atop Mount Colden, which has so enriched your lives.

For those people who because of accidents of history have not yet achieved the measure of security which they perhaps need before they can know the rarest beauties of the Forest Preserve, for them especially and their children, I urge you to protect it, for I am confident that it will not be long—and other determinations of this Convention hopefully may speed the day—when we succeed in applying a small fraction of the genius we apply to flying to the moon to so ordering our economy and body politic that everyone will share some part of our affluence. When that day does come, and those not yet so fortunate are able to pick those blueberries, I beseech you to please, please see that they are not behind a fence, across a thronged road, or leased out. I urge you to defeat the amendment of Judge Froessel."

Robinson sat down to thunderous applause. Her speech had rebutted the charge that the Forever Wild clause benefitted only the wealthy. She had linked the preservation of wilderness to the interests of low-income and Black voters, and she had done it with eloquence. It didn't matter that David Sive had written the words she read, or that the convention ultimately decided to send Froessel's amendment on to voters anyway. An alliance had been forged.

Fortunately for Robinson, Sive, and their colleagues, voters rejected the entire package of constitutional reforms in November. But the activists did not know what the voters' verdict would be on August 31, 1967, at 5 p.m., when a state road crew rolled away the barriers blocking the thirty-mile stretch of Northway connecting Underwood to Keeseville. The highway opened on time and under budget. For the next two months, New Yorkers could zip all the way to Montreal in their V-8 Thunderbirds, rickety old Ramblers, and New Yorker station wagons. They could take in the scenery without the distraction of traffic lights on their way to Montreal's Expo 67, a global celebration of technological progress. In a poetic coincidence, Noah Rondeau died one week before the last section of the Northway opened.

The number of New Yorkers who were keenly focused on "saving" the Adirondacks had grown exponentially. So had the number of visitors. But the state of the public lands of the forest preserve was no longer the environmentalists' only concern.

There were virtually no restrictions on how millions of acres of privately owned land in the park could be developed. If developers built homes and resorts to serve an onslaught of tourists, the landscape Verplanck Colvin wrote about—the "vast appearance of primeval forest stretched over range on range to the far horizon"—would be gone forever.

The leaders of the young environmental movement agreed that it was time to adopt bold plans for the entire Adirondack Park. And that summer, someone did step forward with a plan. He released it one month before the Northway was completed. He had a track record of accomplishments and virtually unlimited funds, and he was the governor's best friend. There was only one problem. He was a Rockefeller.

Chapter 4

# Brotherly Love

Peter S. Paine Jr. got into an argument with Laurance S. Rockefeller in 1967. Laurance, the younger brother and closest friend of New York State Governor Nelson Rockefeller, was visiting Paine's father, a Princeton classmate. But as the three men strolled through the Paine family's property in the Champlain Valley, hunting for grouse, the small talk turned a bit tense. Rockefeller, fifty-seven, was probably taken aback by the cheekiness of Paine Jr., thirty-one, although he was too much of a gentleman to show it. But Laurance remembered it, and that changed the younger Paine's life.

Paine had been criticizing a proposal Laurance Rockefeller had recently made to turn the core of the Adirondack State Park into a national park. It wasn't hard for either man to understand why so many local residents were against the proposal, because it could force thousands of them to give up their homes. But that, to Rockefeller, was a comparatively small cost. He was continuing a family tradition. His father, John D. Rockefeller Jr., had bought out or evicted families to create the Smoky Mountain and Grand Teton

National Parks. Laurance himself had pursued similar plans to create national parks in the Virgin Islands and California redwoods.

What surprised Laurance Rockefeller, according to Paine, was that many environmental activists were also opposed to the idea of an Adirondack National Park. Paine explained that the federal laws that protected wilderness areas were not as strict as the state's Forever Wild clause. Article 14 of New York's constitution was adopted in 1894, and over the next seventy years, camp owners and their lawyers enforced it so effectively that it became nearly impossible for a private citizen to legally cut down a tree inside the forest preserve.

Revoking the Forever Wild clause would be a very tall order, because changing New York's constitution requires the approval of two successive state legislatures followed by a statewide referendum. Paine pointed out that a national park could be abolished by one act of Congress. Even if that didn't happen, the people who decided which parts of the park would be developed, and how they would be developed, would be in Washington, DC, not Albany. But Laurance Rockefeller didn't care about the Forever Wild clause, according to Paine. In fact, he wanted it gone.

Gifford Pinchot wrote that publicly owned natural resources should be managed to provide "the greatest good for the greatest number for the longest time." He was talking about land and water. Laurance Rockefeller's great achievement was to extend that idea to people.

The Rockefeller family directed its giving toward several long-term goals, and one of them was improving public access to parks and open space. Laurance worked for this by creating statistical measures of recreation and its public benefits, then using those metrics to convince legislators to approve spending. In the 1950s and 1960s, improving public access meant building roads and visitor centers.

In Rockefeller's world, the highest and best use of a stunning mountaintop panorama might be realized by cutting a road to the top and putting a parking lot and a snack bar at the summit, so nonhikers could enjoy the view over a cup of tea. After all, Americans in the early 1960s were forty times more likely to say that they enjoyed pleasure driving over hiking. Rockefeller's surveys had proved it.

Peter Paine Jr. was born in 1935, and he spent his childhood summers in the Adirondacks. He loved to visit a place locals called Highbridge. "It's a series of falls on the north branch of the Boquet River, in the Dix Mountain Wilderness," he said.

Paine sat in a small conference room at the office of Champlain National Bank in Willsboro, which was founded by his grandfather and remains in family ownership. He wasn't wearing a suit, though you might expect that attire for a banker; he was lively, almost fidgety, and dressed for the woods in a fleece vest, baseball cap, and boots. "The river narrows down into a cut that's about three feet wide, and then plunges into a marvelous pool that you can't touch the bottom of. I used to go up there when I was a kid," he said, and his blue eyes lit up at the memory. "There was never anybody in sight."

The Paines had been wealthy for several generations. They operated a pulp mill near Willsboro, a hamlet in the Champlain Valley. Their farm and property includes almost three miles of Lake Champlain shore, the last two miles of the Boquet River before it empties into the lake, and one thousand acres purchased by Peter Paine Jr.'s grandfather. Paine did not pay much attention to the Adirondacks or the family property in his twenties. He had been working for a Wall Street law firm in London. Yet tiny Willsboro was his family's homeplace. "I was just off the plane in 1967," he said. "I had just gotten back. I thought the Adirondack problems were interesting."

Both Paine Jr. and Laurance Rockefeller considered themselves environmentalists. But neither man belonged to the Association for the Protection of the Adirondacks. Peter Paine Sr. was Willsboro's town father, and in 1967, the Champlain Valley was outside the Blue Line. As soon as he returned from Europe, Paine Jr. became counsel to the Lake Champlain Committee. He was teaming up with his neighbors to fight a proposal to build a large nuclear power plant across the lake from their land. Yet he found it easy to identify with Robert Marshall, Paul Schaefer, Arthur Crocker, Howard Zahniser, and other founders of the international wilderness movement. All of them shared a love for the remote parts of New York's North Country.

None of these men were famous in those days, either. "Ecology was thought to be for eccentrics," wrote Henry Diamond, Laurance Rockefeller's chief advisor for environmental issues. "Conservation was an afterthought on political platforms, slightly ahead of Esperanto and a single tax." But in 1967, Laurance had already been a champion of parks and conservation for more than a decade. And when he spoke, his beloved big brother, Nelson, listened.

Thanks to Laurance Rockefeller, Peter Paine Jr. would end up devoting a large part of his career to protecting the Adirondacks. As his public profile grew, Peter Paine Sr., the paper mill magnate, would sometimes get phone calls meant for his son. The older man would say, "Sorry, you've reached Paine the polluter. You want Paine the environmentalist!"

Nelson Rockefeller, heir to a vast fortune and governor of New York from 1959 to 1973, loved to hire talented people and watch them attack complex problems by making big, bold plans. "If somebody said 'two words to label Nelson Rockefeller as a politician,' I would use 'task force,'" said R. W. Apple of the *New York Times*. "He loved task forces."

Rockefeller also wanted more than anything to be president of the United States, and he knew that voters all over the country would be energized by government programs that had lofty, long-term goals. It might be hard for twenty-first-century readers to believe, but in the early 1960s, most Americans trusted their political leaders. According to a long-running survey, more than 70 percent of Americans in 1960 said the federal government would do what is right "just about always" or "most of the time." The public's trust started heading down in the late 1960s, and it fell off a cliff in 1973. Since 2010, the number has consistently been below 20 percent.

In 1960, two-thirds of the population of New York State lived in the boroughs and suburbs of New York City. These voters were complaining loudly to their governor about air and water pollution, overcrowding, run-down parks, and overflowing garbage dumps. The groundswell of urban concern gave Rockefeller several opportunities to do things that raised his national profile. In 1960 and 1962, he introduced and passed bonds that financed the expansion and renovation of state parks. At least a dozen other governors followed his lead. Funding parks was a safe strategy in New York. Al Smith, who served as governor in the 1920s, burnished his image by launching the career of Robert Moses, the legendary park builder and power broker. Smith crafted his own presidential bid in 1928 by building a reputation as the champion of the common man. Parks were commonly referred to as "the lungs of the city," and funding them was a visible manifestation of Smith's commitment to the welfare of working people.

In 1964, with concern over pollution growing, Rockefeller moved beyond parks. The governor was spending a lot of time in California early in 1963, during his second bid for the presidency. "While he was out there, it became apparent to him that everybody was talking about the water supply," said Richard Wiebe, who worked for Bill Ronan, one of Nelson Rockefeller's closest advisors. "When he came back he was noodling about and he said, 'Okay, what am I going to do now? Water was such a big deal out there. Why don't we have a water program in New York?' And it was probably Ronan who said, 'Well, we don't really have a water supply problem. We have a dirty water problem.'"

Ronan assigned Wiebe and an associate, Ed Van Ness, to study water pollution and recommend ways to clean it up. "We turned in a five-pager that said, yeah, sewage in the water is a real son of a bitch, and we will need about three months to estimate the cost of building local plants statewide," Wiebe said. "We didn't hear another word about it until around Thanksgiving, at which time Ronan called me and asked us to deliver something in time for the governor's annual message in early January. We pulled together a proposal for a billion-dollar bond issue in five weeks."

Nelson Rockefeller's pitch to voters is preserved in a film called *Little Drops of Water* that intercuts alarming images of drought-depleted reservoirs and filthy creeks with statements from various state officials, including Rockefeller, about what needs to be done. The film holds up fairly well until the fourteen-minute mark, when Oliver Townsend, chairman of the New York State Atomic and Space Development Authority, appears on a Long Island beach, wearing a trench coat, a dark brimmed hat, and black horn-rimmed glasses. Townsend solemnly unveils a scale model of a nuclear-powered desalinization plant and says that it will produce one million gallons of fresh water a day, along with 2,500 kilowatts of electricity. Townsend also told a reporter from the *New York Times* that the state planned to recoup the plant's high cost by selling its radioactive byproducts, such as plutonium.

The Pure Waters Bond Initiative passed by a wide margin. "I think it proved to a lot of people around the country that there are votes in the environment," Wiebe said.

Rockefeller's bond acts were major steps forward for the environmental movement. They paved the way for federal legislation like the Land and Water Conservation Fund (passed in 1965), the Clean Air Act of 1970, and the Clean Water Act of 1972. But Rockefeller loved to pour concrete at least as much as he loved nature. He also pushed grand-scale plans that would be terrible for the environment, like building an expressway bridge across Long Island Sound or making plutonium a few miles away from a public beach. And when the nuclear desalinization plant never got past the drawing board, Rockefeller probably didn't care. Home-run hitters strike out a lot. What matters is the next at-bat.

Rockefeller paid Henry Diamond, Richard Wiebe, and other top advisors very high salaries, supplementing their state paychecks with money from his own pocket, because his main selling point as a presidential candidate was being the smartest governor in the country. He wanted his proposals to meet the standards of late-1960s business management gurus like Peter Drucker and W. Edwards Deming. A Rockefeller commission began by acquiring reliable data from diverse sources and using statistical science to analyze them. Its staff combed through the literature and asked experts to define the best practices.

In the early 1970s, Wiebe was director of the State Office of Planning Services (OPS). Richard Booth, a lawyer fresh out of school, walked past Wiebe's car on his way to a meeting at the OPS office. "The back window was filled with books on government organization and politics," Booth said. "I had been a political science major, so I found that interesting.

"Once the meeting started, I quickly realized that this guy Wiebe could outthink any lawyer I had ever met. He had the New York State statutes behind his desk. He would grab a book and immediately find a law and quote from it. Apparently, he had memorized them.

"During a break, I told him that I had noticed all those books in his back seat, and that I shared his interest in management and organization. He said, 'Well, you know, the Office of Planning Services is not my real job. My real job is being a senior advisor to Nelson Rockefeller. He assigns certain areas to each of us and we are expected to read everything that comes out in that area, summarize it, and report back to him.'" Rockefeller was preparing to be president of the United States. Management, organization, and bureaucratic lines of authority were some of the fields Wiebe scanned for him.

Peter Drucker was an admirer of economist Joseph Schumpeter, who wrote in the 1940s that capitalism depended on a "gale of creative destruction" that is "incessantly destroying the old" while "incessantly creating anew." The problem, of course, is that discarding obsolete practices is not popular with those whose jobs depend on them. But in early 1969, the Adirondack Park was still a few years away from that day of reckoning.

In 1961, Nelson Rockefeller started another task force. He ordered the Office for Regional Development (ORD) to sketch out a long-term development plan for the entire state, and in 1963, he found a talented young idealist to run it.

Harold Jerry was a Princeton- and Harvard-educated lawyer from Platts-burgh who had just been defeated after serving a single term as Elmira's state senator. It had taken Jerry three tries to get elected, and when he finally made it, he found the district a bad fit. Jerry was Roman Catholic, and the Ku Klux Klan remained active in the rural parts of his district. He was also extremely bright, and his sharp wit and impatience often did not serve him well on the campaign trail. "He had a very difficult time dealing with aver-age people," said Howard Kimball, a friend and former Elmira mayor who worked on Jerry's campaign. "He was wonderful when it came to dealing with bankers or businessmen."

How was he when it came to kissing voters' babies? "No," said Kimball. "No. No."

Jerry was tenacious, detail oriented, and committed to the spirit as well as the letter of the law. His reelection campaign failed after the Republican electoral machine in his district turned against him. But it wasn't much of a loss, because Jerry didn't really want to live in Elmira. Leading a task force was a much better match for his talents and taking a nine-to-five job in Al-bany meant that the Jerry family could spend every weekend in the Adiron-dack backcountry.

In 1961, Jerry and his wife Lyn cashed in their savings to buy 1,500 acres north of the Adirondack village of Speculator. Dug Mountain Camp sits on the western edge of the vast, pristine Siamese Ponds region and is 4.5 miles from the nearest public road. The Jerrys fixed up a turn-of-the-century cabin and outbuildings there while raising four children. The buildings didn't have electricity or running water, which they thought was perfect. "Our families thought we were insane," said Lyn, "but we couldn't pass it up."

The ORD was one of Nelson Rockefeller's attempts to get local planners and elected officials to think big. *Really* big. Its report, released in June 1964, tries to chart the state's course all the way to 2024. Here is an excerpt: "Nu-clear bombs and nuclear power plants, giant computers, automated manu-facturing processes, aircraft flying faster than sound, space exploration and satellite broadcasting, the collection of data from other planets, and prepa-rations to send man to the moon—all of these extensions of man's capabili-ties have come in the last twenty years. It cannot be doubted that in the decades ahead even these accomplishments will be surpassed. As the most productive state in the world's most productive nation, New York must keep pace with these complicated developments."

"It had been written by consultants, and it was a mess," said Wiebe, who supervised the effort. "But Harold Jerry was very bright and acerbic. I liked him a lot."

Much of the report's text was organized around a single data point that was ringing alarm bells in think tanks all over the world in 1964. The earth's population had doubled between 1925 and 1960 to reach three billion, and demographers were predicting that it would double again by 2000. The world's leaders were trying to figure out how to feed, house, and educate all those new people without gobbling up every scrap of arable land and fresh water. It's telling that Nelson Rockefeller and many others were convinced they could figure out a way to do it. They disagreed with Thomas Malthus and his disciple, Fairfield Osborn Jr. They believed that with human ingenuity, good planning, and coordination, they could accomplish almost anything.

The report, titled *Change, Challenge, Response*, is beautifully designed. It inspires confidence through 154 color pages of tables, charts, and jet-age illustrations. It carves the state into ten regions and asks local officials to submit annual reports to the governor on their short-term and long-term needs. It asks localities to standardize zoning laws according to guidelines issued by the governor. In the press conference announcing the plan, Rockefeller promised that he would bestow grants and prestige on those who toed the line.

But there are roughly 1,600 local governments in New York State, and their officials have a strong commitment to the tradition of "home rule." Article IX of the state constitution says that localities have "rights, powers, privileges and immunities" that state power can't touch. Conservative local legislators couldn't bear the idea of Albany bureaucrats telling them how to write their zoning laws, even if they didn't know much about zoning. Rockefeller toured the state to support the report and its recommendations, but he needed local officials to buy in, and very few of them did. The whole thing fell flat.

In 1966, a powerful state senator from Long Island insisted that Rockefeller fire Harold Jerry. The senator saw the ORD as a threat to local autonomy, and, more than that, Jerry probably had said something snotty to him. Lyn Jerry tells what happened next. "Rockefeller calls Jerry and says, 'Pick me up at the airport.' On the way home he says, 'Harold, I'm sorry. I've got to let you go, but I'll take care of you.' And he did." The governor gave Jerry a planning job in the Conservation Department, which meant that he could spend even more time outdoors. "It was a nice place to be," Harold Jerry said.

During his long career in politics, Nelson Rockefeller successfully hid the fact that he was dyslexic. By all accounts his intelligence and memory were extraordinary, but for his entire life he found it difficult to read and write. So as governor, he depended to an unusual degree on the advice of people he trusted. And by the time the ORD episode was over, he trusted Harold Jerry.

Rockefeller's Republican Party controlled both houses of the state legislature for most of his time as Governor. His successor, Hugh Carey, described Rockefeller's power by saying, "He owned one party and leased the other." And Rockefeller's immense wealth gave him even more power. The Rockefeller Brothers Fund operated a private think tank that developed the governor's ideas and released them in slick, well-researched packages. Legislators didn't have similar resources, so their opposing arguments often didn't come off as well. Rockefeller's political contributions also made it nearly impossible for the Republican Party's county chairmen to oppose him. And if the legislature refused to give him something he wanted, he could often buy it.

Rockefeller even orchestrated the retirement of New York's legendary power broker, Robert Moses, from the State Council of Parks in 1966. He gave the parks chairman job to its vice chairman, his younger brother Laurance. It was nepotism, pure and simple, but no one challenged the decision. If anything, Laurance was overqualified for the job.

Laurance was more like their father, John D. Rockefeller Jr. He was ambitious but shy, and he preferred to stay out of public view. He was one of the first "venture capital" investors, effecting change by making strategic early investments that were informed by research, and joining with investment partners who created networks of innovation and energy. He quietly multiplied his millions by putting them into promising start-up businesses like Eastern Airlines (in the 1940s) and Apple Computer (in the 1970s). He used similar means to advance the causes of parks, conservation, and medical research. Successful venture capitalists can afford to fail, and they can also afford to wait.

Although Laurance's personality was much more reserved than his older brother's, they had always been best friends, and they loved nothing more than scheming together. As boys, Nelson and Laurance pulled endless pranks on their caretakers and siblings. Nelson's nickname for Laurance was "Bill," borrowed from a Western novel, and he called him that for the rest of his life. Laurance also called Nelson "Bill" for a while, although that didn't stick.

Nelson was the governor. But every week of their adult lives, when it was time for their haircuts, Nelson and Laurance tried to align their schedules so they could go to a private barber together.

In 1924, Laurance (age fourteen), Nelson (age sixteen), and their older brother, John D. III (age eighteen), went with their father on a tour of Western states. They didn't jump in the car like a regular family. They chartered a private train and followed a social schedule, and they were met at each stop like visiting heads of state. The family's host for much of the trip was Horace Albright, a National Park Service administrator who hoped the Rockefellers would use their fortune to buy privately owned land near Jackson Hole, Wyoming, and turn it over to the government. The Rockefellers had already played a major role in buying and developing Acadia National Park in Maine. Albright wanted them to do it again, to save the stunning scenery and wide-open spaces just south of Yellowstone National Park.

It worked. Albright arranged for father and sons to go to Jackson Lake, which has a spectacular view of Grand Teton and Mount Moran. He made an initial pitch there and followed up in several other carefully chosen spots. Two years later, when John D. Jr. took his two younger sons, Winthrop and David, on a similar trip, Laurance asked to go along.

Laurance never forgot those trips, and in the following decades he relied on Albright as a mentor. The Rockefellers began buying land in Jackson Hole in 1926. Grand Teton National Park was created in 1929 and the Rockefellers continued to work with the Park Service through the 1930s, despite protests from local landowners who opposed a government takeover. And Laurance could always call on Albright, who became a consultant to the Rockefellers after he retired from the Park Service in 1933.

When he was thirty, Laurance became chairman of the family corporation that acquired land near Jackson Hole. He signed their last holdings over to the national park a decade later. By that time, the family had also purchased hundreds of houses and farms in North Carolina and Tennessee to create Great Smoky Mountain National Park. That was a long, difficult process, because many families in the Smokies did not want to move, no matter the price offered. Dealing with them, and other opponents, became part of the family's conservation playbook.

In 1955, a Rockefeller-owned company opened three hotels inside Jackson Hole National Park, with an agreement that the hotels would donate any profits to the park. The family's critics portrayed it as a sweetheart deal. Some of them cited the collaboration between the Rockefellers and the Park Service as evidence for a broad conspiracy that also extended into the State Department and other branches of government. But the family ignored the critics, the National Park Service officials were happy to receive the gifts, and the relationship deepened.

Laurance liked to make parks. He and his wife Mary landed their sailboat at Caneel Bay on the island of Saint John, a US-owned territory in the Caribbean Sea, in 1952. They were impressed by the largely untouched tropical forests and reefs they found there. Sensing opportunity, Laurance began buying up land on the island and, in 1956, he gave 4,600 acres to the government as the initial grant for Virgin Islands National Park. The park was officially dedicated on December 1, which was also opening day for a Rockefeller-owned luxury resort on Caneel Bay. That hotel, along with the hotels at Jackson Hole and several others, was managed under the corporate name Rockresorts. The hotel chain helped create an industry that was later branded "luxury ecotourism."

Ecotourism companies ease the hardships of backcountry travel for their customers by turning outings into catered adventures. On October 10, 1965, Laurance and Nelson tried it in the Adirondacks. They took a two-day horseback trip on a new Adirondack trail that went up Cold River to the dam at Duck Hole, one of the most remote spots in the park. They were accompanied by a large group that included rangers, journalists, aides, and the conservation commissioner. The governor arrived and departed by helicopter.

The Rockefeller brothers' host was Bill Petty, who was trying to get them to fund more facilities for horseback riding in the Adirondack Forest Preserve. Petty had learned how to pamper downstate "sports" from his father. He arranged for elaborate meals served by white-clad waiters and lodging in a Conservation Department cabin at Duck Hole that had hot and cold running water and a working telephone. When the governor inspected the remnants of Noah Rondeau's shack he jokingly said, "I think we've got to rebuild this place."

Laurance Rockefeller was not a regular visitor to the Adirondacks. His father left him a camp on Upper Saranac Lake that was near his great-uncle's much more elaborate home, but he didn't go there very much, and in the early 1960s, he donated the compound to one of his father's favorite charities. "My father said that Laurance didn't particularly like to vacation in the Adirondacks," said Peter Paine. "It just wasn't his thing." Or maybe he didn't want to carry around all the baggage left behind by his great-uncle, William Avery Rockefeller II, whose name still made many locals snarl.

The Rockefeller brothers had big years in 1958. Nelson was elected governor for the first time and President Eisenhower appointed Laurance to head another big, bold task force. Post-war America was booming. Working families had more money and leisure time, and they were choosing to spend it in the great outdoors. Visits to national parks tripled between 1945 and 1950, and grew at an annual rate of 7 to 8 percent through the 1950s and 1960s.

The national parks had 26.6 million visitors in 1960, a six-fold increase over 1945's total. But the total acreage in the national park system had increased just 20 percent during that period. Families arrived at Yosemite and Yellowstone and were met with overcrowding, long lines, and litter. Citizen groups and congressmen were calling for action. Eisenhower responded by creating the Outdoor Recreation Resources Review Commission (ORRRC) and asking it to report to Congress on three big topics. He asked it to project the total demand for outdoor recreation for the years 1976 and 2000, to recommend resources that should be developed to meet the projected demand, and to suggest policies and programs that could lead the nation toward those goals.

The ORRRC was the brainchild of Joe Penfold, conservation director for the Izaak Walton League, a national group for hunters and anglers. Penfold was frustrated because the forestry and mining executives who testified before Congress could present ample facts and figures to argue for more timber cutting and mining. When Penfold testified, he didn't have numbers to mount a rebuttal. There weren't any data to show the demand for hiking, camping, horseback riding, public beaches, or days in the park. He knew that tourists were important to local economies in lots of places, but he didn't know where or how much. There was no national inventory of parks, and no survey of open spaces that would make good parks if they could be purchased with public funds. Generating the data that would answer all these questions, and many others, fell to the ORRRC and its chairman, Laurance Rockefeller.

Of course, Laurance was able to hire the best help. He turned to Henry Diamond, who was twenty-five and fresh out of law school in 1958. Diamond said he applied for a job at the ORRRC because he wanted to work in the White House, and he thought that joining the Rockefeller camp was his most likely stepping stone. "It was a very attractive thing to be a part of," he said. As it turned out, Diamond never got to work in the White House. But as he sat in his Washington, DC, office in 2003, impeccably dressed and surrounded by photos of himself shaking hands with every president since Lyndon Johnson except one, it seemed that he might have done even better.

Diamond came to Washington from Vanderbilt University Law School, and forty-five years later, he retained a soft Tennessee accent and a talent for sly jokes with punch lines that snuck up on you. He did not display the photograph of him shaking hands with Richard Nixon, for example.

Between 1958 and 1962, Diamond assigned, revised, and published a steady flow of material from the ORRRC's many contributors. Their report was massive, at twenty-seven volumes and 4,800 pages. Like *Change, Challenge, Response*, it is a period piece that reflects the era's faith in cooperation and statistics. Using economic forecasts, national surveys, and demographic projections, the report estimated that the number of national park visitors would increase 85 percent between 1960 and 1976. (In fact, the number tripled.) The survey results also proved beyond a doubt that millions of Americans in the early 1960s liked to walk, swim, and ride bicycles. But the most popular leisure activity, by far, was taking the family car out for a drive to look at scenery.

The report contained an amazing amount of detail. It had a national inventory of open space compiled from aerial photographs, a list of federal and state agencies that administered public land, and several new ideas that turned out to be enormously influential. "The idea of buying land for parks and open space with public money was not very well established in this country," Diamond said. A few big cities had purchased parkland before the 1960s, but states and the federal government had not. Their parks had been carved out of the public domain or were donations from wealthy families like the Rockefellers.

"One of the things we proposed to make the idea more palatable politically was to sell one national resource, such as offshore oil or surplus property, and put the proceeds into parks and open space," said Diamond. The idea became the Federal Land and Water Conservation Fund, which has made grants of nearly four billion dollars and has protected 2.4 million acres of land since it was established in 1965.

The report also described the use of easements for open space protection. Easements are an ancient legal device, and in the early 1960s they were mostly used to give nonowners the right to cross someone else's land. The report pointed out that nonprofit groups and public agencies could also use easements to buy development rights from landowners, thereby protecting the land in perpetuity as open space while keeping it in private hands.

A handful of conservation easements were in place in 1962, including one in the Adirondacks, but the ORRRC report put the idea before park planners around the country. In 2011, conservation easements protected nearly 30 million acres across the United States. New York's Department of Environmental Conservation protected an additional nine hundred thousand acres through easements in 2015, and about three-quarters of those acres were in the Adirondack Park.

The ORRRC also called for citizen action. After the report was released in 1962, Penfold produced a digest and guide for citizens who wanted to lobby federal, state, and local officials for more recreational development. That also worked. During the 1960s, the National Park Service (NPS) added sixty-nine units and 3.1 million acres, including Canyonlands in Utah (1964), Delaware Water Gap in Pennsylvania and New Jersey (1965), Guadalupe Mountains in Texas (1966), and North Cascades in Washington (1968). The NPS added Redwood Park in California (1968) with significant assistance from Henry Diamond and Laurance Rockefeller. The system also acquired nine national seashores and lakeshores, a response to the commission's finding that Americans were particularly hungry for access to public waterfront.

Henry Diamond's success with the ORRRC earned him a lifetime appointment as Laurance Rockefeller's advisor on environmental affairs. "Their office was wonderful," he remembered. "They always called it Room 5600 in Thirty Rockefeller Plaza, which sounds like a mail drop. But in fact it was three floors of Rockefellers and their support staff. It was a very formal place. There was a lot of office decorum, and the secretaries came to work in hats and gloves. Each brother had an office in the four corners of the fifty-sixth floor. Laurance had the southeast corner, Nelson had the northeast, David had the southwest, and John III had the northwest." The fifth Rockefeller brother, Winthrop, was in Arkansas. He was elected its governor in 1966.

Holt Bodinson went to work at Room 5600 in 1966. "I was Henry's eyes and ears at meetings he couldn't get to," Bodinson said. "He worked on the fifty-sixth floor. You had to get through security to get up there. I worked on the fifty-fourth floor with the conservation staff, and that was quite a place, too."

Bodinson sat next to William "Holly" Whyte, a journalist who was able to retire after he wrote a bestseller called *The Organization Man*. During the ORRRC years, Whyte championed the idea of using easements to protect open space. In the mid-1960s he launched the "street life project," which became another highly influential book called *The Social Life of Small Urban Spaces*. Other colleagues on the fifty-fourth floor included Fred Smith, who worked on the Public Land Law Review Commission; Kenneth Chorley, the point man for the reconstruction of Colonial Williamsburg; and Connie Wirth, who had led a drive to rebuild the National Park Service.

Diamond and Laurance Rockefeller continued to push the open space agenda through the 1960s, notably by helping Lady Bird Johnson on a national "beautification" campaign that cleaned statues, built playgrounds, campaigned against highway billboards, and convened an influential national conference in 1965. But they always kept the Adirondacks in their sights.

In 1961, Laurance Rockefeller had written to Wirth to suggest that the National Park Service study the feasibility of turning the Adirondacks into a national park. Wirth didn't get a chance to do it before he retired, but the idea didn't go away. In 1962, in his capacity as vice chairman of the New York State Council of Parks, Laurance supported a proposed amendment to the state constitution that would set aside 10 percent of the Adirondack Forest Preserve for campgrounds, beaches, and state park-like facilities; 60 percent for hunting, fishing, and other forms of "wilderness recreation" that allowed motor vehicles; and 30 percent for "primitive wilderness."

Laurance was following up on one of the ORRRC's main conclusions. The report found that the United States needed more of what it called "effective acres," which meant recreational areas within a few hours' drive of population centers. The basic problem was (and still is) that most of the nation's public land was in western states, while most of the population was in the east. The Adirondack Forest Preserve could add millions of "effective acres" to the nation's supply of recreational land, but only if its managers could be freed from the Forever Wild clause, which prevented state land from being used to maximize public access to outdoor recreation.

In 1965, Nelson asked Laurance to lead an effort to create a few more effective acres in New York. The target area was the Hudson River, which rises in the Adirondack High Peaks and runs north-south through most of New York State. It is a major recreational site but its lower section, from Albany to New York City, had become industrialized and heavily polluted.

"People who have swum in the river itself say the taste of the water stays in your mouth for days," wrote journalist Anthony Bailey in 1967. Laurance became chairman of the State Hudson River Valley Commission. He was asked to recommend ways to clean up the river and bring New Yorkers back to its shores with picnic baskets in hand.

One windy morning that spring, Anthony Bailey boarded the *Dauntless*, a sixty-five-foot motor yacht that Laurance Rockefeller used to commute from his home near Tarrytown to his Midtown Manhattan office. Bailey's companions were Connie Wirth, "a bulky, bespectacled, and genial man" who was executive director of the commission, and Ben Thompson, a retired National Park Service naturalist who was head of the commission's planning staff.

The three men left Tarrytown and steamed north seventeen miles to the commission's offices on Iona Island. Along the way, they talked about some of the challenges the commission was facing. Wirth said that the Commission's main goal was to enhance the scenic and recreational qualities of the river. The Governor supported that goal, but he also wanted two projects that would make the goal much harder to achieve. The West Side highway would put a fifty-mile barrier of concrete and traffic along the riverbank from Manhattan to Beacon. The Storm King storage project would paste power lines and water tunnels onto the face of an iconic mountain that guarded the entrance to the scenic Narrows. Both proposals had spawned energetic opposition from citizens' groups, whose lawyer, David Sive, was using new kinds of legal arguments that were, to everyone's surprise, holding up in court.

When the *Dauntless* docked at the commission's offices, Bailey found "a score of young men and women working on charts, maps, and overlays. Upstairs, in a room temporarily vacated by two women who were compiling statistics, Mr. Wirth and Mr. Thompson used some of the charts and maps to demonstrate what the commission was doing. As they did so, I felt something of the excitement a planner must feel at marshaling great forces in a conscious shaping of the human environment."

Wirth told Bailey that he felt a sense of urgency, both in the short term, because new development proposals were coming in nearly every day, and also in the long term, because the population of New York State was projected to increase from 17.7 million in 1965 to nearly 30 million in 2000. In fact, the state's population barely budged—in 2019, it was 19.4 million—but that was not the future Wirth was planning for.

Bailey doesn't say whether he and Wirth talked about the Adirondack Park. The Hudson is a rocky stream when it flows out of the park about 160 river miles north of the spot where they met. But to Laurance Rockefeller, the park was a six-million-acre prize because it was within a day's drive of New York City, Philadelphia, Boston, and several other large cities where one-sixth of all Americans lived. And the opening of the Northway would dramatically reduce the time it took to get from coastal cities to the Adirondack Park. The question was what kind of park the Adirondacks would be, and how much of it would remain Forever Wild.

Henry Diamond remembered a day when he and Connie Wirth were returning to New York in Laurance's airplane. "We were flying over the Adirondacks," he said. "Laurance turned to Connie and said, 'Wouldn't it be wonderful if we could make a national park down there?' Connie, who never saw two or three million acres that he didn't think should be a national park, said it was a wonderful idea."

The conversation became animated and detailed, recalls Diamond, and it continued into the airport parking lot. "So Laurance, being Laurance, asked Connie to write a report," said Diamond. Then he got into the back of a waiting limousine and was whisked away.

Wirth recruited Ben Thompson and Roger Thompson (no relation to Ben), the same man who had argued with George Davis over beers. Roger Thompson had managed a timber stand in the Adirondacks before he started teaching at the State College of Forestry. Wirth and Laurance met with him in December 1966, just after he had published a highly critical review of forest preserve management for the State Council of Parks. At that time, Thompson was a staff member for the state senate's finance committee. Laurance asked Nelson to loan Roger Thompson to the study group. A few days later, Wirth and the two Thompsons got to work.

Laurance told the governor and the secretary of the interior what his private task force was doing, but they didn't hold public hearings or post any notices, as a government task force would. "They just poked around," said Diamond. "It kept two or three people busy for two or three months."

Clarence Petty had a hint in advance that something was up. "This fellow called me up about two weeks before the national park report came out, and he wanted the maps that Neil Stout and I had drawn up. We had no idea what he wanted them for. When I read about the proposal in the newspaper, right away it made sense.

"Unfortunately, they ran the boundary of the national park right through the middle of some of the so-called wilderness areas that we had set up. There wasn't much sense in the way they had drawn it. And with Tupper Lake and Saranac Lake and Lake Placid plopped inside a national park, the whole thing looked rather dubious to us."

Timing is everything in politics, and the timing of the Adirondack National Park proposal seemed good. A great deal of debate and political organizing aimed at the Forever Wild clause had happened because of the constitutional convention in summer 1967. The twenty-three-page *Report on a Proposed Adirondack National Park* was delivered to the governor's office in late July 1967, a day or two before Dollie Robinson's speech at the constitutional convention.

Shortly after he received the report, Nelson Rockefeller and his top aides went to a town hall meeting north of Albany. Harry Albright, Nelson Rockefeller's deputy secretary, remembered that the trip made him airsick. "To my stomach's chagrin we flew in a small King Air turbo prop that held no more than six people," he wrote in an unpublished memoir. "After the meeting, our hosts presented the governor with a box of apples. I remember getting back on the plane and munching on the apples while the governor opened his briefcase and pulled out the printed copy of his brother's recommendation to transform the Adirondacks into a national park.

"The governor passed the printed report to me on the plane and described it as 'terrific.' Knowing the governor's strong feelings toward his brother, I assumed that meant we were about to embark upon a program to nationalize the Adirondack Park."

It didn't turn out that way. The initial reaction to the national park proposal was confusion. Although it had been produced privately, many readers thought the report was an official state publication because Laurance was chairman of the Council of Parks. The authors compounded the confusion by putting a New York State seal on the cover of the original printing without asking anyone's permission. When asked about that at a public meeting, Wirth said, "That was stupid on my part. I didn't know what I was doing."

The governor frantically tried to reclaim all the copies and replace them with a second printing that had no seal on the cover, but he wasn't entirely successful, and the episode made a bad impression. It sent a message that in 1967, many of the official policies of New York State were being privately produced by the Rockefeller dynasty.

Laurance's proposal described an Adirondack National Park of 1.72 million acres. It would be the third-largest national park in the United States, although it would only claim about 30 percent of the existing 5.9-million-acre state park. About 1.2 million acres inside the proposed area were already in the forest preserve; the other 600,000 acres of private land would be purchased at a projected cost of about $500 million (in 2020 dollars). Privately owned land was "a latent danger to the public's interests in the area," the report said. As the number of visitors increased, more privately owned open space would be converted to housing developments, amusement parks, and other "inconsistent uses."

"Development was changing the atmosphere of the Adirondacks," said Diamond. "It was uncontrolled, and the laws were extraordinary. You couldn't cut a tree on state land, but in the next acre you could build a Ferris wheel or whatever else you wanted. Laurance thought something should be done, and Nelson recognized the problem."

The national park would protect the state park's most precious assets, from the High Peaks in the northeast to Cranberry Lake and the Fulton Chain of Lakes in the west and Indian Lake in the south. Within the national park boundary, private homes on plots of less than three acres and businesses "consistent with park purposes" would be allowed to remain. Lake Placid, Saranac Lake, and other communities inside the line would draft new zoning laws under the direction of the US Secretary of the Interior. All other private lands, including undeveloped lakeshores, timber stands, and hunting camps, would be acquired quickly through negotiation if possible, with condemnation as a last resort.

The proposal accomplished something that almost never happens in New York State: consensus. Everyone hated it. It wounded hometown pride and state patriotism by arguing that the mix of public and private land was unworkable, and by calling the present state park "a myth." Landowners in the millions of acres of state park that were excluded from the proposal either feared that they were being left behind or that the feds would eventually come after them, too. And state officials wondered what they were supposed to do with all those leftover acres.

The New York State Conservation Council mobilized to stop the proposal because hunting and trapping are almost never allowed in national parks. Timber companies said they would be put out of business. Property rights advocates called it a Rockefeller land grab. And wilderness advocates like Peter Paine Jr. feared the loss of the Forever Wild clause, especially because of a side comment in the report suggesting that a Blue Ridge Parkway-like road through the forest preserve would improve public access.

The proposal was easy to attack because it was sloppy. Assemblyman Glenn Harris, whose district encompassed much of the park, objected that neither he nor anyone else who represented the park had been consulted or forewarned. And if Rockefeller was proposing to ban hunting, he said, why did the state just authorize seven thousand deer hunting licenses for the Moose River Plains?

A few days after the report was released, Laurance Rockefeller and Connie Wirth met with about twenty-five officers of conservation groups, game clubs, and lumber companies. Harold Hochschild, who owned a Great Camp and was a longtime member of the Association for the Protection of the Adirondacks, took notes. Hochschild wrote that Arthur Benson expressed his support for the proposal, which delighted the hosts. "They evidently didn't know or remember his connection," wrote Hochschild. "They were disconcerted at lunch when I told them that Benson is the manager of Frontier Town, the Wild West show near Schroon Lake."

Hochschild told the room that he and other Great Camp owners had no desire to sell their properties or share their lakefronts with the public, and that the millions of visitors to the Adirondacks "would be astonished to learn that Wirth thinks the state park is a myth." He speculated that Rockefeller and Wirth would try to bring the plan to the 1968 state legislature, but that "it was also apparent that they were taken aback by the breadth and intensity of the opposition."

After enduring a three-month barrage of negative newspaper editorials, position papers, club resolutions, and personal arguments from friends including Peter Paine Jr., Laurance Rockefeller addressed a meeting of the park's oldest outdoor organization, the Adirondack Mountain Club (ADK), in Warrensburg. Peter Paine and Henry Diamond both described the tone in the room as "hostile." "The weather was bad, and the plane was late," said Diamond. "The bar had been open for some time, and when we came in there was an audible growl."

Laurance Rockefeller spoke from a prepared text and did not take questions. He backed away from the original proposal, saying that he made it to "stimulate thinking on an important issue—not to railroad anyone into anything." He said that he was content to make changes, such as dropping the parkway idea, allowing hunting in some areas, and negotiating with private landowners, whose concerns he said were "valid." But he also doubled down on his support for the Park Service by attacking what he called "a somewhat ideological, but very real objection to asking the federal government to play a role." That objection was misguided, he said.

"The rounding out and long-term protection of the Adirondack Preserve is a very major undertaking," he said. New York could not afford to buy all that land quickly enough. At current acquisition rates, he said, it would take more than a century to add another million acres to the forest preserve. Federal assistance was needed to save the park before it was too late.

Laurance didn't persuade anyone in the crowd that an Adirondack National Park was a good idea. But he did challenge them to act. Everyone in the room also knew that the Northway had just opened.

"The national park concept is one means of solution, but if there is a better one, I shall enthusiastically endorse it," he said. "Whatever the formula, this much is basic: we must have the same courage, foresight, and imagination of those who served us so well by creating the Forever Wild clause of the constitution. In their time it was a brand-new idea, a bold new concept. Let us join together to meet the challenges of our day so that we may do as well by future generations as the past has done by us."

A few weeks after the national park report was released, Nelson Rockefeller asked the Conservation Department to prepare an official reaction. The commissioner gave the job to his chief planner, Harold Jerry, and told him to consult with Clarence Petty. Clarence got the nod because of the three years he and Neil Stout had spent bushwhacking through the forest preserve, producing a report for the Joint Legislative Committee on Natural Resources showing which parts of the forest preserve might be suitable for formal designation as Wilderness Areas.

The report didn't look good to either of them. Jerry had first learned about the national park proposal on July 30, when Lyn came back from town and threw the Sunday *New York Times* on the table of their Dug Mountain cabin. "Here," she said, "this will make your day."

Lyn knew that her husband, whom she always called "Jerry," liked nothing better than the feeling of righteous indignation. And the more Jerry read, the more he disliked the proposal. "It punched a great big hole in the park as it existed," he said. "It left the state park as an administrative monstrosity. We'd be left with a doughnut that had a vast hole in it, and there was nothing we could do with that."

Jerry and Petty agreed to write the Conservation Department's response, but neither of them had an open mind. They traveled to Yosemite, Yellowstone, Grand Teton, Great Smokies, and other national parks. "We discovered that a great many of the activities in those national parks were carried on by concessionaires, and some of them were very lavish. We found showers, electric lights, generators, and all sorts of amenities that were not in the Adirondack Park," Jerry said. "They were far removed from the Forever Wild clause we were trying to protect."

In January 1968, Jerry and Petty released their report. They had looked at each parcel of privately owned land within the proposed park boundaries and concluded that it would cost far more than Rockefeller had estimated to buy them. They found that the timber industry, which was as important to the Adirondacks as tourism in those days, would be disorganized, "perhaps irretrievably." Tourism-related businesses would also face great upheaval. In addition, 888 single-family homes, 1,962 seasonal residences, and a few multiunit dwellings, totaling roughly 3,000 households, would be forced out unless they were granted exemptions.

What finally killed the proposal was an editorial in the *New York Times*. Its author, John Oakes, was a cousin to the Sulzberger family, which owned the *Times*. Oakes was a regular visitor to the Sulzbergers' Adirondack Great Camp, where he socialized with Harold Hochschild and other AfPA members. He was also on the board of the Wilderness Society. And in 1968, an editorial in the *Times* had great political power.

The Conservation Department's economic arguments were "poor reasons" to oppose the national park idea, Oakes wrote. It was far more important to protect the forest preserve, which he called "the most valuable tangible asset possessed by the State of New York." The preserve was "superbly safeguarded by the 'Forever Wild' provision of the State Constitution," he concluded. He was making the same point that Peter Paine Jr. had made when he had argued with Laurance just a few months earlier.

Nelson Rockefeller announced that he was shelving the national park proposal on the day the *Times*'s editorial ran. But Laurance Rockefeller's challenge still hung in the North Country air, along with a lingering suspicion among North Country folks that the Rockefellers would return.

Looking back on the episode, some observers have speculated that the national park proposal might have been a "false flag operation." In this conspiracy-minded view, the Rockefellers floated an idea they knew would fail, in order to prepare the public for their actual goal, which was the Adirondack Park Agency. Nelson Rockefeller died in 1979, and Laurance declined a request for an interview for this book. But Henry Diamond said that he had asked Laurance about this, and that the charge is not true: "It would have been nice if we had been that clever, but we weren't."

The proposal did get people thinking, however, and Laurance was informed as the discussion moved forward. On September 6, 1967, Harold Hochschild drafted a letter to fellow members of the Association for the Protection of the Adirondacks that described his conversation with Dave McAlpin, a banker and Blue Mountain Lake neighbor who worked in global conservation issues. The two men had talked about forming a committee, "aided by such experts as they may select in various disciplines—game, fish, forestry—to undertake a study of the future of the private lands of the Adirondacks. This would of necessity include the state lands, because of the interrelationship.

"Dave has written [Conservation] Commissioner Kilbourne that there is a move afoot to organize an objective study as indicated above. He has also written Laurance Rockefeller, as I understood him, to the same effect, and expressing the hope that further investigations LR himself may make will be more thorough than those on which the Wirth report was based."

On February 2, McAlpin wrote to Hochschild from Caneel Bay to report that William Rockefeller III, the son of Laurance's cousin and an heir to the Bay Pond property, was staying next door with his wife. "Before they came down, Laurance asked him to serve on the Commission, but after talking it over with his partners (at the law firm Shearman and Sterling), he declined," McAlpin wrote. "It certainly can do no harm if we talk it over with LSR to see whether we can make a constructive contribution."

And on April 18, Harold Hochschild wrote to his brother, Walter: "Laurance Rockefeller told Crocker last week that Nelson is expected to announce the composition of a commission sometime before April 25."

Politics is the art of the possible, and the Rockefeller brothers were skilled in the political arts. Laurance leaned on his brother to appoint a task force to study the future of the Adirondacks, modeled on the ORRRC, and see if they could maximize the "effective acres" of the Adirondacks through other means.

Henry Diamond, who managed Nelson Rockefeller's third presidential campaign in 1968, said that the governor agreed to form the Temporary Study Commission on the Future of the Adirondacks for three reasons. First, the politics were good. Protecting the Adirondacks would play well downstate, where millions of voters lived, even if it might irritate a few thousand who owned property inside the Blue Line. Second, Nelson loved to solve problems and thought task forces were fun. And, of course, there was his relationship with his brother.

"Laurance was one of the few people who could really talk straight from the shoulder to Nelson in the mid-1960s," said Diamond. "Their father was gone. Some of their senior advisors were no longer around. Nelson had been governor for five or six years." Almost everyone he met wanted something from him. "But Laurance could talk pretty straight to him," said Diamond.

So in summer 1968, Henry Diamond called Peter S. Paine Jr., reminded him of Laurance's conversation with him the previous year, and asked him to come to a meeting. Around the same time, Harry Albright called Harold Jerry. Soon after that, Jerry called Clarence Petty. And then Jerry called Larry Hamilton, the Cornell professor. Jerry said that he had a job opening for a graduate student who wanted to work on a land use plan for the Adirondacks. I know just the right person, said Hamilton. Come on over.

Chapter 5

# GOING ROGUE

Harold Jerry sat at his desk on a frigid Monday morning and thought about Friday afternoon, when he could get back to the woods. He imagined his wife Lyn and perhaps one of their children driving north with him from Albany to a spot near the Village of Speculator. They would park their Jeep in near-total darkness, strap on skis, snowshoes, and headlamps, and stride four and a half miles to a cabin that had no electricity or running water. When they arrived, the temperature inside the cabin would be well below freezing. They would stoke the wood stove for a day-and-a-half until they had to go back to civilization. That was their kind of fun.

Jerry was forty-eight years old in 1968, with four kids and a midlevel job as a facilities planner for the State Department of Conservation. He was used to taking orders he didn't agree with and planning new campgrounds and ski areas he'd rather not see built. He lived for the times when he could escape to big, untouched landscapes. He hoped that one day he would get a job that matched his passion. He also had one advantage that most Albany bureaucrats did not have. He was friends with the governor.

Nelson Rockefeller was chasing his dream job, too. He had been governor of New York for ten years, and he wanted to be president of the United States. His third attempt had ended at the Republican Party convention in August 1968, but Rockefeller didn't dwell on the loss. He dominated the state's Republican Party, which controlled both houses of the legislature. He would not face reelection for another two years. He was one of the world's richest men. He still wanted to be president, but he had a lot to do in New York, and a lot of power to do it with.

One of the items on the governor's agenda was drafting a long-term plan for the Adirondacks. The management of one state park might have seemed trivial to a man like Rockefeller, but the Adirondacks is not just any park. It is an internationally famous nature reserve that is as big as Vermont. Millions of people visited it in 1968, and a chorus of prominent New Yorkers, led by the governor's beloved brother, was warning him that its beauty was in immediate danger of being lost to overdevelopment.

Other voices had different concerns. Full-time residents of the Adirondacks did not think of their home as an occasional vacation spot. Most of the Park is private land, and it is an important source of timber, minerals, and water. Full-time park residents struggled to find good jobs. Their problem wasn't overdevelopment, but a lack of economic opportunity. Their voices did not usually reach Albany or New York City, however.

Rockefeller saw another chance to build his presidential resume, or at least burnish his legacy, by "saving" the Adirondacks. His ambitions finally gave Harold Jerry his dream job. They would also be the making of George Davis, and they would give Clarence Petty a capstone for his career as a ranger. But whose Adirondacks would they be saving?

Jerry and a group of commissioners made recommendations that were so uncompromising that Rockefeller was reluctant to endorse them. The commissioners used political brinksmanship at least twice, making threats that forced the powerful governor to capitulate. They proposed development rules so strict that some legal experts characterized them as a government "taking" of private property. And then they organized a lobbying campaign that persuaded the governor to turn their vision into law, over the objections of his brother and several powerful legislators.

Ordinarily, recommendations as wild as theirs wouldn't have stood a chance. But Harold Jerry and his team were relentless. Their timing, strategy, and execution were perfect. In just two-and-a-half years, the Temporary

Study Commission on the Future of the Adirondacks (TSC) gave the "forever wilders" power over the North Country.

Nelson Rockefeller enjoyed racing sailboats. He knew how to take advantage of prevailing winds. And in 1968, something was definitely in the wind.

The proportion of Americans who identified air and water pollution as serious problems increased from 33 percent in 1965 to 70 percent in 1970. In May 1968, Sierra Club Books published *The Population Bomb*, which argued that the earth had already exceeded its carrying capacity and was headed for catastrophe. The book suffered from overheated prose and bad science, but it immediately became a bestseller.

Americans believed that the world was in dire straits that spring. Riots erupted in over a dozen cities after the assassination of Martin Luther King Jr. on April 4, fueling a bitter debate about what needed to be done to address racial injustice. In Vietnam, 543 American soldiers died during a single week in February. The country was tearing itself apart over those issues, and many politicians didn't know where to stand. But who could be opposed to clean air, clean water, and natural beauty? In summer 1968, a new environmental program was likely to find widespread support without getting a governor into trouble.

Ron Pedersen worked for Nelson Rockefeller, whose New York City offices were in a townhouse on West 55th Street. Henry Diamond worked for Laurance Rockefeller, whose offices were in Rockefeller Center, the skyscraper complex his father had built in the 1930s. "Henry used to jokingly say that the idea of the Temporary Study Commission was developed on the back of an envelope, in the back of a car, as he and I were riding between offices," said Pedersen. It wasn't a long car ride, but the idea wasn't complicated. "The obvious government solution to a big problem is to create a committee to look at it, so that's what we recommended," he said.

Pedersen wasn't telling the whole story. Laurance Rockefeller had been discussing a task force for the Adirondacks with Dave McAlpin, Arthur Crocker, and other members of the Association for the Protection of the Adirondacks for several months. A commission was what Laurance wanted, and he wanted it on his terms.

Nelson Rockefeller told his appointment secretary, Harry Albright, to put together the commission by Labor Day. Albright immediately called Harold Jerry and said that three key people—the governor, Henry Diamond, and a man Albright called "Mr. Laurance"—had agreed that Jerry should be its staff executive. Albright promised Jerry that the TSC would not be a typical effort. The governor would appoint the commissioners, none of whom would be current members of the legislature. The commission would work for the governor, and its report would go directly to him.

"Nelson was not an environmentalist, but Laurance was, and Nelson had great affection for his brother," Albright wrote. And the immediate goal of the commission was clear: "We needed injunctive relief. The idea was to freeze development." Rockefeller wanted the report and its recommendations finished in eighteen months, so the legislature could consider its recommendations in spring 1970.

Jerry was delighted to take the job. His current post in the Conservation Department had given him lots of information about activities in the Adirondacks that, in his opinion, needed to stop. Clarence Petty had documented illegal roads, garbage dumps, and cabins on state land eight years earlier that still had not been shut down. Snowmobiles were not regulated or licensed, and their numbers were doubling every year. Jerry had just learned that a state agency had resurrected a plan to build a dam that would flood the upper Hudson River. And although Jerry hated the idea of building big downhill ski centers on state land, lots of high-level people were saying that ski centers would add jobs.

Shortly before he got Albright's call, Jerry had turned in a big project. He had supervised several people who had spent months analyzing and calibrating the slopes of Adirondack hillsides. Jerry knew the conservation commissioner was planning to use his data to identify the best places for new ski areas. As staff director of the TSC, Jerry might be able to squelch plans like those. The wilderness needed him.

Years later, Jerry told interviewer Dick Beamish that he was proud to be called an environmental extremist. "It's all right to be conciliatory, but that's not my role," he said. "I don't see that role for myself, and I never did. We have to have somebody staking out the extreme position, and when I say extreme, I simply mean protecting the Adirondack backcountry. I believe that there shouldn't be any buildings in the backcountry. Otherwise it's death by a thousand cuts. A little bit here, a little bit there, and in the end it's all gone."

Land use planning was a relatively new idea in 1968, and no one had ever come up with a plan for sustainable development in a six-million-acre region where huge public forests were surrounded by even larger tracts of private land. But the TSC did have several things to build on. One was the Joint Legislative Committee's inventory of wilderness areas. The other was Laurance Rockefeller's Outdoor Recreation Resources Review Commission (ORRRC).

In 1968, the ORRRC's successor, the Bureau of Outdoor Recreation, had begun buying undeveloped land to turn into recreation areas. It was guided by the Wilderness Act of 1964, which prohibited almost all forms of development on nearly ten million acres of land. The federal wilderness system was growing every year.

The TSC would be organized along lines similar to the ORCCC. Much of its research would be conducted by private consultants or state agencies. Jerry would be responsible for assigning and organizing their material into a main report and technical appendices. The printing of the TSC report was even supported by a grant from Bureau of Outdoor Recreation.

The job of coordinating all that work and meeting the 1970 deadline would be massive. It would require a director who had a thorough knowledge of the subject, strong connections among natural resources specialists, and exceptional administrative skills. Harold Jerry was a good fit. He was a native of the North Country who could move comfortably in the upper-class enclaves of Albany and New York City. The son of a prominent Plattsburgh lawyer, he had gone to Princeton, served as an Army captain during World War II, and returned to graduate from Harvard Law School. During the war, Jerry had been in charge of the last infantry battalion that was shipped to Europe. He had taken his men through devastated landscapes to occupy Czechoslovakia, although he never saw combat.

Jerry was intelligent, articulate, handsome, and stylish. "He would grandly parade into the state capitol building in a black Chesterfield coat," according to Albright. "He was a bit of a dandy," said Norm Van Valkenburgh, who worked with Jerry at the Conservation Department. "He wore fine Homburg hats and was always dressed to the nines. If he was in his office, you could just walk in and talk to him. In other places, he always carried himself like he was higher than you were. He made you aware of his social position."

The TSC was part of the governor's office, so Rockefeller did not have to follow civil service rules. He could hire and appoint whomever he wanted, as long as it didn't get him into political trouble. Based on his choices, it appeared that he was looking for people who had good college credentials and membership in exclusive clubs.

Rockefeller did not appoint any women to the TSC, which was not unusual in 1968. He also ignored other groups. There weren't any seats for working-class people or elected officials from Adirondack towns. The commissioners belonged to a small cohort whose accomplishments were made much easier because their privilege was so rarely challenged.

The first of eleven commissioners to be appointed was Henry Diamond, who everyone understood was Mr. Laurance's representative. The next was Leo O'Brien, who had been the US congressman from Albany for fourteen years before retiring in 1966. O'Brien had been a newspaper reporter and a midlevel operative in Albany's notoriously corrupt political machine before he was elected to Congress, but he wasn't a thug. "Leo had established a record in Congress as someone who could get things done," Albright wrote.

O'Brien was best known for sponsoring the legislation that made Alaska a state. He had also worked closely with Laurance Rockefeller and the ORRRC to establish Virgin Islands National Park, Fire Island National Seashore, and other federal park projects. He could be relied on to support the national park model. "Apparently Nelson and Laurance both felt that if Leo could get Alaska to become a state, he could get the Adirondacks to become a public park," according to Albright.

The governor wanted O'Brien to be chairman of the TSC, but he held back from making an announcement. Rockefeller was a centrist. Some of his initiatives, such as Adirondack Park protection, would be popular with liberals and Democrats but would alienate conservatives and Republicans, who tended to emphasize the principle of home rule. And Rockefeller needed the support of those Republicans for other issues, especially during elections. He feared that giving the post to O'Brien, an Albany Democrat, would alienate conservative upstaters. So Rockefeller told O'Brien privately that he was his choice for chair, but he did not announce the appointment until the 1968 election was over.

O'Brien used his Albany connections to move the commission forward anyway. He did it "by obtaining funding from his former drinking buddy," wrote Albright. That buddy was Albert Marshall, who controlled the budget of the executive chamber. The TSC asked for an annual budget of $150,000 ($1.1 million in 2020). "Neither Rockefeller, Jerry, nor I could sell the idea of funding the commission to Marshall," Albright wrote. "But if we sent Leo to Al, he would come back with everything we required. This happened time and time again."

Henry Diamond quickly offered Peter Paine Jr. a seat, even though Paine was just thirty-two and had disagreed with Laurance. Paine was picked because his father was Laurance's Princeton classmate, and his family ran in the same social circles as the Rockefellers. In fact, Peter's wife, Patty, had once dated Laurance's son, Larry. Before he accepted the commission seat, Paine asked Laurance to call the managing partner of the law firm where Paine worked, to get his permission.

Rockefeller also pleased liberals by appointing two Black men to the eleven-member commission, in a state where 20 percent of the population was Black. The two were chosen because of their influence with blocs of urban voters. One was Fred O'Neal, a stage and television actor and president of an actor's union. He was also a leader in the civil rights and trade union movements, and he had just been appointed to the executive council of the American Federation of Labor and Congress of Industrial Organizations (AFL-CIO). The other was Julien Anderson, an oral surgeon on the faculty of Columbia Dental School, who had previously served on several Rockefeller commissions.

Rockefeller also appointed a prominent travel writer and television producer, Lowell Thomas, to the commission, perhaps in hopes that Thomas would focus his cameras on the Adirondacks. But Thomas and Anderson were duds. "The only thing we knew about Julien Anderson was that he liked to ski," said Peter Paine. Maybe they weren't interested, or maybe they were too busy, but at any rate, Anderson and Thomas only attended one of the commission's thirty-four business meetings, and it wasn't even the same meeting.

All of the other commissioners took their jobs seriously. Fred O'Neal had spent his life in New York City. He was completely unfamiliar with the Adirondacks, but he attended every commission meeting, did all the reading, and hung around afterward to tell stories about all the places he'd been. "Fred was fascinating," said Peter Paine. "He was imposing—I think he stood about six foot four or five. He had an aquiline nose and was quite handsome, with a very deep voice."

The other five commissioners already knew about the Adirondack Park because they owned summer homes there. The wealthiest and most influential commissioner was Harold Hochschild, who was seventy-six when he was appointed to the TSC. Hochschild had been the CEO and partial heir to a family-owned mining company before he merged it with another firm to form American Metal Climax (AMAX). Hochschild's German Jewish background contributed to his lifelong interest in human rights. He retired after the merger and devoted more time to several causes, including the anti-apartheid movement in South Africa.

Hochschild had also known Nelson Rockefeller since the governor was a boy. And he had a passion for the Adirondacks and its history. He was a long-time member of the Association for the Protection of the Adirondacks (AfPA) and had written *Township 34*, a regional history classic about the central Adirondacks. He had used part of his fortune to build and endow the Adirondack Museum in Blue Mountain Lake. He spent as much time as he could at Eagle Nest, his family's property on two thousand acres a few miles from the museum.

Watson Pomeroy joined the commission shortly after retiring from nineteen years in the state legislature. Pomeroy had chaired the legislative committee that conducted the Adirondack wilderness survey of 1959–1962. He was also a member of the AfPA. Frederick Sheffield, a Yale classmate of Pomeroy's and friend of Hochschild's, was a New York City lawyer who owned an estate near Saranac Lake. Sheffield had been an Olympic rower and served on the board of Saranac Lake's medical research foundation, the Trudeau Institute. Howard Kimball owned a home at the Adirondack League Club, a private fifty-thousand-acre preserve south of Old Forge. Kimball, who had worked with Harold Jerry during Kimball's term as mayor of Elmira, was probably given a seat on the commission because he was a Republican from central New York. He also sat on the board of the Gannett newspaper chain.

Rockefeller also gave a commission seat to James Loeb, co-owner of the *Adirondack Daily Enterprise*, the only daily newspaper published inside the Blue Line. Loeb was not a typical small-town publisher. He had cofounded the liberal lobbying group Americans for Democratic Action with Reinhold Niebuhr. He co-owned the *Daily Enterprise* with Harry Truman's former press secretary, Roger Tubby. Loeb had been John F. Kennedy's ambassador to Peru and the West African country of Guinea. In 1968, he was leading a campaign to establish a community college in Saranac Lake. The *Daily Enterprise* wasn't exactly a hobby—Loeb and Tubby both lived in the park, and Loeb regularly wrote its editorials—but neither man needed the money.

Politicians often appoint fact-finding commissions when they want to avoid an issue. But that was never Nelson Rockefeller's intent with the Adirondack commission. First of all, the commission wasn't entirely his idea. "It was really Laurance's commission," said J. Neil Huber Jr., one of the TSC's staff lawyers. "We knew that Laurance was the one pushing it behind the scenes, even though we never met with him."

The governor also liked nothing better than generating big new ideas. "He liked smart people," said Michael Whiteman, his chief counsel. "He liked to get them together and look at what they came up with." Rockefeller appointed eighty-one study groups of various stripes between 1959 and 1970. He started thirteen of them just in 1968.

Rockefeller had already set up several commissions to look at the potential for coordination between local governments. None of them had produced breakthroughs, mostly because of resistance from local officials. "When you talk about regionalization in New York State, you're talking about screwing local officials in 931 towns and 600 umpty-ump villages, et cetera, et cetera," said Richard Wiebe, whom Rockefeller appointed to head the Office of Planning Services in 1970. The Adirondacks offered a better chance for a regional plan to succeed, Wiebe said, because the state had a lot more authority in the Adirondacks than it did anywhere else.

Despite its clubby aspect, the TSC was an independent group that was not inclined to automatically endorse the suggestions of the governor or his brother. Watson Pomeroy had joined David Sive and others in leading the opposition to the utility project at Storm King Mountain on the Hudson River, a project Nelson Rockefeller supported. And the governor also knew that Loeb would never vote for him. A few months before he was named to the Adirondack Commission, Loeb had agreed to serve as co-chair of New York's committee for the presidential campaign of Robert F. Kennedy.

Peter Paine, of course, had argued with Mr. Laurance. And Harold Hochschild had done more than argue. He had organized other AfPA members to hire a public relations firm to fight Laurance's national park proposal, and he had begun organizing an informal group along the same lines as the TSC a year before the governor gave the idea his blessing.

"The Temporary Study Commission was not one of those exercises where you walk around the table and file it on the shelf," said Peter Paine. "I was a young, noisy lawyer. I loved the sound of my own voice. And there were a lot of lawyers and journalists on that commission. We did not suffer from a lack of people who were willing to express their views."

This was especially true when Captain Harold Jerry was steering the discussions. "I think Harold went into it knowing what he wanted out of it," said George Davis.

The governor announced the commission on Thursday, September 19, 1968, and called its first meeting for the following Tuesday. In a press release, Rockefeller repeated what his brother had said at a meeting in Warrensburg ten months earlier: "As our forefathers sought to protect the natural resources of the Adirondacks for our generation, it is our responsibility to review the potential of these resources under present day situations and to chart the future of the Adirondacks with as much wisdom and foresight as was done for us."

September 19 was a slow news day, but the announcement barely made a ripple. The *New York Times* didn't cover it until ten days later. Loeb ran a five-paragraph Associated Press story on the front page of the *Daily Enterprise*, then added another few paragraphs so he could explain his own involvement. It is unlikely that many of Loeb's readers believed him when he said, "No one should suspect that this Commission is in any way an effort to promote the National Park idea."

At their first meeting, Harold Jerry briefed the commissioners on the Adirondack National Park proposal and reactions to it. "In order to maintain complete objectivity," he wrote, "Laurance Rockefeller and R. S. Kilbourne, the Commissioner of Conservation, were not invited to this meeting." The governor attended the meeting and led an informal, off-the-record discussion. Still, Laurance defined the agenda.

The Rockefellers hinted at their intentions by asking the commission to answer seven questions. He had originally published the questions in January, in a press release reacting to the Conservation Department report produced by Harold Jerry and Clarence Petty, after consulting with Laurance and his advisors. Questions one, two, and three were open ended, but four through seven were leading. All you had to do was switch the order of the first three words, from "should there be" to "there should be," to turn them into orders.

1. What should be the long-range State policy toward acquisition of additional Preserve land?
2. What measures could be taken to assure that development on private land is appropriate and consistent with the long-range well-being of the area?
3. What should be the State policy toward recreation development in the area?
4. Should there be federal participation in any phase of the plans, including a limited park or wilderness area?
5. Should there be greater management flexibility in some portions of the area?
6. Should there be even stronger safeguards for the wilderness portions?
7. Should procedures be developed for a more flexible policy regarding consolidation of public lands?

The commissioners must have wondered how they could possibly answer such broad questions in sixteen months. And their concerns were heightened when their agenda was immediately interrupted. From the beginning, the TSC was sidetracked by incomplete information and the actions of other state agencies.

The hot issue that fall was a proposed 220-foot dam just downstream from the confluence of the Indian and Hudson Rivers. The Gooley Farm Dam would flood thirty miles of wild river and fourteen thousand acres of forest, creating a twenty-two-square-mile lake in an area that was almost completely undeveloped. The dam had originally been proposed in 1922 by the state's Water Power Commission and had not been actively considered for decades, but a severe drought in the mid-1960s had reduced New York City's drinking water reservoirs to dangerously low levels.

After downstate officials lobbied hard to resurrect the dam project, the state quietly started to move. Commissioner Kilbourne asked the US Army Corps of Engineers to make detailed topographical surveys of the Hudson River Gorge in summer 1968. Nobody told Harold Jerry that the survey had been ordered. He learned about it only after a visitor to the gorge noticed a survey stake. The hiker told his friends, and the word got around.

Once they learned what was going on, Jerry and a subset of the commissioners felt an urgent need to block or modify those plans. In public, they said that long-term decisions about the Adirondacks should be placed on hold until the TSC was done. But they were also proceeding from a different set of values.

Shortly after the TSC formed, "Peter Paine called me and said that he wanted to meet with some of us when he was passing through town," said David Newhouse, a Schenectady environmentalist who was chair of the conservation committee of the Adirondack Mountain Club. "It turned out that he wanted to ascertain the purity of our positions and our thinking. He wanted to know if we were with him on their environmental positions. We persuaded him that we were. At the end he told us, 'If you ever say anything about this meeting, I'll deny that it ever occurred.'"

Rockefeller asked the commission to consult with advisors, so Jerry began reaching out to groups and industries with ties to the Adirondacks. They didn't announce that list for another year. The official advisors included representatives from forestry, hospitality, recreation, local government, hunting and angling, and other fields. But the TSC's files contain extensive correspondence with representatives of environmental groups that goes back to the commission's first days. Environmentalists shared Jerry's worldview, and he used them as an important source of back-channel communication and news.

From the beginning, full-time residents of the park complained that they were being ignored. The day after the appointments were announced, Loeb wrote an editorial noting that he was the only full-time resident on the commission. The "composition of the commission reflects one basic fact which [we] . . . might as well recognize and accept," he said. "The Adirondacks do not belong to us, but rather to all of the people of the state and the nation."

Rockefeller had learned the hard way to respect local officials' insistence on home rule. He responded to the complaints by sending Lieutenant Governor Malcolm Wilson to Elizabethtown to meet with State Senator Ron Stafford, whose district included most of the park, and Richard Lawrence, whose family owned a New York City–based publishing company.

Lawrence had lived in Elizabethtown since 1946 because his second wife, Elizabeth Hand Wadhams, belonged to one of the North Country's most prominent families. Dick and Elizabeth Lawrence had many ties to child welfare and education charities in the North Country. They were also friends with the Paines, and Lawrence had run Rockefeller's reelection campaigns in the North Country in 1962 and 1966.

Rockefeller offered commission seats to Dick Lawrence and Robert Hall, the publisher of the weekly *Hamilton County News* and other newspapers.

Hall was then preparing the first issue of a new magazine called *Adirondack Life*. Rockefeller also had reason to believe that Hall would be comfortable supporting big, long-term planning efforts. Hall had been a reporter for the newspaper of the American Communist Party, the *Daily World*, before becoming disillusioned with the Soviet Union in 1956 and moving to Warrensburg.

Hall and Lawrence would fall in with Hochschild, Paine, Pomeroy, O'Neal, Sheffield, and Loeb to push an agenda that was very different than the one favored by Laurance Rockefeller's team. The other commissioners would stand aside. And despite his background and continuing influence on public opinion, Hall was never called out for his communist past. The commission convened before the era of personality politics began, and besides, no one in Albany or New York City cared very much about what happened way up in Warrensburg.

Harold Jerry had only sixteen months to produce the TSC's report, so he started his new job under pressure. But when it came to hiring his staff, he moved carefully and slowly. He wanted fresh thinking—people who had not been "captured by the system," according to one staff member—and he also needed people he could drive hard. Jerry would ask his thirteen staffers and fifteen consultants to prepare research for thirty-four business meetings, eight three-day field trips, six public hearings, and thirty meetings with advisors and citizens' groups. Most of that activity would be packed into fourteen months.

On the morning of Thursday, October 17, 1968, Jerry held a meeting in Cornell University's Roberts Hall. The dean of Cornell's State College of Agriculture had invited graduate students who were interested in forestry, biology, landscape architecture, economics, geology, and other fields to hear about potential jobs with the TSC. But Jerry also went to Cornell to meet a specific person.

Larry Hamilton, the Cornell professor, had called Arthur Crocker, secretary of the Association for the Protection of the Adirondacks, to tell Crocker that the AfPA ought to support his new graduate student, George Davis. "We wanted to be involved in the Temporary Study Commission as soon as we heard about it, but we didn't have the money to hire Davis," said Crocker. "And then, what do you know, Harold Jerry got him. Harold Jerry was very important to me." And Crocker was also important to Jerry. As the TSC moved forward, Crocker stayed in touch to offer help and advice.

For George Davis, the TSC was love at first sight. He had been at Cornell's graduate program for about six weeks, after five years as a US Forest Service ranger, and he was trying to figure out how to finance his thesis. He wanted to write a long-term management plan for the Adirondack Park. That was going to require a significant amount of fieldwork, and he didn't know how he was going to pay for it.

"I was impressed with Harold Jerry," Davis remembered. "I saw that the Temporary Study Commission meant a great deal to him personally. At that point in my life, I also thought that anyone who knew the governor was way up in the stratosphere, so I was in awe of him. Then we talked one on one, and I saw a bit more of his human side. After that, I was ready."

George Davis had been married in 1965. In the fall of 1968, he and his wife, Joan, had a three-year-old daughter and a newborn. He was earning $3,580 as a graduate student ($26,400 in 2020), and he was concerned about making ends meet. As Jerry spoke, Davis scribbled on a legal pad. He wrote "OPC" in large letters on top of the first page. The acronym stands for "Office of Planning Coordination," which Nelson Rockefeller had established to draft "a comprehensive plan for the development of New York State" based on regional land use plans. It sounded like a job Davis wanted.

Jerry offered Davis a temporary appointment at an annual salary of $12,000 ($88,300 in 2020) plus benefits. "Here was a man offering me the chance to do exactly what I was struggling to do at Cornell, for three times as much money," Davis said. "So as soon as classes ended, I put the thesis on hold and moved to Albany." On January 21, he wrote to a Forest Service contact and said, "I hope to get my thesis from this Commission work."

As soon as Jerry understood what the TSC had been asked to do, it became obvious that Rockefeller's spring 1970 deadline was unrealistic. Jerry knew how to collect data and make it into reports, but in this case, he had very little to go on. All previous efforts to pass regional land use plans in New York, including the Hudson Valley Commission, were either incomplete or failures. Hawaii had completed a statewide land use plan, but its methods could not be applied to the Adirondacks. The park was bigger than Hawaii, anyway. St. Lawrence County alone was bigger than Delaware. But spring 1970 was the deadline Jerry had been given.

As he was courting George Davis, Jerry was also persuading the Conservation Department to loan Clarence Petty to the TSC. That wasn't hard, either. "Harold was a hell of a good guy," Petty said. "He liked the woods. I took quite a few trips with him."

Petty recalled a time when Jerry asked him to come with him to the top of Mount McNaughton. The summit was about four miles from the nearest trailhead. There was no trail, and the mountain had been heavily affected by the Big Blowdown. Petty knew a relatively easy way to the top, but Jerry insisted that they follow a route that had been described by hikers in the 1940s. "It was the damnedest blowdown you ever saw," Petty said. "Harold lost his wristwatch, and I tore my shirt. We looked like we had been clawed by grizzly bears. We got to the top and checked the register. Only four other people had been there in the last year, and they all had written, 'Never again.' I looked at Harold and said, 'You can see why.'"

But Jerry always stuck to a hard line. "In the field artillery, you learn that it doesn't do any good to study territory from afar," he said. "The only way you'll know the ground is by going out and looking at it." So when George Davis showed up at the offices in December 1969, Jerry introduced him to Clarence Petty and gave them simple orders: "The first thing I said to them was 'Get out of the office, stay out, and don't come back.'"

Davis and Petty started hiking in earnest as soon as mud season began in April 1969. They spent a year walking through the back woods of the Adirondacks. Instead of writing his thesis, Davis filed reports on what they saw. And that was only one part of what he did for the TSC. "His work ethic was incredible," Jerry said.

After he met Davis at Cornell, Jerry drove on to Syracuse University and talked with Robert Anderson, a professor at the law school who had just published *American Law of Zoning*, the first comprehensive legal survey of that topic. Anderson told him about Neil Huber, his best researcher, who had just graduated. Jerry contacted Huber and lured him away from his job. Huber started when Davis did, just after Christmas. Jerry was so choosy that it took him six months just to get his staff together.

Davis didn't wait to start working, however. He heard that Cornell was beginning a project called the New York State Land Use and Natural Resources Inventory (LUNR), a flyover of the entire state that would produce 140,000 black-and-white photos. The project's director, Don Belcher, had analyzed aerial pictures of South Pacific beaches to rate their potential as troop landing sites during World War II. Belcher went on to teach engineering at

Cornell and develop the field of remote sensing. The LUNR planes calibrated their altitudes to match the 7.5-minute maps produced by the US Geological Survey. Four centimeters on one of these maps equals one kilometer on the ground. The photographs yield the most information if they are taken in summer, when people are working outdoors and trees can be identified by their leaves.

Davis learned from Belcher that LUNR's planes were just beginning to collect photos. Adirondack counties were last on the schedule. Davis wrote to Jerry, who used his connections to make sure that the Adirondacks were photographed as soon as the leaves came out in 1969, so they could be of use to the TSC.

The commission leased office space on the sixth floor of 41 State Street in Albany, a short walk from the state capitol. Many commission meetings were held there; others were held at the governor's New York City offices at 22 West 55th Street. At the second meeting in November, the commissioners approved twelve broad study topics: legal and constitutional questions, wildlife, forestry, water, recreation, public and private land use, transportation, local government, the park's economy, federal policies, a schedule of tours for the commissioners, and a catchall Jerry called "aesthetic, geologic, scenic, historic, and scientific aspects of resources and recreation."

Jerry would eventually assign forty-nine specific studies, fourteen of which were done by paid consultants. George Davis was responsible for twenty of them. Peter Birckmayer, a Cornell-trained economist who lived in Albany, took fourteen. Neil Huber took nine. Harold Dyer, a recreational specialist who was loaned to the TSC by the Taconic State Parks Commission in May 1969, took four. And Richard Estes, a recent graduate of the University of Pennsylvania planning school, joined in March as Harold Jerry's assistant. He also took two reports. The TSC staff also included Clarence Petty, on loan from the Conservation Department; Arnold Putnam, a natural resources planner; Andrew Barothy-Langer, a cartographer on loan from the state transportation department; and five secretaries, four of whom were women.

The commissioners spent a lot of time that fall dealing with unexpected crises. As soon as the TSC was announced, it started receiving letters from people who were opposed to the Conservation Department's proposal to build Gooley Dam. Environmental groups were bringing another crisis-driven campaign to its climax.

In May 1967, Senator Robert F. Kennedy and Stewart Udall, the secretary of the interior, had paddled in the tenth annual Upper Hudson White Water Derby to promote a federal law that would create a national wilderness system for rivers. The law did not pass that year, but it was reintroduced after Kennedy was assassinated. President Johnson signed the Wild and Scenic Rivers Act into law in October 1968, which added attention and media coverage to threats to the Hudson River Gorge posed by the Gooley Dam. Letters were arriving by the dozens, so the commissioners approved a form response. That wasn't enough for Peter Paine, who stated (in the minutes) "that he felt strongly that the views of the commission should be solicited before any final decision was reached."

Another trouble spot was a pending report on winter recreation that suggested seven potential sites for new downhill ski areas. Jerry had submitted the data for this report shortly before he went to the TSC. The report would soon be released by the State Office of Planning Coordination (OPC). The commissioners asked the OPC to hold the report until the TSC could make its recommendations, but the OPC said it was too late. Paine and several other commissioners urged acting chair Harry Albright to ask the governor to give the TSC an opportunity to express its views before the state made any big policy changes related to the commission's assignments. Albright said he would.

George Davis moved to Albany shortly after Christmas and immediately started vetting report assignments. "One of the problems with New York State government has been that most of the state agencies are inbred," he said. "They pride themselves on the quality of their work, and they often don't feel the need to learn what people outside of New York State are doing. We discovered that Vic Glider, who was in charge of the Conservation Department's big ski areas, had never been to a ski area in Vermont. That was just amazing, as far as we were concerned."

Davis recruited Doug Clarke, a biologist from Ontario, to write the report on wildlife management. Clarke was an exceptionally good writer, and his report is easy for lay people to understand. He got the job for that reason, but also because the mix of wildlife in the Adirondacks is similar to that of southern Canada.

"Harold Jerry believed that you should steal good ideas from wherever you find them," Davis said. "So we used outside consultants, sent staffers to conferences, and inspected out-of-state areas that had problems similar to ours."

Davis said that the two years he spent working for the commission were "greatly enjoyable" because "we could look at almost anything we wanted."

As the staff delivered a stream of high-quality material to the commissioners, the commissioners became fans. Davis, Paine, and other alumni described the commissioners and staff as teams that brought out the best in each other.

"I really didn't know the Adirondacks very well in 1968," said Peter Paine. "I didn't know a great deal about the Forever Wild clause, the fights over the dams, and this, that, and the other thing. Many of us had to learn a whole lot and learn it fast. But we had commissioners like Watson Pomeroy, who had a profound knowledge of the forest preserve, and we were also blessed with an exceptionally competent staff. We ended up having a great deal of admiration for them, although it was not a staff-driven exercise—not by any stretch of the imagination."

As 1969 began, most of the staff was in place, reports had been assigned, and the commissioners had gotten to know each other. The group was also being pushed by a huge tailwind of public concern. On January 28, 1969, one week after Richard Nixon became president, an oil spill fouled the beaches of Santa Barbara, California. Images of dying birds and sea otters drove the public's demands for the government to act.

On January 31, the TSC held its first meeting in the Adirondacks, in Lake Placid's Olympic arena. The agenda was packed. The commissioners approved a five-page interim report to the governor that broadly outlined their research program and schedule. They also met George Davis for the first time, and they listened to his plan for an inventory of all the privately owned land in the Adirondacks. It sounded like a crazy idea. In 1969, almost all records of private land were on paper and kept in far-flung county courthouses. But Davis wanted to try, with the assistance of Conservation Department staff and interns, and the commissioners voted to let him go ahead. Richard Lawrence underlined "Private Land Inventory" in his copy of the agenda and put a big "(!)" next to it.

Lawrence had lived in a small Adirondack town for thirty-four years, so he had a better understanding than other commissioners did of what George Davis would find when he visited a typical town office and asked for their records. He knew that some of the offices were a mess, and even the well-run places might not be inclined to help a stranger from Albany. Also, Lawrence was frank in his belief that Adirondack towns couldn't handle land use planning, and he had an idea about what needed to be done instead. The state needed to create an independent commission to control development on private lands.

"Harold Jerry's original idea was that the commission would only recommend changes to the Conservation Department for the management of the forest preserve," Lawrence said in an interview with William Kissel in 1998. But Lawrence told Jerry that improving the management of the forest preserve wasn't enough. The commission also needed to recommend rules for development in the private land.

"Jerry asked me to explain my position to the staff, so I came down to Albany and had a meeting with them," Lawrence said. The idea he suggested was outlandish: a state agency that controlled the uses of private land in a region larger than Rhode Island, Delaware, Connecticut, New Jersey, or New Hampshire. "I got blank stares from everyone except Clarence Petty, who said, 'Dick, I see what you're talking about.' I could have kissed him.

"Another thing I said early on was that we had to keep the idea of a state agency very quiet. If it leaked too early, we would just get clobbered. So we didn't bring it up with the other commissioners right away. We moved toward it gradually, and one by one, they came along."

Another important event at the Lake Placid meeting happened after a five-hour bus tour of the area disembarked on Saturday. The Lake Placid Chamber of Commerce held a cocktail party at the Olympic arena so the commissioners could meet with local leaders. Leo O'Brien, who had been officially appointed TSC chairman in December, started drinking there. Then he went to a bar and kept on drinking. In those days, there wasn't as much disapproval attached to getting drunk in public. But "I have known some drunks," said Peter Paine, "and from the first time I laid eyes on Leo, I could see he was a bad drunk. He would get out of control at the worst possible moment."

"We were all staying at the Golden Arrow Motel," said Lyn Jerry. "Someone came back and said, 'If you want to see a drunken congressman, come on down to the bar.'" Several people remember Leo singing, laughing, telling dirty jokes, and gossiping about the governor with his new friends. Some say that he found a sled hitched to a pack of dogs, jumped aboard, and took off down Main Street. "I remember him sitting on the curb in front of the hotel on the main street of town," said Howard Kimball. O'Brien needed someone to help him find his bed.

Leo's behavior had not been a problem at the Albany meetings because he didn't have to stay overnight. He depended on his wife to control him. But

Mrs. O'Brien did not go on overnight trips with "Oby," as she called him. He couldn't control his addiction when she was not around.

The next morning, Leo was too hung over to enjoy the snowmobile rides that Harold Jerry had arranged. Very few of the commissioners had ever seen a snowmobile. Afterward, the commission and staff got in two chartered planes and flew back to Albany and New York City. The snow-covered mountains are beautiful from the air, but they probably were not noticing the scenery. Harold Jerry, the staff, and the commissioners were thinking about everything that had just happened, how much they had to do, and, now, whether they could depend on their leader.

By March 1969, most of the staff was in place and the commissioners had taken the roles of leaders and followers. "Peter Paine was probably the single most important person," said Howard Kimball. "He had his head screwed on properly. He knew what was going on, and he did what he set out to do. He was always asking questions." Paine was the whip who drove the process forward. He usually voted with Hochschild, Lawrence, Sheffield, and Hall.

Paine was also fond of pressing his arguments forward by making long digressions during meetings, which might have persuaded some but certainly irritated others. "I think Peter is very well characterized by what Henry Diamond is reported to have said at a commission meeting after Peter had carried on at some length over some issue," said Ron Pedersen. "Henry rolled his eyes and said, 'Another painful peroration from Peter Paine.'" "Peroration" is a debater's term for the concluding part of a speech that typically is intended to inspire enthusiasm in its audience.

At the March 4 meeting, George Davis reported that he was still struggling to find ways to inventory every parcel of privately owned land in the park. The Conservation Department was not enthusiastic about cooperating. The commissioners considered scaling back the effort or seeking private funds to hire more workers, and they agreed to meet again in two weeks because they had so much to do.

Two weeks later, the staff had found a workaround. They proposed to use data from the State Board of Equalization and Assessment, which exists to determine a uniform rate of increase or decrease in property taxes charged by local governments and schools. The board collects records on every tax parcel in the state, including the address of the owner, assessed value, and acreage. The records also describe how the land is used in nineteen categories including farm, residential, estate, commercial, seasonal dwelling, resort, forest land, and tax exempt. And the board also owned a computer.

In those days, computers did not have internal memory. They were IBM tabulation machines about as large as a small sofa. Each tax parcel had a paper card that was encoded with information manually, on another machine, by an operator who punched holes in the card. The staff reported that these "Hollerith cards" needed to be recoded to add the acreage of each land parcel in Adirondack counties, and that some statistical tricks would probably be needed to estimate missing data. The job would cost $10,000 ($70,000 in 2020) and take one person four months to do, but it could be done.

The commissioners were dazzled and delighted. A month earlier, they had been introduced to snowmobiles. Now they were learning how computers worked.

And there was more good news. A Conservation Department official told the commissioners that the Gooley Dam proposal was fizzling out, for two reasons. Senator Bernard Smith, chairman of the Senate Conservation Committee, had introduced a bill to stop the dam that was moving toward passage. Smith represented Long Island and was a friend of pro-Forever Wild groups, and he also owned a cabin near the Hudson River Gorge. It also helped that the drought that had threatened New York City's water supply had broken, so the reservoirs were full again. The Conservation Department was looking for alternative ways to secure more water for the city, the official said. Smith's bill passed in April, ending the dispute.

In April 1969, the TSC met again in New York City. The staff delivered another encouraging report about the big computer run. Watson Pomeroy asked Jerry to distribute an exceptionally good article from the *Syracuse Law Review*, "Permissible Uses of New York's Forest Preserve," that had been written by a recent graduate, William Kissel. But the big item at that meeting was a report from George Davis on what "wilderness" meant, and how the commissioners might want to enhance it.

"Wilderness is like God, love, or beauty, in that it means different things to different people," Davis said. "It is an emotional response, definable in a person's mind based on previous experience." Some attempts at "wilderness management" had been made, he said, such as the federal wilderness standards that had been passed in 1964, but the key question was highly subjective: "How do we manage a state of mind?"

Davis suggested an outline for a classification system for the forest preserve. The basic idea was that the Conservation Department's existing definition of "Forever Wild," which allowed some building and motorized access,
would be acceptable for some of the public land, but that other categories
needed stricter standards. Davis had been developing those standards by reviewing the work of the Pomeroy Commission and talking to its lead scout,
Clarence Petty. He had also been talking to Harold Jerry, who had been talking to David Sive, David Newhouse, Arthur Crocker, and other environmentally minded friends. The commissioners were impressed and stimulated.

After the meeting, George Davis and other staffers went to a bar to celebrate. Davis and Petty were pals by then, so Davis played a trick on him.
"Just being around the commissioners was nerve-wracking, because you always had to be on edge and ready to answer questions about whatever it might
be," Davis said. "So at night, we'd want to unwind.

"We went to a place called The Horse's Tail and talked Clarence into
going with us. We didn't tell him we were going to a bar, of course, because
he would never do that. We told him we were going out to get some fresh
air, and of course he made comments about what fresh air was like in New
York City. But we got him there. We got a round banquette table in the corner and put Clarence in the middle. He was trapped.

"For the next three hours, we all sat there and drank and drank and
drank. Clarence had plain water. But I always had the feeling, and I don't
think that he would ever acknowledge this, that he sort of liked the experience. It was so foreign to anything else he had seen."

Davis was also in high spirits because it was the start of fieldwork season.
He and Petty would spend at least half of their paid time hiking or traveling
between April and October 1969. They continued to go out regularly during
the cold months, and in 1970, with the report deadline bearing down on him,
Davis still spent at least thirty-four days in the field between June and October. He filed forty-seven detailed reports describing what he saw. Neil Huber and George Dyer also went out and added even more eyewitness evidence
of conditions in the field. That was the kind of data Captain Jerry liked best.

Petty required Davis to get up long before dawn, because he insisted that they
start hiking as soon as it was light enough to see. Thirty-five years later,
George Davis paused and smiled when he thought about it. "What a job!" he

said. "Walk around, drive around, canoe around, whatever you wanted. And my guide was somebody who knew the area better than anyone else alive.

"We looked at private forest land to see the amount and type of timber being cut, and we looked at farms in the Champlain Valley, but mostly we looked at the state lands," he said. And Davis, twenty-eight, was surprised at the speed and endurance of Petty, sixty-four. "I thought, how can a man of this age possibly be so young?" he said. "That impression stayed with me the whole time."

Hiking equipment was much heavier then, but Davis and Petty were fortunate to begin their travels just after the debut of freeze-dried food. One field report mentions a dinner of "Beef Stroganoff a la Davis, garnished with mosquitoes." The dinner conversations were much more enjoyable than the food. "Clarence was such a good-hearted person," Davis said. "He took his teaching job seriously, but he would also listen. I wanted to use different criteria for wilderness than he had used during the Pomeroy Commission, and once I explained it he was willing to go along. He was the perfect partner, except that he didn't drink beer. He was no good at that."

Davis has a favorite story about the day he and Petty surveyed the Pepperbox Wilderness, a remote area on the park's western edge. "We left the motel about five o'clock in the morning," he said. "We walked all through the Pepperbox, which is a huge swamp basically, and probably the wildest place I know of in the Adirondacks.

"We got out of the woods around three-thirty and drove to the little community of Big Moose. There was a bar, and it was hot, and I had been out there sweating and swatting mosquitoes, so I pulled in to have a beer.

"Clarence says, 'What are you doing? You can't do this. It's only four o'clock. You don't get off work until five o'clock.' I said, 'Jeez, Clarence, I started at five a.m. Isn't eleven hours enough?'

"He said, 'The people in the bar won't know that, and you have a state car. You can't park that in front of a bar and then drive it after you've had a beer.'

"I told him I was going to do it anyway. So after we park, he goes to the trunk and gets out his bright orange Conservation Department raincoat, which is unmarked. It was a beautiful blue-sky day, probably eighty degrees, and here's Clarence wearing a raincoat just to cover up his shirt.

"Into the bar we went, and he got branch water. That's exactly the way he ordered it. I had my beer and we left. I think Clarence and I learned something about each other that day. He's a man of principle, but he knew how to bend when he didn't have any choice."

The fieldwork was governed by the seasons. Some swampy areas were easier to survey in winter, when they were covered by ice. Higher elevations were only available when they weren't blanketed by snow and subjected to high winds. But the list of places to see was so long that they had to take chances.

Harold Jerry envied the crew of Davis and Petty, and he was eager to join in the adventures. "We had a rule that no field trip would ever be canceled, and we never broke that rule," said Jerry. "Early in the season [May 1969], I went with Clarence and George to climb Mount Marcy in the snow. We were going to go up the Mount Van Hoevenberg trail and sleep at the Four Corners lean-to. In those days, state employees could call the Albany airport and get the weather forecast. So I called from the motel the night before and the guy's exact language was, 'Brother, your luck has just run out. A front is coming in, and it's going to bring heavy rain for thirty-six hours straight.' He was exactly right." George Davis's reports note that more than 2.5 inches of rain fell during their trip.

"The snow was still deep, but it was rotten, and you'd fall through to the rocks underneath," Jerry said. "My snowshoes were new and didn't break on the first day, but their snowshoes broke twelve times. Each time we'd have to stop, cut a tree branch, and tie it to the frame."

It rained all night, making it difficult to build a fire. Once the fire got started, they couldn't keep smoke out of the lean-to, so they chose clean air over warmth and put the fire out. "My snowshoes finally broke on the way back" the next morning, said Jerry. "George and Clarence were both elated. It was the most miserable, wretched trip of my life."

Other trips were far more pleasant. "One of the best days was when we looked at the region that became the Saint Regis Canoe Area," Jerry said. "I'll never forget when I went in there because we all just marveled at the lucidity of the water. You'd measure it by lowering something called a Secchi disk. I could still see the disk clearly when it was twenty or thirty feet deep."

The goal of the fieldwork was figuring out sensible rules and standards for the forest preserve. Old-school Conservation Department rangers liked the idea of naming a place a "wilderness," because in the 1950s, it meant they wouldn't have to do much work there. In this view, the few people who illegally drove in or built shacks in those areas were not worth pursuing because the territory was so vast. Most Americans would not put up with the hardship required to see the backcountry.

The great park builder Robert Moses spoke for both Rockefeller brothers when he said, "The rank and file need reasonable access, running water, and simple sanitary facilities." In 1954, Moses denounced "the locking up of [the Forest] Preserve on a basis imposed by extreme fanatical conservationist minorities." He urged that the state "modify the senseless and obsolete restrictions which make the Preserve now little more than a wilderness museum."

In 1969, it was Moses's assumptions that had become obsolete. Although the backcountry wasn't any easier to reach, it was showing signs of overuse. It wasn't that hordes of hikers were overwhelming the Adirondacks. The register at one popular trailhead, Cascade Mountain, for Saturday, August 9, 1969, shows eleven hikers signing in and six signing out. The following Friday, August 15—the opening day of the Woodstock music festival—eight hikers signed in at the Tahawus trailhead, and twenty signed out.

The problem was that hikers in those days had a much larger impact. They left behind piles of garbage, cut trees, turned hiking trails into herd paths and jeep roads, and generally left places looking abused. It was particularly bad in the High Peaks. Harold Jerry even asked the Adirondack Mountain Club to stop the practice of honoring "46ers" who climbed every peak of four thousand feet or more, but the group refused.

What was needed was a shift in values, so that hikers would change their behavior to leave no trace of their visits. Davis and Petty went to national wildlife refuges, national forests, and national parks to look for ideas, and came back with two good ones. The first was customer service. Unlike the High Peaks, the Great Gulf Wilderness Area in New Hampshire was well posted with trail signs that kept people from going off route. The Forest Service also did a better job than the Conservation Department of posting and explaining the rules. The second big idea was ecosystem-based management, which had been in place for years at Great Smoky Mountains National Park. By regularly monitoring indicators such as water quality and trail conditions, National Park Service rangers could find and correct problems faster.

Davis's field reports also focus on aesthetics because, as he had told the commissioners in April, the goal of wilderness management was to inspire feelings of natural purity and solitude in visitors. Davis had a clear, forceful writing style, and he did not hesitate to express his opinions. His field notes for the Mount Marcy trip say that the amount of litter was "appalling," and "it was obvious that no campaign was being waged to combat the problem.

At no point in the entire trip did we notice a 'Pack Out What You Pack In' or similar sign.

"Our first view of beautiful Avalanche Lake was the most aesthetically depressing point of the trip," he continued. "The beauty of this lake can only be appreciated by those who have seen it. [But] where the main trail crosses the outlet, a telephone line has been strung across both the trail and the lower end of the lake. In addition, a three-foot diameter spool of wire was left lying along the side of the trail. It is inconceivable that anyone would choose this location for a telephone line."

By the end of the summer, Davis had become a vocal critic of the Conservation Department, with lots of evidence to back up his charges. He saw dozens of trails eroded or put in the wrong places, and buildings where no buildings should be. In his reports, he regularly launched into "painful perorations" that rivaled Peter Paine's.

It didn't hurt that Davis spent his evenings talking things over with Petty, who had the moral standards and skills of a superhero. One of their last trips together, in January 1971, was to the Hudson River Gorge area. Davis had a last-minute conflict, so Petty decided to walk in alone on the first day.

"I got up to the motel that afternoon around four o'clock, and Clarence's car was already there," Davis said. "That was unusual, because Clarence would usually still be working. It had been a bitterly cold day—thirty-four degrees below zero that morning. I went in and found Clarence all bundled up, with his clothes strung all over his room. He had made a wrong move when he walked onto OK Slip Pond. He had gone through the ice with snowshoes on.

"If I had done that, at thirty-four below, I would have just said goodbye. But Clarence was able to catch himself on the edges and work himself out while wearing snowshoes. This was not easy, and he spent a lot of time in very cold water.

"Now, when something like that happens, you're supposed to take your boots off and wring your socks out as much as you can. But it was so cold that his boots instantly turned to sheer ice, and there was no way to untie them.

"So what does Clarence decide to do? He decides to walk out. The pond is ringed by cabins. I would have broken into one of them and started a fire. But instead, Clarence jogged four miles with frozen snowshoes while wearing a suit of ice. He managed to start his frozen car and get the heater going, so he survived. But he wouldn't break into someone else's cabin, even if his life was at stake."

The Rockefellers knew what the TSC was up to. Harry Albright was in touch with Harold Jerry almost daily, and Henry Diamond sent Holt Bodinson whenever he couldn't attend a meeting. At some point in mid-1969, it became clear to the Rockefellers that the commission might not recommend the things that Laurance wanted. They were considering a regional zoning plan, which Laurance approved of. But instead of opening up more public land to recreational development, they were discussing ways to make the state's interpretation of the Forever Wild clause even stricter.

"Things became tense between the Rockefeller brothers because of this issue," Peter Paine said. "I think Henry Diamond and Harry Albright got caught in the middle of that tension."

In June, the TSC met at Harold Hochschild's New York City offices in Rockefeller Center. They approved a "prospectus" that described their work plan and methods in detail, and they planned public hearings for Old Forge in July and Lake George in September, followed by Rochester, Utica, New York City, and Saranac Lake. They didn't have nearly enough time to conduct the hearings, consider what they had heard, and report with recommendations by the end of the year. But the group couldn't worry about what might happen in six months. There was too much work to do immediately.

The commissioners soon found out that the Rockefeller brothers weren't the only ones who felt strongly about the Adirondacks. About 250 people packed into the Old Forge High School gym on July 8, a Tuesday night, exceeding everyone's expectations. A school board meeting was going on upstairs. Leo O'Brien notified the crowd whenever the school board was preparing to vote, so spectators could shuttle between meetings. Speakers were asked to limit their statements to five minutes, but many of them didn't, and the meeting went on for hours.

The TSC had sent out notices asking people to respond to the governor's seven questions, and the speakers also knew a few other things. They knew that Laurance wanted a national park. They knew that New York City wanted their water. And they knew that the governor liked big plans. He had already condemned and destroyed 1,200 historic buildings in downtown Albany, displacing seven thousand residents, and in 1969 he was building a complex of state office buildings on the site that would ultimately cost $2 billion

($12.2 billion in 2020). The futuristic complex would include five skyscrapers; one of them would be the tallest building in the state outside of New York City, clad in stone imported from three continents. So naturally, Adirondackers were concerned about what Rockefeller had planned for them.

Jim Loeb covered the Old Forge hearing for the *Adirondack Daily Enterprise* while also participating as a commissioner. The first three speakers were from downstate water authorities. Loeb reported that the audience sat silently as they explained the city's precarious situation, its lack of alternatives to the Hudson River, and its need for impoundments upstream from sources of pollution. Then a succession of local speakers told the New York City folks to get lost, Loeb said, and each of them was greeted with loud applause.

"I refuse to prostitute the Adirondacks and make them something odorous and cement," said Robert Lindsay, president of the Fulton County Fish and Game Club. "Leave it alone," added Kenneth Crane, the owner of a summer home on Limekiln Lake. "Pay attention to the people here tonight. We know a lot more about this than people from Buffalo do. We are not about to be taken in by selfish interests.

"We have heard rumors about federal participation where they come and kick you off your land. That is why the crowd is here tonight. The people didn't come here tonight to listen to the problems of the New York City water supply. . . . If there is federal participation, you will reap a harvest of bitterness you will never live down." Loud applause followed.

"We need no part of the federal government to make this park when once a year they will rob you so that the rest of the year you are broke," said Floyd LaDue, a resident of Old Forge. "Now they want to come in and take the trees, lakes, streams, and the good air and ruin them. I say this Forever Wild was one of the things that came into this country. Let's nail it down! . . . If New York City is so hard up for water, why don't they go out their back door with a dipper? Because they have polluted their waters. Now they want to rob us." More loud applause.

The TSC hearings in Rochester, Utica, and New York City were dominated by camp owners, hikers, hunters, and others who supported a strict interpretation of the Forever Wild clause. Speakers in Old Forge, Lake George, and Saranac Lake held more diverse views. Almost all of the speakers from inside the park defended home rule and their own interests. Foresters said that state lands were being wasted under "single-use management," the industry term for wilderness, and would be healthier and much more

useful if selective cutting and motorized recreation were allowed. Local officials and businesspeople favored anything that would increase tourism.

Robert Lindsay and other hunters liked the Conservation Department's
current policies, which favored them over other groups. Jack Plumley, an
Oneida County legislator who was happiest at his camp on the Mad River,
went to the microphone in Old Forge and read the passage from William
Chapman White's book *Adirondack Country* that is quoted on page 27 of this
book. "Leave it alone," he said, to loud applause.

Each hearing opened with a long statement by Harold Jerry or a commissioner describing the TSC's research into every acre of the park. But most
of the speakers at the three hearings held inside the park (which were transcribed) spoke only about state-owned land. When they mentioned privately
owned land, it was usually to object to Laurance Rockefeller's proposal to
buy or condemn it, and their tone was similar to Kenneth Crane's "come and
take it" threat. Only a few speakers supported zoning, and even fewer talked
about the need for regional land use planning. The idea of zoning was foreign to them. Many of them didn't know that they lived in a park, or that
state laws could overrule local laws.

One of the few who did know was William Roden, who owned a few
rental cabins on Trout Lake. Roden wrote a popular column for sportsmen
that was syndicated by Warren County publisher and TSC Commissioner
Robert Hall. The two men may have talked things over, because at the Lake
George hearing on August 22, Roden called for a new agency that would
administer regional zoning of private land and place tighter controls on signs
and shorelines. For every five members of the agency, he said, three should
be elected by people who live inside the Blue Line. And the cost should be
borne by taxing the park's property owners.

"Just remember all ownership must be covered, all owners treated the same,
and local control and administration," Roden said. "Those are the ingredients
for successful Adirondack Park zoning, just as they are for zoning everywhere."

None of the speakers at the Old Forge hearing were women. Three
women spoke at the Lake George hearing, however, and all of them favored
regional zoning. They were Winifred (Winnie) LaRose, a real estate agent
from Lake George; Mary Prime, a landowner who was active in community affairs in Lake Placid; and Margaret Lamy, a Lake Placid native who
had spent eighteen years working for Loeb as a newspaper reporter before
taking a job at Harold Hochschild's Adirondack Museum in 1968.

Lamy told the crowd that she was disturbed by the many speakers who told the TSC that "outsiders" didn't have the right to "come into this region and tell us what to do. This attitude strikes me as ridiculous," she said. "How can the interests of 110,000 people living inside the Blue Line outweigh those of the 18 million people of the rest of the state who not only own part of it, but whose taxes support it at all levels through payments for the operation of local government, schools, and the Conservation Department?"

Lamy said she was more concerned about "the destruction of the wild character of this region" than she was about "the complaint of Adirondackers about how hard it is to make a buck." She said that the eighteen years she had spent covering local governments had convinced her that they could not handle the challenges the park faced. She envisioned a park where a core wilderness region, centered around the High Peaks, would be surrounded by a "doughnut" administered by regional commissions, where open space would be protected while development would be allowed on private land.

"A master plan for the region as a whole is an absolute essential," Lamy said, "and I don't see it developing in the scattered planning efforts now going on." What was needed, she said, was "stricter controls combined with a working partnership between state and local officials."

Thirty-four years later, as she sat in the lobby of the Hotel Saranac, Lamy's voice rose as she recalled that time. "The local politicians totally ignored the study commission," she said. "They held all kinds of meetings and hearings, and the politicians just sat on their hands and didn't pay any attention. I used to cover those board meetings. Honestly, I wondered if a lot of those guys ever read a newspaper anyway. It might sound funny now, but it was deadly then."

Lamy said she spent her life arguing with park residents who were quick to oppose any extension of state power, "but if they need a boat ramp or something built, well then the state ought to do it. That's the double standard we live with."

Jim Loeb knew what was coming. "Whatever the final Commission recommendations are, they will be greeted with considerable hostility," he wrote in an editorial after the Old Forge hearing. "This is inevitable, because no set of meaningful recommendations could possibly satisfy everyone."

The TSC held its July meeting the day after the public hearing in Old Forge. After approving seven more consultant contracts, they watched a slide show George Davis had put together on his fieldwork. By this time, Davis and Petty had spent twenty-four days in the field, and he had accumulated a long list of specific recommendations. Even more were coming in from Harold Dyer, who was on loan from the Taconic State Park Commission.

Dyer had been inspecting Conservation Department campgrounds on the edges of the big roadless areas at Siamese Ponds and Silver Lake, and he recommended that the state acquire several parcels to eliminate tar-paper shacks, views of mining activity, and other scenarios that clashed with the commission's vision of quiet and seclusion. And Dyer couldn't resist taking a swipe at the amusement parks he saw on private land on Canada Lake. Their merry-go-rounds, Ferris wheels, and "carnival setups" were "the type of 'tourist trap' that should be discouraged," he wrote.

The other big agenda item in July was whether the TSC should ask Nelson Rockefeller for more time. O'Brien, Diamond, and Pomeroy were sent to request an extension. The governor didn't say yes at that meeting, but word soon arrived that Rockefeller would attend the dedication ceremony for the Adirondack Museum's brand-new building in Blue Mountain Lake on August 1, 1969. The museum was entirely funded by TSC Commissioner Harold Hochschild, who everyone knew favored the extension. Anticipation was high.

At the ceremony, Rockefeller praised Hochschild and the museum. He touted his investment in recreational projects inside the Blue Line, and his support for the bill that banned Gooley Dam. Then he announced that he was extending the TSC's term until December 1970, "which will assure us ample time to allow every interested group and every individual a full opportunity to be heard."

Rockefeller was happy to extend the deadline because he had come up with bigger, better environmental items he could tout during his 1970 reelection campaign. He was asking Henry Diamond to propose ways to combine departments from different state agencies into one huge agency that was devoted to environmental protection. The formation of the State Department of Environmental Conservation (DEC) would be announced on Earth Day, April 22, 1970. Around that time, Rockefeller also told his speechwriter, Hugh Morrow, to slap together a book. Morrow gave a stack of the governor's speeches and position papers to a freelance writer and paid him to clean them up. *Our Environment Can Be Saved* was released a few weeks before the election, with Nelson Rockefeller listed as the author.

The governor also agreed to the extension because it was a way to avoid potential problems. By August, he understood that the recommendations of the TSC were not likely to win him any friends among upstate Republicans, so it would be better to push them through in a nonelection year. And Rockefeller also dared not offend Harold Hochschild, who possessed a potent weapon he could use against him at any time.

John Oakes, editorial page editor of the *New York Times*, was a member of the Association for the Protection of the Adirondacks, a board member of the Wilderness Society, and a persistent critic of the governor's environmental record. "He was always pushing us by saying we weren't doing enough on the environment," said Albright. Oakes was also a close friend of Harold Hochschild's. It would be much harder for Rockefeller to compete in New York City and its suburbs if he was getting slammed by the *Times*, and he knew that Hochschild had the influence to make that happen. "That was critical," Albright said.

Harold Hochschild arrived late to the public hearing at the Lake George High School gym on August 22. As he raced to take his seat, he tripped and fell, hard, on the wooden floor as Harold Jerry was speaking. The crowd gasped but Hochschild, seventy-six, immediately got up as if nothing had happened. After Jerry finished, Leo O'Brien introduced Hochschild, "who just made the nicest slide into first base since Ty Cobb."

O'Brien was a skilled politician, and his regular column in the *Albany Times-Union* kept him in the spotlight. He knew how to run a meeting, "but he got drunk all the time," said Howard Kimball. "And he was always so hung over the next day. At one point, I just said the hell with it and drove back to Elmira."

But the staff kept moving ahead. The day after the Lake George hearing, they approved a contract for a report called *Centralized Framework for Planning and Land Use Control*. The day after that, the commissioners took a field trip to the Hudson River Gorge. Lyn Jerry remembered that Fred O'Neal hiked in wearing wing-tip shoes. And in September they met in Warrensburg, without O'Brien.

Hochschild, the "temporary chairman," arranged for a new documentary film called *Multiply and Subdue the Earth* to be shown at that meeting. The film opens with a shot of white rats climbing over each other in a lab enclosure while the narrator solemnly reads from a study that links overcrowding to "deviant behavior." The film also includes an interview with the planner Ian McHarg, who explains his method of analyzing water supply, soils, and other natural features to determine the limits of land development.

O'Brien returned for a meeting in Old Forge on October 24, where the commissioners planned out the rest of their time through December 1970. The fact-finding stage of their work had been largely completed, and the focus was changing to writing and decision making. Public hearings were also continuing, and Harold Jerry asked for a discussion of "public relations aspects of the commission's work."

The next day, several commissioners took their last field trip. Clarence Petty arranged for float planes to take them to the heart of the 245-square-mile West Canada Lake wilderness. "We took a nine-mile hike, and I remember trying to keep up with Watson Pomeroy and Clarence Petty," said Peter Paine. It was just like the old days.

Leo O'Brien did not go on that hiking trip. After the commission meeting on Friday, he went to a local bar, got loaded, and started telling ribald stories about Governor Rockefeller to the patrons. It got so bad that Paine and others dragged O'Brien out of the bar that night, put him in a car, and told their staff lawyer, Neil Huber, to drive him two-and-a-half hours back to Albany. "That was OK with me," said Huber. "I don't like hiking anyway. I prefer golf."

O'Brien had lost whatever respect the commissioners had once had for him. "Many of them were not big drinkers," Huber said. "Harold Jerry didn't drink at all." Jerry was probably disgusted by O'Brien's behavior. But there was also a bigger problem.

The public and the commissioners had agreed that the federal government should play no role in the Adirondacks. But O'Brien could not give up on the idea of a national park. At the public hearing in Rochester, which was very lightly attended, O'Brien threw the floor open for discussion and tried to propose a multistate compact for a "regional national park." The idea had not been discussed before, and it had never been tried. It went nowhere. O'Brien did not share the vision that Harold Jerry and his staff had nurtured in the other commissioners.

"I think Leo was a political appointee, and he was in over his head," said Huber. "I always wondered why he was in charge." And by the end of October, Jerry had a solid majority of the commission behind him, including one commissioner who had known the governor when he was still wearing short pants.

Chapter 6

# Order Must Be

Harold Hochschild eased into the cool water of Eagle Lake and moved away from the shore. He looked back at the trees and rocks that were familiar and soothing, and his cares receded. As a younger man he would spend summer afternoons swimming five miles or more in Blue Mountain Lake, pausing to sun himself on his neighbors' docks and narrow beaches. Even now, the highlight of his summer days was swimming whenever the temperature of Eagle Lake reached sixty degrees.

Hochschild was small (about five feet, two inches), extremely nearsighted (he wore his eyeglasses when he swam), and seventy-seven years old in 1969 (he wore gray or dark blue trunks, not tights). At the insistence of his beloved wife Mary, he was always accompanied by someone in a boat—but he insisted that it be a small boat with a silent electric motor, kept at a distance. He also said that he didn't need the boat. He had the muscle tone and endurance of a much younger man, and swimming six-tenths of a mile was not hard for him. It seemed that one thing age had brought him was an abundance of memories.

As he glided along, regularly switching between five different strokes, Hochschild remembered evenings when his family and their neighbors tied their boats together in the middle of Blue Mountain Lake. They listened to their favorite tunes on a portable Victrola as they watched the moon rise behind silhouettes of mountains.

Harold Hochschild was born on May 20, 1892, the day the Adirondack Park was signed into law. His father, Berthold Hochschild, and three other families had bought two thousand acres on the north shore of Eagle Lake in 1904. When his father died in 1928, Harold and his siblings inherited the land, along with an 1899 building he called the Clubhouse because it was originally built for a golf course. In 1937, Harold's brother Walter built a far more elaborate compound nearby; it consisted of a large main house, a guest house, and a boathouse sheathed in split cedar logs and paneled with spruce from fallen trees on the property. But Harold preferred to live in a cottage that had been built for him in 1924. It was much smaller and paneled in dark wood. Despite its stunning views, it had small, old-fashioned sash windows. And it had lots and lots of books.

"Mr. Hochschild was a neighbor, but not in a social sense," said John Collins, whose family owned rental cabins nearby. "He was a lovely gentleman, but he was from another world."

Hochschild was a legendary host. "I have a recollection of being served one of the best lobster salads I ever had for lunch," remembered Michael Whiteman, counsel to Governor Rockefeller. "It was very elegant, and we drank a lot of wine. Then we went out in his boat."

Whiteman remembers Hochschild backing his mahogany Hacker-Craft away from the dock on Eagle Lake, pointing the bow toward the narrow channel that connects Eagle and Blue Mountain Lakes, and gunning the motor. "I had not had that much wine for lunch in years. I thought, 'How am I going to manage this?' Then he drove us across the lake and gave us a personal guided tour of his museum."

"He seemed to know everybody," said Eileen Rockefeller Growald, who met Hochschild when she was a college student in 1974. "He loved young people, and he loved to mix things up. I went to a few of his New Year's Eve parties. He had a tradition of inviting camp owners from Blue Mountain Lake to come over after dinner. He would show old black-and-white movies, like Charlie Chaplin movies or *Casablanca*, and there would be dancing and music."

Hochschild would invite about twenty houseguests and another fifteen neighbors into the great room of the Clubhouse. When the clock struck twelve, everyone stepped outside, yelled "Happy New Year!" and blew tiny horns into the vast silence of an Adirondack winter night.

Hochschild was informal but courtly, fun-loving but courteous, and committed to the German ethic of *Gemütlichkeit*, which translates roughly as "coziness." His goal for Eagle Nest was to create social settings where everyone could enjoy life together, as long as they were invited and well-behaved.

The merger of his mining company with another company in 1957, coupled with his retirement as CEO, had left him extremely wealthy and free to do as he pleased. He plunged deeper into his passions. Chief among them was the Adirondack Museum, with its mission "to expand understanding of Adirondack history and the relationship between people and the Adirondack wilderness." The museum (renamed the Adirondack Experience in 2017) has a large art collection, several thousand artifacts, and a well-curated archive that verified many of the facts in this book. Germans often use a phrase to describe how they view society—*Ordnung muss sein*, "order must be"—and Hochschild realized that ideal inside the museum.

Hochschild swam up to a large rock about thirty feet from the opposite shore of Eagle Lake, touched it, turned, and pushed off for home. He was loose and warmed up now, and the cool water felt like a silent embrace. When he did the breaststroke, he saw aquatic plants, floating seedpods, and occasionally a small, startled fish. When he did the crawl, he closed his eyes and retreated into his memories. But his favorite was the backstroke, when he could look at the magnificent backlit clouds, and all the trees, plants, and birds living in perfect harmony.

Hochschild returned to the dock and dried off, refreshed. The swim had done its magic. The day before—August 1, 1969—he had been the guest of honor at the opening ceremony for the museum's new building, which he had built with his own funds. He was proud of the accomplishment, of course, but he also found it unpleasant to be singled out. His nerves were raw when he came back to camp, but now, with the sun setting, he felt as serene as the surface of the lake.

At the museum, Hochschild had introduced Governor Nelson Rockefeller to the crowd. He had shifted uncomfortably in his chair as Rockefeller praised him. But he had smiled when the governor announced that he had granted the Temporary Study Commission (TSC) a one-year extension, to give "every interested group and every individual a full opportunity to be heard before the commission."

Several other members of the TSC were in the audience with Hochschild. They knew that the commission needed a new chairman, and that Hochschild was the natural choice. They did not know then that in less than six months, Hochschild and Rockefeller would square off for a political duel, with the future of the Adirondack Park hanging on the outcome. One last time, Hochschild needed to summon up all his gravitas—his charm, his negotiating skill, his knowledge of the park, and all of the favors he had accumulated over the decades—to persuade his fellow commissioners to endorse his vision of a new order for the Adirondacks, and then to pass that vision into law.

Hochschild was "a tiny little man," said Whiteman, "and your first impression of him might be that this is a quiet, introspective person. But as soon as you started talking to him, it became clear that this guy was a dynamo. He had goals, he had organization, he was determined, and he just kept going. Nothing phased him."

As the TSC did its work, American concerns about environmental issues were peaking. On January 1, 1970, President Nixon signed the National Environmental Policy Act, which required projects using federal funds to submit a new kind of report—an "environmental impact statement"—for approval. Three weeks later, Nixon pledged "to make reparations for the damage we have done to our air, to our land, and to our water" during his State of the Union speech. In December, he signed a major expansion of the Clean Air Act.

But Nixon didn't really care about cleaning up the environment. According to his chief environmental advisor, John C. Whitaker, he supported these measures because he needed to keep up with his rivals in the Democratic Party. He was especially wary of Maine senator and presidential candidate Ed mund Muskie, who was largely responsible for the original Clean Air Act and its expansion.

"There was an arms race to get out in front of environment because it was so important to the voters," said Oliver Koeppel, an attorney from the Bronx who used strong environmental positions to score an upset victory in a special state assembly election in March 1970. Koeppel said that when he showed up in Albany, "environmental stuff was all the rage."

Nelson Rockefeller played this game too, and true to form, he played it for high stakes. In fall 1969, he asked Henry Diamond, Ron Pedersen, and Michael Whiteman to draft a plan that would combine the two thousand employees of the State Conservation Department with five hundred State Department of Health employees to make a new mega-agency called the Department of Environmental Conservation (DEC).

Pedersen identified three reasons for the reorganization. "First, we were reacting to powerful social forces," he said. "Second, the demands of the Pure Waters Bond Issue of 1964 and other concerns, such as solid waste and landfills, were forcing the Health Department to focus on environmental questions as issues of public health. And third, the Conservation Department needed a shake-up.

"Taking care of state parks outside the forest preserve had become a major state function. The state parks system was run by the Council of Parks, which was chaired by Laurance Rockefeller and was a division of the Conservation Department. The Conservation Department had three big divisions: Parks, Fish and Wildlife, and Lands and Forests. We felt that Parks needed its own boss because the Conservation Department wasn't serving everybody. The State Conservation Council [a statewide organization of hunters and anglers] thought it owned the department. That needed to change."

On January 7, 1970, the governor introduced a long slate of environmental initiatives in his annual Message to the Legislature. The ideas ranged from noise control to cleaning up junked cars, but it was the DEC that grabbed all the attention. After the speech, Pedersen ran into State Commissioner of Health Dr. Hollis Ingraham in a state capitol hallway. "The governor had said that he wanted to strengthen the Health Department, but what he proposed was like pruning away half of a tree," said Pedersen. "Ingram was livid. He lit into me." The Conservation Council and several environmental groups also opposed the DEC, he added, because they feared losing their existing relationships. "There was considerable turmoil," he said.

The governor's 1970 message is forty-three pages long, and it doesn't mention the Adirondacks. But if figuring out the future of the park was just a small game piece to Nelson Rockefeller, it was more than a full-time job for the TSC's staff and commissioners. Executive Secretary Harold Jerry had set an ambitious agenda, and even with a one-year extension, they still found it difficult to keep from falling behind.

The staff began sending the commissioners reports and recommendations that would be distilled into eight technical reports and one main report. Harold Jerry generated the material, and Peter Paine drove the process. In November, Paine told the commissioners that the TSC was moving into a new phase. Important decisions were being made, and it was critical for them to attend every meeting in order to keep informed.

The commissioners approved at least ten reports in November and December 1969. They also began shaping a response to the governor's second question to the TSC: "What measures could be taken to assure that development on private land is appropriate and consistent with the long-range well-being of the area?" In November, they reviewed a report from a consultant, former Oneida County planner Edward Rissi, on regulations that controlled land use and development in the United States. By the end of that discussion, most of the commissioners had agreed in principle to propose an independent planning and regulatory agency for the Adirondack Park.

The agency's purpose would be land use planning, which sets the desired future development patterns in a given area. Most zoning laws are local laws that determine how specific parcels of land should be used. But the embryonic agency would be more concerned with a much larger area. It would have jurisdiction over 3.45 million acres of private land, a region slightly smaller than Connecticut. It was also drafting a master plan for 2.24 million acres of public land. That is the size of Yellowstone, which was the nation's largest national park in 1970. The agency's task would be to get more than a hundred towns and villages in the Adirondacks, plus one enormous state agency, to follow consistent rules, either voluntarily or by force of law.

In November 1969, few people knew the difference between zoning for use and zoning for density. No one had ever written two land use plans for a 5.7-million-acre region before, and especially not at the same time. No one had ever tried to enforce them, either. But that was the commission's vision.

Of course, the Conservation Department already had a small staff of professional planners. Harold Jerry had come from that office. All the counties in the park had planning departments, as did about 10 percent of towns and villages inside the Blue Line. Several regional planning agencies also existed. But there was very little cooperation between these offices, and almost all of their work was concerned with zoning in cities and villages.

Richard Lawrence believed strongly that Adirondack towns and counties were not up to the planning challenge. In November 1969, he had been pushing that point on the TSC for almost a year. Environmental activists like Charles Callison, vice president of the National Audubon Society, wrote letters reinforcing Lawrence's view. By the end of the year, staff lawyer J. Neil Huber Jr. was working on a detailed proposal for a new agency. "My principal suggestion is that the commission earnestly consider the advisability of the establishment of a permanent planning and zoning commission for the forest preserve counties," he told the commissioners on February 9, 1970.

The commissioners also understood that their recommendation would have to be made carefully. Jim Loeb wrote to Jerry to support the idea of an agency but added that "if any study [like Edward Risse's] is ever made public, somehow it will have to be translated into the kind of English which normal people understand, and not only planners and technicians." Loeb also said that he felt strongly that park agency members appointed by the governor had to come from different political parties, because "if the agency became a political instrument, it would be disastrous."

The question about appropriate uses of private land was one of seven the governor had asked the Temporary Study Commission to address. The other six questions were about state-owned land. And the launch of the DEC meant that the commission had to adjust to a major shift in state bureaucracy.

In January 1970, Harold Jerry learned that the governor was planning to give responsibility for campgrounds and other public facilities in the forest preserve to the new Office of Parks and Recreation, which was governed by a commission whose chair was Laurance Rockefeller. Many people in the Conservation Department liked this idea, according to Pedersen. They were hook-and-bullet guys who didn't want to manage ski centers and ball fields. But Jerry, Hochschild, and others saw the change as a mortal threat.

Hochschild feared that if Mr. Laurance's people were allowed to operate public facilities in the forest preserve, he would use his influence to increase the number and size of those facilities, adding roads and other things the TSC didn't want. If the DEC's domain was limited to land that was governed by the Forever Wild clause, the two agencies would quickly develop turf battles. An independent agency for the Adirondack Park might be able to negotiate with the DEC, but it almost certainly would become irrelevant if a third party were involved. That would be even more likely if that third party were controlled by the governor's brother, who was almost universally hated in the Adirondacks. Laurance had proposed the Adirondack National Park just two years earlier, and the memory remained fresh.

On January 21, 1970, the commission met in New York City. Governor Rockefeller's secretary, Harry Albright, attended with all of the active commissioners except Leo O'Brien. Hochschild was elected "temporary chairman of the meeting." That night, Hochschild hosted a private dinner at the Century Club. "The purpose of the dinner was for the commissioners to tell Harry Albright that Leo O'Brien had to be replaced by Harold Hochschild," said Peter Paine.

Albright was prepared. Leo was an old friend of his, and Albright had already met with him to lay down the new rules. "I convinced him to give me a presigned letter of resignation, which we would accept if he fell off the wagon again," Albright wrote. "Any commissioner could call in the resignation at any time. Armed with the letter, I was ready for the confrontation. What I wasn't ready for was the Century Club. This Albany boy had never seen such a fancy spread. There was tray upon tray of smoked salmon, capers, caviar, all kinds of cocktails, and then a formal dinner party with three wines. Although I felt like a fish out of water, it didn't stop me from making a spirited defense of Leo's virtues.

"I don't know if the commissioners were listening, but I do know we were all drinking. Some of this group of distinguished New Yorkers, with the exception of our host Harold Hochschild and a few others, came as close to being universally crocked as any group I have ever seen before or since. Each commission member demanded Leo's demise. I remember someone standing up on wobbly feet and assuring me that alcohol was 'a horrible thing for a public figure.' It never occurred to any of these speakers that they were all similarly public figures, and that they were similarly crocked."

But O'Brien's inebriation was just a symptom of the commission's real problem, which was weak leadership. And solving the problem by appointing a strong leader like Harold Hochschild "did not go down very well with the governor, for several reasons," said Paine. "Harold was wealthy, and Leo was a good old Irishman from Albany. I think they were concerned about that image. Harold was also not awed by Nelson Rockefeller in the slightest. He had great wealth of his own, and he was used to dealing with prime ministers and finance ministers because of his mining business. Rockefeller was also sixteen years younger. Harold was one of the few people Rockefeller could not talk down to."

Hochschild had a long list of powerful political and social connections he could call upon to oppose Rockefeller if that became necessary. Many of Hochschild's friends were major donors to the state Republican Party. And as an organizer of the opposition to the national park idea, Hochschild had recently tangled with Laurance and come out on top. An ally had warned Harold to be careful of the Rockefellers during that national park fight, because they "simply hated to lose."

But those things were assets to Jerry, Paine, and other commissioners. They knew where they wanted to go, and only Hochschild could get them there. The TSC considered Hochschild its chairman from that evening on.

The next day, the commission held a public hearing in New York City that was dominated by environmentalists, many of whom spoke against giving the State Council of Parks a role in the Adirondacks. Arthur Crocker, Arthur Savage, and others were joined by Mrs. George Dalziel, the state president of Federated Garden Clubs, a women's organization that played a major role in the Adirondacks. Al Forsythe of the Sierra Club told the commission that miniature golf courses, travel trailers, hotels, and ski areas were incompatible with "the higher uses of our wild lands."

"The area is already overdeveloped," Forsythe said. "There are more roads than optimum. Motor campsites and plush accommodations are anachronisms among the rare beauty of the region."

Looking back on that day, Arthur Crocker said that he was greatly relieved to hear that Hochschild, who had been a trustee of the Association for the Protection of the Adirondacks (AfPA) since 1951, had been appointed chair. But the January meeting also launched two months of increasingly tense communications between the TSC and the governor's office.

The new chairman was a clear signal to the Rockefeller brothers that the TSC was not going to deliver the recommendations they had hoped for. Laurance wanted the Adirondacks to be opened up to the public, like a national park. Hochschild was a stalwart supporter of a strict interpretation of the Forever Wild clause. The TSC was going to recommend large wilderness areas and other strict controls on how public land could be used. Laurance wasn't happy about it, and he told his men to say so.

Two of the governor's aides attended the TSC's February 4th meeting. Ron Pedersen briefed the commission on the DEC proposal, and Henry Diamond suggested that the TSC take a close look at Maine's Allagash River, a "wilderness waterway" that was protected federally, managed by the state, and the recipient of federal funds to acquire additional land. Leo O'Brien had advocated a similar position.

Then Diamond kept talking. He questioned the need for an independent state agency. "I remember the scene as if it were yesterday," Harold Jerry said. "The commissioners were seated in several rows. Harold Hochschild and I were facing them. Henry Diamond, who was sitting in the back row, piped up and said, 'The thorough studies the staff is now doing are not what this commission was asked to do. We were supposed to make a quick survey and come up with recommendations for solving immediate problems, not try to plan the future of the park for all time.'" Diamond was saying that the TSC should wrap things up quickly.

The room had been darkened for a slide show, so the commissioners' faces were not visible to each other. As soon as Diamond stopped speaking, Fred O'Neal stood up. "Now Fred knew nothing about the park when we began, but he had done all the reading and he went on every field trip," Jerry said. "He had become an expert on the park; he was a man of great intelligence and perseverance. He had this great big, deep voice, but he didn't speak very often. Without turning around to face Henry Diamond, who was sitting right behind him, Fred said, 'I was not put on this commission to pull Nelson Rockefeller's coals out of the fire.' Then there was dead silence. Nobody said a word."

After Diamond's proposal and O'Neal's response, the commissioners passed two resolutions. The first stated that at present, "Any federal participation in the management of Adirondack Park property does not seem desirable." The second opposed the idea of giving Laurance's Office of Parks and Recreation any role in the Adirondacks.

The next day, Hochschild wrote to Pedersen to ask for a meeting with the governor. He said that at two recent hearings, conservation organizations had expressed "the deep apprehension, which we share, at the proposed change in the special status of the Adirondacks and at the proposed split in the responsibility for the Adirondacks hitherto borne by the Conservation Department."

The commission's vision had come into focus. Six of the eleven active commissioners—Hochschild, Paine, Lawrence, O'Neal, Watson Pomeroy, and Frederick Sheffield—wanted an independent agency that was part of the executive chamber to manage development of private land in the park. These six also tended to support the many ideas suggested by Harold Jerry and his staff, which consistently aimed at protecting the natural integrity of wild areas, promoting quieter forms of recreation, shifting the park's economy toward nature-oriented tourism, and tightening regulations on motorboats, snowmobiles, logging equipment, and other gasoline-powered machines.

Commissioners Jim Loeb and Bob Hall went along with the majority, although they occasionally voiced concerns about what a wilderness-first approach would mean for full-time park residents. Howard Kimball had broader objections but couldn't articulate an alternative, so he remained silent. And O'Brien was in favor of a federal role, but he had been muzzled. That left Laurance's man, Henry Diamond, who was increasingly concerned with setting up the DEC. Diamond would play a key role as messenger and broker as the TSC proceeded. His importance to the commission would only increase after he resigned in April.

Pedersen met with the commission again in the Village of Saranac Lake on February 16. The minutes record the TSC's position: "the preservation of the environment has a higher priority than the satisfaction of recreational needs." The commissioners held their last public hearing the next day, inviting the public and any of the thirty-nine official advisors who had not met with them yet to attend.

The advisors had been appointed in September 1969. They were a diverse group that included foresters, owners of small businesses, planners, and local elected officials. Harold Jerry checked in with them and used their positions to shape and articulate the commission's proposals, but not to change the vision. About a dozen of the advisors represented environmental groups, and by the time the list was officially announced, Jerry had already been working closely with those people for several years.

Jim Loeb chaired the public hearing in Saranac Lake because, he said, "I'm a hometown boy." Leo O'Brien quietly attended both days, along with about 250 local people. The speakers held diverse opinions, and the overall tone was courteous. Several of them mentioned Laurance Rockefeller, just to say that they didn't trust him. Earl Kwook, the owner of a lakeside home, told Loeb that if the state parks people started running things, the TSC might be ignored. Loeb replied that if that happened, the commissioners promised to "get up on our hind legs and say something about it."

Kwook didn't know that, in private, the commission was fighting for its life. After the Saranac meetings, Hochschild wrote to Pedersen. "When our

Commission was appointed by the Governor the Adirondacks was, and still is, under the sole supervision of the Conservation Department. The administrative system now envisaged by the Governor will be entirely different. It may be, therefore, that in the Governor's view the Commission has become an anachronism. Such things happen. If, on the other hand, our mission has not, in the Governor's mind, been superceded, the members of the Commission will, I know, appreciate it if he will take the time to meet briefly with us to clarify the situation."

The governor wrote to Hochschild on February 23 to say that he fully supported the commission and was looking forward to its recommendations. After hearing Pedersen's report from Saranac Lake, he had decided that the Conservation Department's Division of Lands and Forests should continue to manage all the land, trails, and public camping areas in the Adirondack Park. However, he thought the winter recreation areas at Whiteface, Van Hoevenberg, and Gore Mountains should be operated by a new agency, the Office of Parks and Recreation, along with the newly opened parkway to the top of Prospect Mountain, near Lake George. The DEC "will be in a far better position to undertake its massive task if it is not also responsible for providing for the great numbers of people which, in season, daily use the specific facilities noted," Rockefeller wrote.

Hochschild was not satisfied. He feared the long-term consequences of giving Mr. Laurance's new agency any role in the forest preserve. On February 27, he replied to Rockefeller that the commissioners were "bewildered" by the proposal to split jurisdiction. "We find it difficult to chart our own course in view of the proposed transfer of authority from an experienced organization to a new and divided jurisdiction. Under the circumstances it may be wondered whether any practical purpose is served by continuing a study such as ours." He asked the governor again for an in-person meeting. He didn't get one.

On March 2, Hochschild wrote a press release that said the State Council of Parks proposal to operate Adirondack facilities, "about which [the commission] was not consulted, holds dangers for the Adirondack environment." The commissioners urged that the decision about jurisdiction be postponed until the TSC made its report public at the end of the year. Hochschild did not send out the press release yet. It was his *coup de grace*.

Peter Paine remembered that Hochschild laid down the gauntlet at a commission meeting in Albany on March 6. "Harold was a very soft-spoken person," said Paine. "I mean, he was graciousness personified. But he said to Henry Diamond, in substance, 'If you insist that we wrap this thing up the way you're proposing it, here's my response. I have here the signed resignations of every member of the commission,' and he showed them to Henry. Then he showed Henry the press release that was ready to go to his friends at the *New York Times*. And then he said, 'I suggest that you go back and talk to Mr. Albright and the governor, and perhaps reconsider your course of action.'"

Hochschild wasn't bluffing. On March 11, he told the commissioners that he had spoken to Henry Diamond that morning. Diamond had told him that the DEC bill was being drafted, that he was hopeful, but that he could not provide absolute assurance that Laurance Rockefeller would play no role in the Adirondacks.

"I told him the commission felt it had not been fairly treated," Hochschild wrote, "and that I hoped the bill could be changed to our satisfaction so that it would not become necessary for us to issue a statement." He added that his company's public relations man was ready to send the materials out if that proved necessary, and that it would be important for Bob Hall and Jim Loeb to run stories in their newspapers on the same day as the *New York Times*. Then he left on a five-day trip to San Francisco.

The threat of bad press in New York's newspaper of record was potent, especially during a tough reelection campaign in which environmental issues were paramount. After Hochschild showed his weapon, Nelson Rockefeller made a political calculation and calmly threw away his brother's dream of adding millions of "effective acres" for recreation. When Rockefeller submitted the DEC bill to the legislature on March 16, his accompanying message said that the DEC would retain complete control over the Adirondack and Catskill Preserves, including all recreation areas, and that "any consideration of change" would come from the TSC, an "outstanding group of citizens" whose recommendations "should offer invaluable guidance."

Hochschild kept pushing. He met with Ron Pedersen, Harry Albright, and others on March 25 to review the legislation and asked Harold Jerry to write a long memo giving the TSC's reaction to it. Jerry followed the bill through the legislature. He reported again on April 10 that the Catskill and Adirondack Forest Preserves had been placed in a regional category over which the Parks Department had no control, and "the modifications made by the governor's office do not seriously interfere with the intent of our amendments." Rockefeller signed the legislation on April 22.

The crisis had passed, leaving Hochschild firmly in control. The governor didn't give him everything, though. In April, Hochschild was addressed as "Mr. Chairman" by Diamond and other commissioners, but the minutes refer to him as "Vice Chairman" in May and "Acting Chairman" in October, even as the report was sent to the printer. Only in the printed report is Hochschild named "Chairman" and his leadership finally acknowledged. Nelson Rockefeller might have done this to avoid the embarrassment of officially demoting O'Brien. It's just as likely that he did it because he hated to lose.

In spring 1970, Nelson Rockefeller was losing. Polls showed him trailing his Democratic opponent, Arthur Goldberg, whose impressive resume included the US Supreme Court. There were far more registered Democrats than Republicans in New York State, and after twelve years, many voters were tired of Rocky. The DEC was a big part of the governor's comeback plan. On Earth Day, April 22, as the cameras rolled, Rockefeller rode a "nonpolluting vehicle"—a bicycle—in Brooklyn. That was "messaging." Then he announced the formation of the DEC and appointed Henry Diamond to be its first commissioner. That was the deliverable.

Henry Diamond could have made life difficult for the TSC in countless ways. But his new job meant that, at long last, he no longer depended on Laurance Rockefeller for his power. Even at the height of the conflict, Diamond stayed on friendly terms with Hochschild. Diamond himself had learned courtliness while growing up in Tennessee. He didn't take political disagreements personally, especially minor ones. He mostly agreed with Harold Jerry's "extreme conservationist" policies and when he didn't, the differences were in degrees. Also, "Harold Hochschild was a very nice man," Diamond said. "I think that helped."

When the leadership struggle was finally resolved in mid-April, the commission was left with three months to deliver the technical reports to the printer, and six months to deliver the main report so the governor could get a printed version at the end of the year. They still had to settle on their recommendations. But they had majority agreement on the most basic issues, and Harold Jerry had kept the staff and consultants working during the crisis.

George Davis presented a big bundle of work at the March 7 meeting in Albany, including a proposal for five different categories for land management in the forest preserve, a proposal to delineate "wild, scenic, and recreational" rivers, a list of especially important tracts of land, and proposed regulations for airplanes and motorboats. Davis, twenty-seven, who had been plucked away from Cornell only one year earlier, had clearly risen in stature. The commissioners accepted his work without comment and added that "the management guidelines are the only way to preserve the quality of the environment of the park from the impact of ever-increasing use. The creation of land use classes and individual management plans will allow maximum public enjoyment of each parcel without destroying it."

Hochschild's company, American Metal Climax (AMAX), hosted the meeting of April 3–4, 1970 in its boardroom at 1270 Sixth Avenue in New York City. The AMAX building is an Art Deco landmark and is part of Rockefeller Center; Radio City Music Hall is on its ground floor, and Laurance Rockefeller's office, and 30 Rockefeller Plaza, was just around the corner. Every subsequent meeting of the TSC was held in that boardroom or at the homes of Harold Hochschild, Richard Lawrence, and Peter Paine.

The commissioners approved another batch of reports and also discussed the creation of the Adirondack Park Agency (APA), the wild idea Richard Lawrence had sold to the staff. Several commissioners pushed their opinion that the agency should also have jurisdiction over the public lands—that their new agency, in other words, should have the power to tell the DEC how to manage the forest preserve.

Commissioner Watson Pomeroy did not attend the April meeting, so Hochschild called him afterward to brief him on what happened. Pomeroy believed that "we are leaving far too much to the proposed park agency," Hochschild wrote to the commissioners on April 7. "He thinks we are not going to get it, and that we should therefore lay down more specific guidelines for the proposed Department of Environmental Conservation." Hochschild suggested that "we make an objective assessment of our chances of getting the park agency, taking into consideration the help we may get from the various conservation organizations and other sources. If we decide to play for all or nothing, we should at least be aware of what we're doing."

The May 5–6 meeting was the first meeting attended by former Conservation Department Commissioner Stewart Kilbourne, whom Rockefeller appointed to replace Henry Diamond when Diamond took over the DEC. Hochschild asked Kilbourne to state his views about the proposed Adirondack Park Agency for the minutes. Kilbourne said, "The future of the Adirondacks requires that there be an independent agency in overall control of the private and public land in the Adirondack Park, with the Conservation Department playing a significant role in relation to public land." Nine of the eleven active commissioners now agreed that the park agency should draft a land use plan for private land, and Kilbourne added another vote to those who wanted the proposed agency to also control the forest preserve.

Peter Paine pushed the idea of more control. "Dick Lawrence long ago suggested that we examine the idea of a single agency for the whole park," he wrote to the commissioners on May 15. "The care, custody, and control of the Forest Preserve is now a very minor part of the new [DEC]. The whole thrust of the Department will be in the fields of air and water pollution and solid waste disposal, where vast efforts will be required. The Adirondacks are not likely to receive too much time, attention, and money." Paine suggested that a park agency controlling "the *whole* park, both the private and public lands, might be the best political answer. Any two-headed monster, no matter how skillfully constructed, is going to create friction, inefficiencies, and rivalries" (italics in the original).

The commission considered a dozen reports during its May 5–6 meeting, many of which included recommendations. Members also authorized one new study (on fire towers) and refused Jerry's request to cancel two studies (on canoe routes and seasonal residences). They told Jerry that if he missed the print deadline, the reports could be circulated in other ways, and if he ran out of money, they would find it somewhere. They approved ten reports and deferred action on two, including the crucial report that contained Neil Huber's first draft of legislation creating the Adirondack Park Agency.

The creation of the Adirondack Park Agency was one of three measures that Harold Jerry considered essential to "saving" the Adirondacks. The other two were specifically focused on the large tracts of private land that defined the park's character.

The commissioners agreed that the largest tracts of privately owned land in the park, which were managed for timber production, should never become the sites of large housing projects, ski areas, or other intensive forms of development. But they also knew that the state was unlikely to ever have enough money to purchase this territory outright. They asked Neil Huber and others on the legal staff to suggest methods, legislation, and financing that would give state officials new ways to control development in the backcountry.

Huber began thinking about the legal devices known as easements. An easement is a tool in land use law that belongs to a legal category known as "servitudes," which grant limited rights to nonowners of land. A "positive" easement allows the holder to do something, such as cross the owner's property with a road or trail. A "negative" easement gives the holder the right to prevent a landowner from doing something, such as impounding a stream or digging too close to a neighboring property. Easements can be purchased or given as donations. They often reduce the value of the land, so the federal government allows the value of easements donated to charities to be counted as tax deductions.

In 2021, the business of buying and selling easements is well established. State laws and court decisions have made the process clear. Lawyers often explain the concept this way: when someone receives a deed to a piece of land, they are really receiving a bundle of rights. These usually include the right to build roads, cut timber, build houses, and prevent trespassing. When landowners sell or donate easements, they sell or donate some of these rights while retaining others.

But none of this was clear when the TSC was forming its recommendations. The common law of servitudes had evolved over centuries, and the laws on the books were head-scratchingly ambiguous; they owed more to history than to logic. They were a mess, and most legal experts in the early 1970s said that they were too flimsy to support the particular form of easement that Huber, Jerry, and the commissioners wanted. Huber began preparing new laws that would clear things up, so the state could permanently protect private land from development.

The TSC envisioned a "scenic easement," a negative easement held by the state in perpetuity (i.e., forever) that would prevent a landowner from building roads or structures. The goal of this easement would be to preserve a property's scenic value for the public. The specific terms would be open to negotiation; for example, the easement could permit public trails or roads to cross the property. It would probably also allow the owner to continue cutting trees, hunting, and using existing buildings in privacy.

The state already held one such easement that met this description, at Elk Lake, about ten miles southeast of Mount Marcy. It had been donated by the conservation-minded Ernst family, which still owned the land, so the arrangement had never been tested in court. The TSC wanted hundreds more easements like these, and they knew they could not get them until the law became clear enough to stand up to legal challenges. They wanted to create a market for conservation easements.

"The great benefit of an easement is that it preserves an option for the future," said Harold Jerry. "As long as the land is not developed, there's always a possibility of bringing it into state ownership and keeping it open. I would have no problem at all with paying $900,000 for an easement, even if the total value of the land is only $1 million, because the easement is enough.

"Once the land is developed, it's gone forever. The chance of the state acquiring land with buildings on it is very remote because the character of the land has been changed, and also because the cost of the property is much higher. But as long as there's an easement on the land, the option is always there for future acquisition. Moreover, the easement itself maintains the atmosphere of the park. People can look at it, see it, and, in many instances, walk through the land and enjoy it just as much as if it were state owned."

Scenic easements would not mean much if the state didn't have money to buy them. So the staff also prepared a report recommending that the state issue bonds for land protection. The first draft of that report called for $98 million, with 21 percent allocated to simple fee acquisition, 57 percent for scenic easements, and the remainder for construction and maintenance.

The TSC also worked up recommendations dealing with the taxation of private forests, aid to local governments, and other incentives intended to encourage the preservation of open space.

But the three essential components of their recommendations for private land were the independent agency, easement laws, and the bond act, according to Jerry, who wrote to Albright that "these three bills are interdependent. One will not work properly without the others."

The commission and staff met again in New York City at the end of May. Nelson Rockefeller, his feud with Hochschild officially forgotten, joined the group for its first hour. The governor knew exactly what he was getting into, according to Richard Lawrence's notes, written on the margin of his meeting agenda: "Keep zoning quiet until after the election. Impact on land values of zoning. How will area people take this?"

When they resumed in Hochschild's offices, the commissioners had a general discussion about how much they should say in public. They decided not to send a spokesman to an upcoming public hearing in Plattsburgh that had been called by a likely opponent, Assemblyman Andrew Ryan. And they approved eleven more staff reports with recommendations, including Neil Huber's report on the structure of the proposed Adirondack Park Agency. But they did not agree on whether the new agency should have the authority to manage the forest preserve.

The next month was a hard one for the staff, who worked with a hired writer to get the technical reports, which ran to 300,000 words, in shape to go to the printer. Partly for that reason, the July 6–8 commission meeting included time for relaxation and celebration. Commissioners and staff met in Elizabethtown as the guests of Richard Lawrence. In addition to the business meeting, the weekend included dinner at Lawrence's home, a hike to a waterfall with coffee and doughnuts provided by a local Girl Scout troop, a tour of a historic fort, a Lake Champlain cruise to dinner at Peter Paine's house in Willsboro, and a bus trip to Whiteface Mountain. They had three months left to finish the main report.

The group reconvened at Eagle Nest on August 13–14 to begin approving the main report, with commissioners arriving and departing on a chartered float plane. They agreed to meet again at Eagle Nest on September 4–5, and then at Hochschild's New York City offices on September 17 and October 6. They had to be finished by then, said Jerry, or they would not be able to publish the report in December.

Editing by committee rarely works well, and the commissioners found it hard going as they reviewed the text. The minutes describe their line-by-line review and detailed discussions of the fine points. But several commissioners had more basic objections. After the August meeting, Jim Loeb wrote to Hochschild to complain that the report on the economy of the park was superficial and lacked concrete recommendations. "The general thrust is that industry is bad and we should oppose it," he said. "My feeling is that some industry is bad for the Adirondacks but there are good industries, such as research pharmaceutical, which should be promoted. If the people of the Adirondacks are completely dependent on a few months of seasonal business, the Adirondacks will become a slum."

Loeb also asked Hochschild whether the report could indicate recommendations where the votes were not unanimous, because all members would not "agree with every point and every sentence." He wanted to avoid minority reports or dissents, which "are reserved for major matters and I hope there won't be any." No dissents were written. George Davis said that the commissioners voted on each of the 181 recommendations, but these votes were not recorded.

Howard Kimball was alienated by the whole process. "It was a great mistake not to include more local residents and local officials," he said. "I'll never forget that August meeting at Harold Hochschild's house. We arrived, and here comes a butler and here come the maids. Oh my God. What the hell is this? Aren't we supposed to be talking about the future of the Adirondacks? And here's a guy who just gave $10 million to finance a museum up there that nobody had ever heard of? It seemed out of touch to me." Kimball didn't attend the last three meetings. Leo O'Brien only came to the one on October 6.

In fact, five members did not return to Eagle Nest on September 4, but it hardly mattered. The commissioners had appointed Hochschild editor in chief, with power to rewrite material in consultation with Lawrence and Paine. Hochschild was unsatisfied with the quality of the consultant's writing, so he redid it. "The report is in Harold's hand," said Paine.

Hochschild was possessive about the text. He enlisted his niece's husband, Claude Boillot, as a proofreader. At the end of the process, he wrote to Boillot that "most of the staff members, including the executive secretary, are men extremely able in their respective fields who never learned to write good English. This is a common deficiency in American professional and business circles."

Several big decisions were left until the end. The commissioners increased the size of the proposed bond issue to $120 million. They debated the draft statute for the Adirondack Park Agency, still unable to agree on whether to recommend that the agency have the authority to govern the forest preserve. They also made a last-minute decision to recommend that the state be given the power to buy the right of first refusal on key pieces of private land.

A right of first refusal guarantees that a potential buyer will be first in line to make an offer if a property ever goes on the market, although it does not oblige the landowner to accept the offer. This recommendation would come back to bite the TSC, although members seemed unaware at the time that it could become controversial.

The TSC made its final text changes on October 6 and 7 and chose "The Future of the Adirondack Park" for the report's title. The next day, Hochschild and Paine met with Harry Albright, who had talked to Henry Diamond. Albright urged them not to recommend that the park agency have the authority to review and revise the DEC's budget.

"Harry's position may be summarized as follows," Hochschild wrote to the commissioners. "The report is excellent. There is at least a chance that

Figures 1 and 2. *Top, left to right:* New York State Joint Legislative Committee on Natural Resources staffers Clarence Petty, Neil Stout, and Chairman Watson Pomeroy make dinner during a research trip in 1961. The committee conducted fieldwork that mapped Adirondack roadless areas, a job that had not been done since 1880. *Bottom left:* Harold Jerry (*left*), executive secretary of the Temporary Study Commission on the Future of the Adirondacks, with staff ecologist George Davis on a research trip in June 1969. The two men became friends during their work for the commission. (Clarence Petty Collection. Courtesy of the Adirondack Experience, Blue Mountain Lake, NY.)

Figures 3 and 4. Paul Schaefer (with ax) and David Newhouse were lifelong enthusiasts for the wild Adirondacks. The two men worked with a small group of Schenectady-based environmental activists for decades before becoming a powerful force in New York State politics in the mid-1960s. (Schaefer photo courtesy of David Gibson; Newhouse photo courtes of the Newhouse family.)

Figure 5. Harold Hochschild, seventy-eight, chairman of the Temporary Study Commission on the Future of the Adirondacks. Hochschild used his wealth, cunning, connections, and diplomatic skill to advance his vision for the Adirondack Park. (Photo by Yousuf Karsh, 1970. Courtesy of the Adirondack Experience, Blue Mountain Lake, NY.)

Figures 6, 7, and 8. *Top*: Governor Nelson Rockefeller (*right*) and his younger brother Laurance rode the Cold River Trail through the High Peaks Wilderness on October 10, 1965, led by Conservation Department Ranger William Petty (*left*). The Rockefeller brothers were lifelong best friends. Laurance perpetuated a family tradition of park building and urged Nelson to carry out his wishes. *Bottom*: Nelson (right), sixteen, and Laurance, fourteen, dressed as cowboys during a family vacation to western national parks thirty years earlier. (Courtesy of the Rockefeller Archive Center, Sleepy Hollow, NY.)

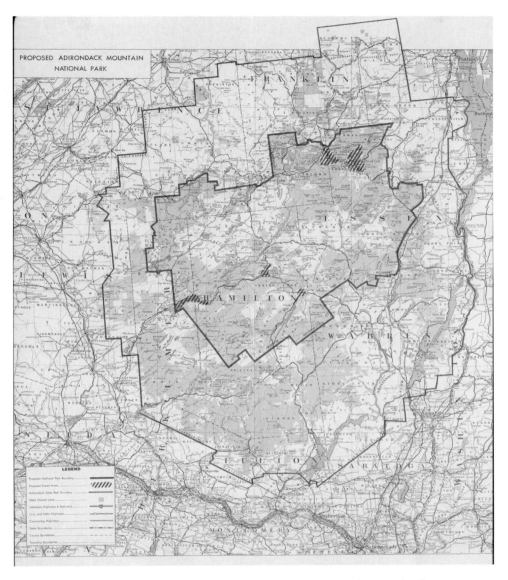

Figure 9. Laurance Rockefeller's August 1967 proposal for an Adirondack National Park achieved something that almost never happens in New York: consensus. Everyone hated it. (Courtesy of the Adirondack Experience, Blue Mountain Lake, NY.)

**ADIRONDACK STUDY COMMISSION MEETS WITH GOVERNOR**
Left to right, Richard Estes, staff planner; Heil Huber, staff counse[l]
James Loeb, Saranac; Frederick Sheffield, New York; Commission[er]
Henry Diamond; Watson Pomeroy; Chairman Harold Hochschil[d]

ov. Rockefeller; Fred O'Neal, New York; Peter S. Paine, Jr.,
illsboro; George Davis, staff ecologist; Stewart Kilborne; Harold
rry, executive director. Seated:Arnold Putnam, staff;Robert Hall,
arrensburg; Richard Lawrence, Elizabethtown.

Figures 10, 11, and 12. *Top*: in 1971, Nelson Rockefeller congratulated members of the
Temporary Study Commission, including staff counsel Neil Huber (misspelled in clipping)
on their report. Assemblyman Glenn Harris (*bottom left*), representing Adirondack counties,
lead the opposition. The commission's goal was to preserve Adirondack open space and limit
so-called "honky tonk" developments like the Village of Lake George (*bottom right*).
(Courtesy of the Adirondack Experience, Blue Mountain Lake, NY.)

Figure 13. The staff of the Adirondack Park Agency poses in front of the APA's Ray Brook headquarters in the spring of 1972. The staffers were underfunded, overworked, and full of passion for their cause. *Back, from left:* George Davis (assistant director), Oleta Marshall (secretary), Harry Daniels (executive director), Anita Riner (planning assistant), Gary Duprey (field ecologist), Clarence Petty (field ecologist), Don Smith (janitor), Richard Estes (planner), Jack Mills (planner), and Carol Gorbea (secretary). *Front, from left:* Gary Randorf (field ecologist), and Yoshi (last name unknown, intern). (Courtesy of George and Anita Davis.)

Figures 14 and 15. *Top*: Adirondack Park Agency board and staff members pose during their November 19–20, 1971, meeting in Old Forge, New York. Activities included field trips, a business meeting, and dinner at the Ferns Restaurant presented by the Webb Town Board. A year later, the same town board sought a court injunction to stop the agency's work. *Back, left to right*: Peter Paine Jr., George Davis (staff), Neil Huber (staff), Richard Estes (staff), Richard Persico, James Bird, Whitman Daniels, and William Foley. *Front, left to right*: Chairman Richard Lawrence, Richard Wiebe, Ronald Pedersen, and Mary Prime. Not pictured: Joseph Tonelli. *Bottom*: Ed Needleman (*left*) and Robert Kafin were lawyer-advocates in the Adirondacks. Contracted by the Sierra Club Legal Defense Fund, they watched the APA board closely and did a masterful job of keeping environmental groups informed. (APA photo courtesy of the Adirondack Experience, Blue Mountain Lake, NY; Kafin and Needleman photo courtesy of Robert Kafin.)

# ADIRONDACK PARK
## STATE LAND MASTER PLAN

**STATE OF NEW YORK**
**ADIRONDACK PARK AGENCY**

**NELSON A. ROCKEFELLER, GOVERNOR**
**JUNE 1972**

0 ........... 5 ........... 10 miles

| | | |
|---|---|---|
| Wilderness | Wild Forest | ● Scenic Vista |
| Canoe Area | Intensive Use | Adirondack Park Boundary |
| Primitive Area | Private Land | |

Prepared by Cartographic Services Section of the Office of Planning Services

**Figure 16.** The map for the 1972 State Land Master Plan zoned the Adirondack Forest Preserve into wild forests, primitive areas, and the most restrictive category: wilderness. (Courtesy of the Adirondack Experience, Blue Mountain Lake, NY.)

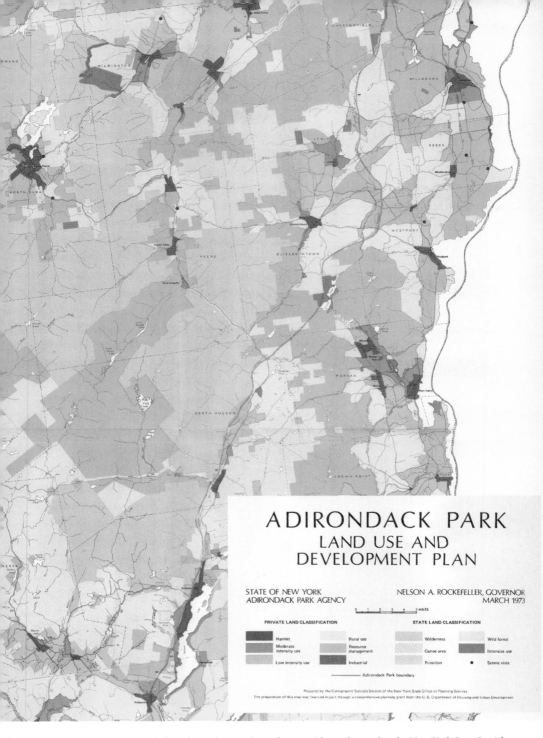

# ADIRONDACK PARK
## LAND USE AND DEVELOPMENT PLAN

STATE OF NEW YORK
ADIRONDACK PARK AGENCY

NELSON A. ROCKEFELLER, GOVERNOR
MARCH 1973

0  1  2  3  4  5 MILES

PRIVATE LAND CLASSIFICATION

Hamlet

Moderate
intensity use

Low intensity use

Rural use

Resource
management

Industrial

STATE LAND CLASSIFICATION

Wilderness

Canoe area

Primitive

Wild forest

Intensive use

Scenic vista

——— Adirondack Park boundary

Prepared by the Cartographic Services Section of the New York State Office of Planning Services
The preparation of this map was financed in part through a comprehensive planning grant from the U. S. Department of Housing and Urban Development

Figure 17. The map for the Adirondack Park Land Use and Development Plan, submitted to the New York State Legislature in March 1973, incorporated significant innovations in regional land use planning for both public and private land. But its complexity and the poor public relations surrounding its release caused a political explosion and led to years of conflict with park residents. (Courtesy of the Adirondack Experience, Blue Mountain Lake, NY.)

Figure 18. On January 20, 1973, eight hundred local residents packed the high school auditorium in Saranac Lake for a raucous eight-hour public hearing on the land use plan. "That was the beginning of the rebellion," one said. (*Adirondack Daily Enterprise*, January 22, 1973.)

Figure 19. As captured by Saranac Lake newspaper columnist Bill McLaughlin shortly after the hearing, locals used sarcastic humor to voice their disapproval of what he called the "invasion from Albany." (*Adirondack Daily Enterprise*, January 26, 1973.)

Figure 20. Nelson Rockefeller signs the Adirondack Park Agency Act on May 22, 1973, as (*left to right*) staff photographer Al Nusco, APA Chairman Richard Lawrence, Assembly Speaker Perry Duryea, and Senator Bernard Smith look on. (Photo by Paul Schaefer. Courtesy of the Adirondack Research Library of Union College and Protect the Adirondacks!)

the Governor, Henry Diamond, and Laurance Rockefeller will accept the concept of the Agency and its planning and policy powers. Don't jeopardize this chance by insisting on something that will be to Henry Diamond like a red flag to a bull." Peter Paine remembered that at the end of that meeting Harry Albright said, "Now I have a job to do. I have to convince Laurance that this is what he really wants."

As the commission worked through the final draft, Nelson Rockefeller's political machine was also doing its work. He spent $6.9 million on his reelection campaign, five times as much as his opponent, and two-thirds of that was his own money. His assault included an overwhelming barrage of television and radio ads, along with the early use of a new weapon: mailings that were tailored to a voter's interests. People who supported environmental causes got a mailer that listed Rockefeller's environmental accomplishments. And there were a lot of those people.

Rockefeller was also good at campaigning. "He liked people," said George Pataki, who was a 27-year-old advance man for the governor in 1970. Pataki was elected Governor of New York in 1994. One of his first jobs in politics was stocking Nelson Rockefeller's motel rooms with the governor's favorite snacks: Oreo cookes, a brand of fortified wine called Dubonnet, and Fresca, a sugar-free, grapefruit-flavored soda.

"Once there was an event where Rockefeller was going to stand at a podium and announce something, probably a local grant," Pataki said. "We went ahead and got everything set up. There was a construction project going on across the street. When the governor showed up, he got out of the car and headed straight for the construction workers. None of the papers mentioned the grant the next day, but they all ran the photo of the governor wearing a hard hat and sitting on a bulldozer.

"I learned a lot from him. He would go to meetings with important people, and he would pay just as much attention to the guy who turned the lights on. The janitor also had a vote."

By mid-September, Rockefeller had pulled even with his Democratic opponent. By mid-October, he was ahead of Arthur Goldberg by eleven points. On November 3, he beat the Democrat by nearly six hundred thousand votes, and despite a strong challenger from the Conservative Party, Rocky got 52.4 percent of all votes cast. He even got to within seventeen thousand votes of Goldberg in heavily Democratic New York City.

Ten thousand copies of *The Future of the Adirondack Park* arrived at the offices of the TSC in mid-December. The governor received his report, signed by all the commissioners, on December 15. Other copies were sent to state legislators, local officials, and anyone else who wrote to request one. Jerry predicted that all the copies would be gone within three weeks. Hochschild then arranged for the Adirondack Museum to print and sell a second edition.

The first outside reader was a journalist. Hochschild instructed Jerry to leak a copy of the report to *New York Times* reporter Bayard Webster on November 3 and said, "I have confidence in his discretion." As soon as the printed report arrived, another copy was sent via special delivery to Hochschild's old friend, Wilderness Society board member and editorial page editor John Oakes.

The *Times* coverage was made to order. Two weeks before the official release date, Webster wrote a preview that quoted Jerry, Hochschild, and Paine, and even included a plug for the Adirondack Museum. "The Park is now a meaningless entity," Jerry said in the article. "It's almost a fiction. All we want is to see that the Park has a compact entity of its own and to come up with a comprehensive plan for a workable Park."

"Harold Jerry told me that we had to be published above the fold on page 1 on a Sunday, and we did that on January 3, 1971," said George Davis. The next day, the TSC enjoyed a glowing editorial endorsement. Its report was "a model of clear and compelling argument," wrote Oakes, who urged that the Adirondack Park Agency Act be passed into law.

The good news kept coming. "Every single daily newspaper in the state of New York supported the report," said George Davis. "We were getting rave reviews." Robert Hall distributed 7,500 copies of a sixteen-page tabloid that summarized the report in his newspapers, vastly increasing its readership in the North Country. Most of the stories quoted Hochschild's summation: "If the Adirondacks are to be saved," he wrote, "time is of the essence." Hochschild even got a note from Bayard Webster, congratulating him on "a thoroughly magnificent job."

Hochschild's private opinion was that the entire process had been haphazard. "Of our thirteen members, two showed up for one meeting each and never returned," he wrote to Boillot. "They signed the report at the Governor's request without knowing what was in it, because the Governor didn't want to ask them to resign.

"The Commission was chronically bankrupt. Eventually we got enough money to end our work, but it was always in doubt until the last minute. During our second year everything was done in a rush because the designer and the printer wanted more time than we expected. I never saw the proofs of the final bound report."

"I remember the only time he ever got mad at me," said Harold Jerry. "When the report was being printed (at Wilcox Press in Ithaca, New York), we sent George Davis there to watch it come off the presses. He called me just before the presses rolled and said, 'There aren't any captions for the photographs.' So I dictated all the captions over the phone, and I failed to mention that to Harold.

"A month or so later, when the printed copies were delivered, I got a very irate phone call from Mr. Hochschild. He said, 'You had no authority to proceed on your own, and some of these captions are very bad. For example, one of them says, 'A myriad of waterfalls abound.' A myriad means ten thousand, and there are not ten thousand waterfalls in the park.' That was the only fracas I got into with him. His standards were very, very high."

Jim Loeb's press summary of the TSC report begins with a strong lead: "The Adirondack Park . . . faces an imminent crisis of unregulated development. Unless its development is intelligently planned, the wild forest character of the park, a unique resource unmatched in the eastern United States, will be doomed."

Few people read all eight technical reports, which, when put together, are about as long as an eight-hundred-page novel—think *Anna Karenina*—and a lot less dramatic. But the reports capture a monumental amount of fact-finding and analysis. And thanks to Hochschild's writing skill, the main report lays out a complex argument in logical order, written in language ordinary people can understand.

The commission put ten recommendations at the head of its list because they were intended to guide all the others. The first was that "an independent, bipartisan Adirondack Park Agency should be created by statute with general power over the use of public and private land in the Park." The subsequent recommendations added details. They recommended that the APA work with local officials and regional planning agencies as it developed a comprehensive plan for the park. Adirondack towns should be encouraged to develop their planning documents and abilities to the point where they could take over the permitting of developments, after they demonstrated their competence to the agency.

The report recommended that the Department of Environmental Conservation retain operational management of the forest preserve, but the agency have the right to review and comment on aspects of the DEC's budget having to do with the park before the budget was submitted to the governor. In other words, two new agencies, the APA and the DEC, would need to figure out a working relationship. And the APA would also have to work out its relationship with the officials of local towns. "A creative partnership between the APA, and DEC, and local governments is, in the Commission's view, the best method of achieving its objectives," Loeb wrote.

"There was some talk about how to appoint the members of the APA," said Peter Paine. "The governor appoints three, the senate majority leader appoints one, the speaker of the assembly appoints one, or whatever. We all said no to this. The governor is the one person who is most susceptible to statewide influence, and this entity needs to be his creation. We felt that the agency would be more likely to remain honest if it reported to someone who represents the entire state, because local pressures for development and accommodation were inevitably going to arise. The APA had to be a creation of the governor."

Land use planning was a fashionable topic in think tanks and graduate departments in 1971, but the recommendation to create the APA was also based on an unprecedented data collection effort. "I think it was the first time anyone had ever analyzed every piece of privately owned land in a large region," said George Davis. The research revealed that two million acres, or more than half of the private land in the park, was owned by just 626 entities. Fourteen of them owned more than ten thousand acres. The upshot was clear. Most of the work of safeguarding the park's open space could be done by negotiating with a small number of people.

The public land report relied on the field research Clarence Petty had done first with Neil Stout in 1959–1961 and then, eight years later, with George Davis. It proposed classifying 52 percent of the forest preserve as "wild forest," with standards that were roughly equivalent to those followed by the Conservation Department. The remainder would be "wilderness" (43 percent) and "primitive" (5 percent) and would follow standards that were stricter than those of the federal wilderness system. Less than 1 percent of the forest preserve was claimed by campsites, boat launches, ski areas, and highways. Article 14 of the state constitution, the Forever Wild clause, would not change. It would continue to determine how each of these areas could be used.

Several recommendations for the forest preserve were cutting edge in 1971. George Davis's work introduced the idea that subjective criteria, such as the feelings inspired by untouched hillsides and vast silences, were valuable and should be included in forming state policies. And the Canadian wildlife biologist Doug Clarke's research supported recommendation no. 65, which said that the state should reintroduce native species, such as martens, eagles, spruce grouse, loons, and ravens, to their historic ranges. This was an early push toward the now-common practice of wildlife restoration.

"We could have introduced wolves," said Harold Jerry. "Doug offered to give George Davis and me twelve wolves, enough to reintroduce them into the High Peaks. But it would have been illegal, so we turned him down. It was a terrible mistake. We should have taken him up on it."

Some recommendations cleared up outdated policies. Recommendation no. 68, for example, was to eliminate bounties paid for killing coyotes in the park. Others were decades ahead of their time. Recommendation no. 178, the $120 million bond issue, said that a large share of it should be used to acquire "scenic easements," a legal device that required enabling state legislation. Recommendation no. 181 said that private donors should establish an Adirondack chapter of The Nature Conservancy to acquire easements and gifts of land. The conservancy chapter was created quickly. It found lots of willing sellers, many of whom had already been identified by the TSC's research. But the bond issue funds were quickly claimed, additional money proved hard to come by, and state laws simplifying scenic easements did not pass for another twelve years.

The TSC's research on economics and local governments disappointed Jim Loeb and others because it did not find any easy ways to attack the region's chronic poverty and shortage of good jobs. In fact, the studies showed that one measure advocated by many local officials—opening up the forest preserve to logging—wouldn't create any new jobs. "Loggers probably wouldn't lose their jobs quite as fast, but we found that existing sawmills and pulp mills would be able to handle the increased yield if the forest preserve was cut, so no new jobs would be added," said George Davis. He added that a lot of the timber in the forest preserve does not have commercial value, because 40 percent of the forest preserve is more than two miles from any road. The expense of building a road big enough for a log truck was high enough that those trees weren't worth the trouble, at least not in 1971.

The economic and local government reports are the weakest of the eight, even though poverty is a serious, chronic problem in the park. In 1971, 8 percent of the residents of all New York counties outside of New York City received public assistance or Medicaid payments. The share was higher than average in eleven of the thirteen counties that fall partially within the Blue Line, and in some of these counties, it was a lot higher. Eighteen percent of the residents of Franklin County received welfare payments in 1971, and 19 percent were on welfare in Hamilton County.

The TSC's staff economist, Peter Birckmayer, was a strong supporter of Lyndon Johnson's antipoverty programs. "The pockets of poverty he saw in the Adirondacks really bothered Peter," said his widow, Jennifer. But Birckmayer left the TSC as soon as its research was completed, and other staffers and commissioners pointed out that helping disadvantaged people was not a critical part of their mission. That omission turned out to be costly.

The TSC's report came out in the early years of a national shift away from high-paying jobs in manufacturing and toward lower-paying, less secure positions in services, such as health care, education, food services, security, and personal care. This shift was as painful to working-class families in the Adirondacks as it was everywhere else.

The Adirondacks "is a very poor area," said George Davis. "The data showed that the region didn't have the labor force, markets, or transportation systems you need to make economic development successful. Nor were we likely to get any of those things anytime soon. We had forestry, a little bit of agriculture in the Champlain Valley, and the tourist industry. Those are not going to be the best industries to base an entire economy on, but that is what we found. We needed to move ahead on that base."

The commission prescribed a bitter pill. To protect the area's most valuable asset in the long run, new rules had to be imposed that would make it harder to do business in the short run. It recommended continued controls over outdoor advertising; the creation of a wild, scenic, and recreational rivers system to control development along river corridors; and the regulation of motorboats and aircraft in the park. It said that ski areas, improved campgrounds, and other intensive recreation facilities should be located on the fringes of the park, and preferably outside its boundaries. It recommended remediation for some of these measures, such as compensating localities for losses in tax revenue caused by the acquisition of easements. But the economic news was bad, and the commission delivered it straight.

The TSC articulated a long-term vision of the park that emphasized bio-diversity, open space, sustainable development, and ecological restoration. It borrowed techniques from diverse places, some of them previously unknown and many of them highly useful. Some of its recommendations were ignored, and others took decades to accomplish. But just two years after the report's release, Courtney Jones wrote that "it has become one of the most impor-tant source books ever produced on the Adirondacks; in the foreseeable future, no serious study of the park as a whole will be undertaken without reference to it. No one who reads it through can avoid a better understand-ing of the area's problems."

In many ways, the report was written for an audience of one. And what got the governor's attention was that a lot of its recommendations were new. "Nelson Rockefeller was not an environmentalist, but he loved innovation," said George Davis. "And we brought him ideas that had never been tried elsewhere on this scale. So here was an opportunity for him to break new ground that was also politically popular.

"We briefed him on the final report in a two-hour session. We sold him on it. And once he was sold on something, there was no stopping the man."

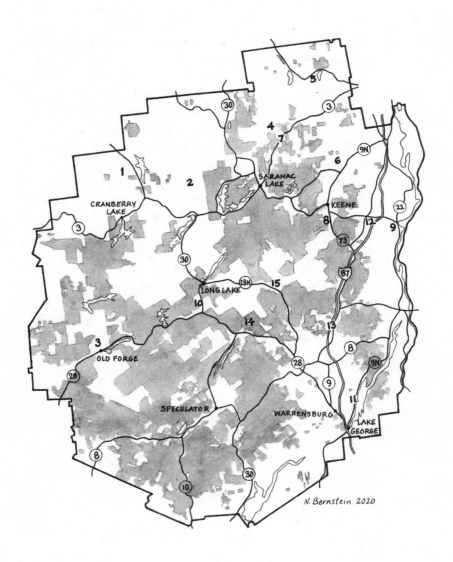

N. Bernstein 2020

Map 2.  This map illustrates state-owned land (shaded) and planned second-home project sites (labeled 1–15) in 1971–1972. In May 1971, Senator Ron Stafford and Assemblyman Peter Berle asked the Adirondack Foundation of Westport, New York, to compile a list of second-home developments planned on private land within the Adirondack Park. Shortly after Foundation Chairman Courtney Jones submitted his list of fourteen sites, the Horizon Corporation announced plans for a development much larger than any of those he had identified.

(Map by Nancy Bernstein. Sources: Liroff, Davis, and Lyman. *Protecting Open Space: Land Use Control in the Adirondack Park*, p. 24; *Plattsburgh Press Republican*, May 27, 1972.)
  1. Horizon Corporation, 24,000 acres, 6,000 to 9,000 lots, west of Route 56 in the Town of Colton
  2. Ton-Da-Lay, 18,500 acres, 4,000 lots, north of Tupper Lake along Floodwood Road
  3. DeCamp Tract, 10,000 acres, 5,000 lots, North Branch of the Moose River, immediately north of Old Forge
  4. Loon Lake, 3,500 acres, 900 to 1,000 lots, northeast of Saranac Lake
  5. Boise Cascade, 3,248 acres, north slopes of Lyon Mountain, west of Dannemora
  6. Ausable Acres, 4,000 acres, Town of Jay
  7. Subdivision of 500 units, Town of Franklin
  8. Adrian East and Adrian West, 500 acres, Town of Keene
  9. Westport Associates, 300 acres, 10 units, Town of Westport
10. Finch Pruyn, Minnow Pond, 200 units, Blue Mountain Lake, Town of Indian Lake
11. Subdivision of 95 units, Lake George, Warren County
12. Garondah Lodge and adjacent Gaylord property, 250 units, Town of Elizabethtown
13. Subdivision of 26 units, Town of Schroon
14. Finch Pruyn, subdivision at Gooley Club, Town of Minerva
15. Finch Pruyn subdivision, Town of Newcomb

Chapter 7

# "Pass the F*cking Thing"

William Doolittle sat in his Saranac Lake office one winter morning in 1971, trying to figure out what he had gotten himself into. He was thirty-four. He had worked at newspapers for more than half of his life, and he had a good job at New Jersey's newspaper of record, the *Newark Evening News*, when he suddenly got the chance to own a paper. He raised $50,000 by tapping into his savings and taking out a loan, and now here he was, the new editor and publisher of the *Adirondack Daily Enterprise* and the weekly *Lake Placid News*.

Saranac Lake (population 5,000) isn't exactly a red-hot media market. Doolittle said that the *Daily Enterprise* is "a daily paper in a weekly town." But the seller, Jim Loeb, was offering a stable operation with no competition at a bargain price. The Doolittles didn't know much about Saranac Lake when they pulled their kids out of private school over the Christmas break, bound for a cold, snowy new home. In fact, Doolittle never even visited the newspaper office before he bought it.

"We bought it in New York City, at my attorney's office," he said. "After the closing, Jim and I drove up to Saranac Lake through an enormous snowstorm. I had no idea about Adirondack politics. I had never heard of the forest preserve."

Loeb filled Doolittle in as they crawled along through the storm. Politics in the North Country wasn't anything like the affluent suburb Doolittle came from, Loeb said. It was loud and personal. Loeb's readers included a lot of hard-core conservatives who basically put new government programs in the same category with rat infestations. The right-wingers were particularly strong in Lake Placid (population 2,500), the tourist town nine miles east of Saranac Lake. "Jim said that the Lake Placid chapter of the John Birch Society held the same views as the local Democratic Party," according to Doolittle.

Doolittle heard several reasons why Loeb was selling the papers after seventeen years. He and his co-owner, Roger Tubby, had developed serious political differences. They couldn't stop arguing about the Vietnam War, which Loeb thought was a disaster. Loeb was also leading a drive to establish a new community college in Saranac Lake. The other board members of the college couldn't decide whether to buy a permanent site from local developer Frank Casier, who was demanding a very high price, and the arguments had gotten personal. Loeb, who strongly favored the site, had become the target of nasty, public insults. He resigned from the college's board in September, then returned after his friends bought a large ad in his own newspaper begging him not to leave. It was all getting to be too much.

Loeb was also finishing up two years of work on the Temporary Study Commission (TSC). He had a pretty good idea of what local reactions would be if the report's central recommendation, the creation of a powerful Adirondack Park Agency, was passed into law. But Doolittle claims that Loeb didn't say a word to him about the TSC or the APA during that long car ride.

Doolittle's first issue as owner was published on December 23, 1969. The TSC report was released to the public a week later. Very few North Country people realized that something big had begun to move. Doolittle certainly didn't. His longtime reporter, Evelyn Outcault, published an editorial welcoming the report on January 4. "The [Adirondack Park] agency would have planning and land use control powers over private and public lands," she wrote. "It is a recommendation which will frighten, if not horrify many of our local residents. It is needed."

Doolittle got used to hearing those horrified reactions. And when he went to meetings where TSC commissioners and environmental leaders pushed the Adirondack Park Agency bill, it gave him a bad feeling. Some of the presenters reminded him of the arrogant student leaders who had pushed him around when he was muddling through Harvard.

After the report was released, local officials warned that the APA was a terrible idea that would bring economic ruin. "We're being asked to throw the switch at our own electrocution," said James DeZalia, chair of the Board of Supervisors in Essex County, which includes a few affluent enclaves (like Lake Placid) surrounded by vast, sparsely populated areas where rural poverty is common.

Strong local opposition can have an outsized influence on the New York State Legislature because of its traditional commitment to the principle of local self-determination, or "home rule." State laws with an impact that falls primarily on one geographic area often do not pass if people from that area object loudly enough for Albany legislators to notice.

As snow season turned into mud season, Governor Rockefeller still had not submitted the package of Adirondack bills the TSC had called for. Time was running out for the legislature to act when environmental activists and TSC commissioners organized an all-or-nothing run for the goal. They blitzed state legislators to convince them that the future of the Adirondack Park was a statewide concern, and that the opposition of the North Country's representatives should be overruled. Claims like DeZalia's were either exaggerated or completely inaccurate, they said. The vast majority of jobs and privately owned properties in the park would not be affected by the bill. Even North Country residents were overwhelmingly opposed to the large vacation home developments the bill was designed to prevent.

The TSC report had shown that tourism was a major source of jobs inside the Blue Line, and it was also the only industry that had a realistic shot at growth. The bills proposing the Adirondack Park Agency and other measures were intended to protect the very thing that visitors were paying to see. The commissioners envisioned a park where public and private lands would be curated to preserve the feeling of wilderness.

The commission's arguments were backed up with reams of data, but many North Country people didn't accept them. They saw the APA as a violation of home rule. They were insulted, and the bill's chances largely depended on how many locals would become angry enough to fight back.

After the Temporary Study Commission report was released on January 3, 1971, George Davis and Peter Paine hit the road. "I would run the slide projector, and Peter would talk," Davis said. "In most of the state it worked really well, because Peter has such a dynamic personality. His enthusiasm brings people in. We were out there for three months, building up support all over the state. It was extremely enjoyable, because we were selling something we believed in.

"But in the Adirondacks, Peter Paine's style did not work as well. The people up there tended to see Peter as an outsider. He is a graduate of Princeton, Oxford, and Harvard, and he practices law on Wall Street. Those things aren't always admired in the North Country."

The most respected voices in small North Country towns are often those of "natives," defined as people whose families have lived in the area for generations. A lot of Adirondackers who hadn't read the report relied on second- or third-hand accounts of it from their neighbors. And the rumors spread.

Paine, Davis, and Robert Hall gave a one-hour presentation to an overflow crowd of three hundred in Lake George shortly after the report was released, followed by two hours of questions and answers. Winifred LaRose, an attendee who supported the commission's recommendations, wrote that the audience was hostile at the beginning, "but it became obvious as the commission unfolded its story that the sentiment changed from hostility to enthusiastic support."

Well, maybe. A reporter wrote that during the question-and-answer session, a woman asked Paine, "Will the report prevent us from leaving our home and small farm to our children?"

"This is one of the most prevalent rumors," Paine replied. "Your fears are totally groundless. From the standpoint of private land ownership, some of the rumors going around are incredible." But, the reporter added, "the question in various forms was raised again and again."

The rumor had formed around a speck of truth. Just before the TSC sent its report to the printer, the commission decided to add recommendation no. 58: "The Conservation Law, Section 1-0503, should be amended to give the Department of Environmental Conservation the power to acquire remainder interests and rights of first refusal in real property." What the commission meant by "right of first refusal" was a voluntary agreement between a landowner and the Department of Environmental Conservation (DEC). The state would pay a fee in order to gain the right to make the first offer, should the land ever go on the market. The seller would not be obliged to accept the state's offer.

The commission's intent was to add one more way to protect undeveloped lakes and sweeping vistas that were privately owned. But they were being too clever for voters, and they also may have been naive about how state governments sometimes choose to exercise their power. What Adirondackers heard, after the story got around, was different. There was no "refusal." The Rockefellers were going to seize their homes. They had suspected it all along.

Unfortunately, the commissioners didn't have the time or the budget to win the hearts and minds of working people in the North Country. And the governor had not submitted a bill yet, so there was no way to disprove the rumors. Instead of persuading the public, Harold Hochschild and other commissioners focused their attention on people who were blocking the bills.

On February 2, 1971, nine members of the TSC met for the first time since October 1970 (Leo O'Brien and Howard Kimball were absent). Peter Paine reported that he and Hochschild had met with the first key individual, Department of Environmental Conservation Commissioner Henry Diamond, on January 22. Diamond had endorsed the idea of the APA controlling development on private land, Paine said, but he balked at giving the agency the power to supervise how the DEC managed the forest preserve. This is entirely understandable, Paine wrote, because Diamond was in charge of the DEC, and "he has a bureaucracy to defend."

More troubling was Diamond's apparent support for a new proposal. The State Council of Parks had asked the governor to give their chairman an ex officio appointment to the Adirondack Park Agency. Paine and Hochschild replied that such an appointment would be disastrous, because Adirondackers regarded the current parks chairman, Laurance Rockefeller, with "intense suspicion" due to his 1967 proposal to turn the Adirondacks into a national park. Diamond didn't back away from his desire to put Laurance on the APA. Paine told the TSC that he and Diamond would keep talking.

The commissioners also discussed their upcoming meeting with legislative leaders. New York gives an unusual amount of power to three people—the governor, speaker of the assembly, and senate majority leader—to set the legislative agenda. The commissioners knew that representatives from New York City and other urban areas would be inclined to support their bills if they came to a vote. But the powerful triumvirate would not put the bills up for a vote unless the commissioners could get them past another three people. One of them was Henry Diamond. The other two were Adirondack legislators.

The most influential legislators representing the Adirondack Park in 1971 were Assemblyman Glenn Harris and Senator Ron Stafford. Harris covered Fulton, Hamilton, and parts of Franklin Counties, which are home to a fraction of the park's residents. But Harris was also chair of the Joint Legislative Committee on Environmental Management and Natural Resources. He was the author of many bills that regulated fishing, hunting, snowmobiling, and other Adirondack pastimes. In 1969, he worked closely with Rockefeller's advisors as chief sponsor of the legislation that created the Department of Environmental Conservation.

Seven other assembly members represented parts of the park. Two of these played important roles in the APA legislation: Andrew Ryan, representing the Adirondack counties of Clinton, Essex, and Warren; and Dan Haley, representing Franklin and Saint Lawrence Counties. But Glenn Harris's territory and interests were primarily focused on the park. He also led the "Appleknockers," an informal group of upstate Republican legislators who reliably took conservative positions. All the Adirondack assemblymen were Republicans except for Haley.

Glenn Harris grew up in the southern Adirondacks during the Great Depression, hunting and fishing for his food supply. He did well enough in school to go to college, then returned to his hometown of Gloversville and bought a bar-restaurant nearby called the Snow Drift Inn. Harris's political career began in 1953, when he was elected to the Arietta Town Council by promising to pave the road that went past his bar. He got his nickname, "Landslide Harris," when he won his first race by seven votes.

Another distinctive aspect of New York's legislature is that most of its seats are "safe." In Harris's district, Republicans outnumbered Democrats roughly three to one. Harris was built like a fireplug and was not an eloquent speaker, but he excelled at serving individual voter requests. He always paid attention whenever a voter in his district contacted him, according to his second wife, Beverly Sawaya Harris, because "he never forgot that one vote matters."

So after he was elected to the assembly in 1964, Landslide lived up to his nickname. He served for twenty-six years and never faced a serious challenger.

Harris was also ambitious—he wanted to move up in Albany—and his ambitions depended on maintaining good relationships with the state's two most powerful Republicans. "He loved Nelson Rockefeller," said Beverly, whom he met while they were both working on Rockefeller's 1966 reelection campaign. "And he was buddies with Perry [Duryea, speaker of the assembly]. They went fishing together."

They probably traded saltwater and freshwater trips. Duryea, who represented Long Island, had a family-owned lobster fishing business. Harris was a licensed Adirondack guide. Duryea was fifty years old in 1971; Harris was fifty-two. Duryea would appoint Harris to the position of majority whip, responsible for mobilizing Republican votes on major issues, in 1973. That would put Harris fourth in line in the assembly's power structure.

The voters in Harris's district consistently gave him the same simple instructions. They wanted to keep taxes low and avoid state regulations while getting as much state aid as they could. Harris said that when the APA proposal was announced, "I told the governor that the people in my area just can't see setting up an [Adirondack Park] agency to override local home rule and zoning laws. The governor told me, 'We have to have something, Glenn, or the land developers are going to run away with the Adirondacks.' I told him that just wasn't true." But there was never any "personal enmity" between Harris and Rockefeller, according to the governor's attorney, Michael Whiteman. That would have been a bad career move for Harris.

The members of the TSC knew that Glenn Harris would never support their recommendations, and they were not surprised in February when Harris asked Rockefeller to delay the vote on the APA bill for a year. But Peter Paine, Harold Jerry, and others took care to maintain a cordial relationship with Harris. In June 1970, Paine wrote to Harris to thank him for a piece of environmental legislation, and added, "The clear message the Commission has had from the Governor is that none of our recommendations should be released in a manner that would get them into this year's political campaign. To someone as well versed as you are in Adirondack politics, this warning is hardly necessary." Harris didn't spill the beans.

Harris and Senator Ron Stafford walked a fine line because they served two masters who often disagreed. They had to succeed in Albany, but they also had to answer to voters who lived in the Adirondack Park. Stafford found the balancing act easier than Harris did. "He was a tall, impressive character," said Andrew Halloran, who was Stafford's aide in the early 1970s. "I liked him. Everybody liked him."

Stafford was only thirty-one when he was elected in 1966. He was an orphan who had been adopted by a family in Dannemora, a blue-collar town where the jobs were in mining, logging, and the state prison. "He was my fraternity brother at St. Lawrence University," said Peter Van de Water, an administrator at St. Lawrence. "I liked him, but we used to call him Always Number One, because he didn't pay attention to anything except his own goals." And Stafford was fidgety. "He might know you well, but if you'd see him, all he would ever say is 'Hi, howareya?' He was a politician to the core."

It might be hard to believe now, but in 1971, people who had intense political disagreements were often able to stay friendly with each other. As the park controversy moved along, Van de Water became the leader of an effort to defeat a large second-home development. One day, Stafford called and asked that he stop. "I said I wouldn't, and that I hoped it wouldn't hurt our friendship," Van de Water said. "He said we were big boys, and we could still be friends."

Ron Stafford was the same age as Peter Paine, and the two men had mutual respect for each other's power. Stafford represented six of the twelve Adirondack counties (Clinton, Essex, Franklin, Warren, and parts of St. Lawrence and Washington). Paine had wealth and connections that were rare for someone in Stafford's district. So when Paine wrote to Stafford on January 6, it had an impact. "As the Senator representing almost all of the Park, you will be an absolutely key man," Paine said. "I hope you will seize this opportunity to show some real leadership and look beyond the bounds of the local interests of the immediate Adirondack constituency, however it may react to this Report, to the larger implications for the state as a whole."

The commission also had an ace in the hole in their dealings with Stafford. One of Stafford's first jobs after law school had been in the Plattsburgh law firm where Harold Jerry's father was a partner. Stafford was charming and had no family, so the Jerrys treated him like a second son. Stafford treated Harold Jerry like an older brother. When Stafford remarried, Jerry was his best man. Jerry was proud of a photo of the two of them together that Stafford had signed, "To Harold, a True Friend."

In public, Ron Stafford was solidly opposed to the APA from the get-go. But he was also a regular visitor at Harold and Lyn Jerry's wilderness camp, and, according to Lyn, the two men had a private understanding. Stafford didn't like the idea of a new state agency throwing its weight around in his district, and he was going to say so in his speeches. But he wouldn't oppose the governor's wishes on this issue.

"Ron had a little switch in his back, and he could flip it on and off," said Michael Whiteman. "He would be carrying on like fury about something, and then he'd stop and look over at you and smile as if to ask, 'How am I doing?'"

The TSC arranged one of its meetings in July 1970 specifically to make Stafford feel welcome and included. He and Henry Diamond were invited to Elizabethtown for a private discussion, dinner at Richard Lawrence's house, and an evening presentation on the problems that were arising from large second-home developments in Vermont. Paine invited Stafford with a specific goal in mind, and he knew just how the senator liked to be treated.

The commission wanted to expand the Blue Line so it would have jurisdiction over fifty thousand additional acres in the northeastern corner of the park, including Valcour Island, a historically important 968-acre parcel in Lake Champlain that was five miles south of Plattsburgh. Valcour Island's open space was threatened by a proposal for a big marina that the TSC thought was inappropriate. But they would never be able to get the boundary changed without Stafford's blessing.

Stafford, whose earliest memories were of an orphanage, was bowled over by the wealth, warmth, and acceptance of Dick Lawrence, who was old enough to be his father, and Harold Hochschild, who could have been his grandfather. He said yes to everything. He even suggested that the Blue Line be extended all the way to the Canadian border.

"The meeting was highly worthwhile," Harold Hochschild wrote to Peter Paine the next day. "It's just as well that Dick hadn't spiked that iced tea with rum. If he had, in another half hour we'd probably have annexed the Province of Quebec."

The essential task for a state legislature is passing a budget, and New York's 1971–1972 budget was a difficult and humiliating experience for Nelson Rockefeller. He was in the midst of several monumental construction projects, including state university campuses, low-income housing in New York City, and a lavish plaza of state government buildings in Albany. Journalists referred to the construction boom as Rockefeller's "edifice complex."

In 1971, the bills for these construction projects were coming due, but tax revenues weren't growing like they had in the mid-1960s. Rockefeller proposed big tax increases, and the state assembly staged a revolt. By the time it was all over, Perry Duryea had forced Rockefeller to settle for less than half of the taxes he had originally asked for. Rockefeller was also forced to cut $760 million (9 percent) from his original spending request. The cuts were especially deep to welfare spending, which cost Rockefeller his friendships with several Black leaders, including baseball legend Jackie Robinson. And the antitax Republicans kept making demands. As midnight approached on April 1, the deadline for submitting the budget, Rockefeller was still in meetings with Republican legislators in the state capitol, ironing out the details.

The budget fight was an irritating distraction for a governor who hated to lose, and it took precious time away from his pet projects. The TSC couldn't move without him. In March 1971, Commissioners Frederick Sheffield and Peter Paine tried unsuccessfully to get Laurance Rockefeller's support. "[Laurance] Rockefeller's original recreation plans and his personal office staff have never deviated from their goals," Sheffield wrote to Hochschild. "They are therefore intending to ignore almost entirely the Temporary Study Commission's report, in spite of the very high degree of support it has received."

Support might have been high, but it wasn't universal. Businessmen in the Adirondacks hated the TSC's recommendations. They wrote to the governor that its ideas "will not preserve the ecology of the Adirondacks, will not meet outdoor recreation needs, [and] will not sustain the depressed economy of the region." That letter was signed by Lyman Beeman of the lumber company Finch Pruyn, which was planning a large vacation home development near the Hudson River Gorge; A. Richard Cohen, the owner of Old Forge Hardware; Francis Donnelly of the New York State Forest Practices Board; International Paper's Gerard Pesez; and Arthur Benson, the owner of Frontier Town in North Hudson, precisely the kind of "honky tonk" amusement park that Hochschild and his friends deplored.

On April 22, Essex County Supervisor James DeZalia said in the *Warrensburg-Lake George News* that "people acquiring property by purchase, gift or inheritance must apply to the Agency for a permit to continue its former use," and "the state must have first option to buy any property offered for sale in the region." Neither of these things were true, but it was impossible to disprove a rumor when there was no bill to refer to. Hochschild wrote to a supporter who had uncovered another rumor on April 22 and could only say, "We shall do whatever we can to dispel further misunderstanding on this subject as soon as the Governor sends the bill to the Legislature." Then he urged his supporter to write to the governor.

During one stressful moment late in the life of the TSC, Harold Hochschild tried to dispel his sour mood by writing a satirical letter to the commissioners. Hochschild wrote about his last night's dream, in which he had read a newspaper article from April 16, 2071. The dream was so vivid, he said, that he was able to transcribe the imaginary article verbatim.

> The controversial law establishing the Adirondack Park Agency was passed by both houses of the legislature at 1 a.m. today in the closing hours of this year's session. The statue relates to the Adirondack Park, 500,000 acres in area, of which 90% is privately owned. The Forest Preserve, the State's portion of the Park, has diminished during recent decades through the sale of a number of lakes and mountains to private individuals who have erected ski towns and built large motels, among them the famous Adirondack Palace Hotel and its 150-foot swimming pool on the summit of Mount Marcy, connected by a funicular railway with the mini jetport at Lake Colden. The 50,000 acres of land still owned by the State, however, boast the best snowmobile trails.
>
> Numerous organizations claim the credit for the creation of the Adirondack Park Agency. Historical research has, however, traced its origin back to the work, a century ago, of a now forgotten group, the Temporary Study Commission on the Future of the Adirondacks, and its staff. The recommendations of this group were received with such hostility that they fled the United States. The last survivors were traced to Afghanistan, where they were said to have spent their final days coloring maps of that country under the delusion that they were coloring maps of the Adirondacks.
>
> A movement is now under way to honor these unfortunates by placing a bronze memorial tablet in the marble lobby of the handsome 30-story building of the Department of Environmental Conservation which stands on the shore of Lake Diamond, formerly known as West Canada Lake.

The low point might have come on March 30, when funding for the TSC ran out. "This will be my last letter," Harold Jerry wrote to the commissioners. "The furniture is being moved out today, the telephones are being disconnected, and by tomorrow the offices will be empty. There is no doubt that the last two years have been the most enjoyable of my life from a professional point of view.

"Regardless of the outcome of the Commission program, I have the satisfaction of knowing that the report is sound, and that for years to come every act in the Adirondacks will be judged against the criteria we have established. . . . Whatever happens to the Adirondacks, your consciences are surely clear."

Rockefeller immediately appointed Jerry to another job. Around that time, Hochschild went to Rockefeller to ask directly whether or not the commission's legislative proposals had any chance. Rockefeller was blunt. "I'm no environmentalist, I'm a power broker," he said. "I'll support the bill if you can show me there's real statewide support for it."

Hochschild, who would celebrate his seventy-ninth birthday in May, decided to continue funding the TSC from his own pocket while also acting as its staff. It had already been his obsession for two years and eight months. With eight weeks left, he went all in.

Michael Whiteman is a founding partner of Whiteman Osterman & Hanna, one of Albany's most powerful law firms. With his dark pinstriped suit, bow tie, shaved head, and piercing brown eyes, he has the look of an Albany insider. Over a half century in practice, he has navigated hundreds of bills through the New York State Legislature. But he still has fond memories of 1971, when he was thirty-three and had just been promoted to the top tier of advisors in the executive chamber.

"We had regular Sunday evening and Monday morning meetings with the legislative leaders," he said. "There was lots more informal discussion in those days—'If you can't do this, what can you do'—lots of give and take. And Rockefeller almost always came to those meetings much better prepared than the legislators did, because they didn't have large staffs back then." After the budget was passed, Rockefeller must have sensed an opportunity. He told Whiteman to take the draft legislation Neil Huber had written for the Adirondack Park Agency and turn it into something that could pass.

On April 5, Hochschild met with Whiteman and Harry Albright to assess the bill's chances. The state legislature had just begun a two-week recess, and it would return on April 19. Whiteman told Hochschild that this legislature was so financially pinched that it would never authorize a bond act or any significant expenditures, but that it might be possible to pass bills that didn't carry a big price tag. He added that an APA bill might pass if Henry Diamond got his wish to retain control over the forest preserve. Hochschild accepted this revision.

Hochschild said that if the park agency were given authority over the development of private land, it was important that it be given that power immediately, because of the danger that private landowners would rush to build before the law took effect. It's difficult to stop a construction project, he said, after earth is moved and concrete is poured. Whiteman said he would take care of that. Finally, Whiteman told Hochschild that Glenn Harris and Ron Stafford were pivotal. If they were actively opposed, he said, it would be difficult for the bill to pass.

So the APA bill could happen, but only if its supporters worked quickly. "We should bring to bear all the influence we can on Stafford, Harris, [Senate Majority Leader] Brydges, and Speaker Duryea," Hochschild wrote in a confidential memo to the commissioners on April 6, with a copy sent to Arthur Crocker. He called on the commissioners and environmental leaders to organize a three-part campaign: letters to all legislators, special efforts to mobilize voters living in the districts of Harris and Stafford, and "letters to the Governor and Messrs. Brydges and Duryea from large contributors to the Republican Party."

The next day, the state president of the American Federation of Labor and Congress of Industrial Organizations (AFL-CIO) wrote a strong letter of support to the governor that was drafted by Fred O'Neal. A week later, Commissioners Hall, Hochschild, Stewart Kilbourne, Lawrence, Loeb, and Paine met with eleven leaders of the environmental movement, who had already rallied their troops. One of them, Marge Lamy, said that despite the vocal opposition, many Adirondack Park residents favored the bill and could be persuaded to write to Stafford and Harris. Crocker and others said they would contact the big donors.

The majority of state legislators saw supporting the APA bill as an easy way to please a big, well-organized group of voters. The environmental leaders also had a good crisis to organize around. Many of them had been priming their members for months with ominous notices about proposed second-home projects that would change the character of many sections of the park if they were all approved. One leader, Courtney Jones, counted fourteen thousand acres that were being planned for housing development. First on the list was Ton-Da-Lay, an 18,000-acre site near Tupper Lake that could contain up to seven thousand housing units. Louis Papparazzo, Ton-Da-Lay's developer, was dropping by the offices of state legislators. Papparazzo was accompanied by the man who had sold him the land, Franklin County Republican Committee Chairman "Red" Plumadore, who was ready to grease the political skids.

New land deals and proposals were turning up every few weeks. Activists said that Adirondack towns could expect the same problems experienced by small towns in southern Vermont that had allowed large second-home developments to be built near their ski areas. The Vermont towns were struggling with severe water, sewer, and traffic problems. They were being forced to raise taxes to build infrastructure that would only be used a few weeks a year.

Saving the environment was still a powerful political issue. On April 22, 1971, the second Earth Day, the anti-litter group Keep America Beautiful unveiled a public service campaign with the tag line, "People start pollution. People can stop it." The television ad was tersely narrated by William Conrad, the star of *Cannon*, a popular show about a tough private detective. It featured images of the Sicilian actor Oscar Corti, who used the stage name "Iron Eyes Cody" and hid the truth about his ethnic background to protect his career franchise, which was playing Native American characters. Corti is dressed in full buckskins with a feather in his hair. He sheds a tear after trash is thrown from the window of a car and it lands at his feet.

Americans went absolutely nuts for this ad. Cleaning up litter became a national craze. And thousands who had been moved by "the crying Indian" also wrote letters supporting the Adirondack Park Agency.

Rockefeller was convinced. On May 10, he submitted eight bills to the legislature. The bills would expand and protect the park boundary; establish a wild, scenic, and recreational rivers system; clarify laws regarding the state's right to hold scenic easements; and compensate local governments. But only one of the bills had a chance to pass before the jam-packed session ended. It created "an independent Adirondack Park Agency, to be responsible for the development of a comprehensive plan to guide future use of public and private lands within the Park and to provide interim safeguards against improvident uses of the lands within the Park that would threaten its future value."

Five days earlier, Hochschild had sent a description of the package to the TSC commissioners: "The bill does not give us all that we had hoped for, particularly as to the public lands. We are convinced, however, that it is the best we can get and that we should accept it." He added as a postscript that

"at our request, the highly controversial but essentially unimportant recommendation regarding first refusal rights has been dropped."

Bill Doolittle couldn't afford to pay for his own reporter in Albany, so state
government news came to the *Adirondack Daily Enterprise* on the Associated
Press's teletype machine, an electric typewriter with a radio link. In 1971,
these devices were about the size of stand-alone drinking fountains, and they
typed on yellow paper with a clack-clack-clack sound that was distinctive to
newsrooms. When the teletype finished typing a story that the Associated
Press thought was important, it would ring a bell. The story about the APA
bill didn't ring the bell.

Doolittle wasn't focused on Albany, anyway. He was trying to turn the
paper around so it would start making money. And he didn't see anything
wrong with stronger protection for the Adirondack Park, which was generally understood in Saranac Lake to mean only state-owned land. He enjoyed
skiing, hiking, and long-distance bicycling. He was also liberal on most issues, and he supported antipollution laws. But what he really cared about,
he said, was the welfare of working-class people.

Doolittle's mission as a journalist was inspired by his stepfather and mentor, Ralph Ingersoll. In a long and varied career, Ingersoll had published
*PM*, a daily newspaper in New York City that took its left-wing principles
so seriously that it did not accept advertising. Doolittle's favorite reporting
assignments were covering civil rights demonstrations and strikes. "Always
be a traitor to your class," Ingersoll had told him.

A few weeks before Rockefeller submitted the APA bill, Peter Paine and
Dick Lawrence had met with about one hundred people at the local town
hall. There had been a lot of shouting. The idea of regional zoning was "to-
talitarian," one man had said. Another said, "Let the state take care of the
state lands and the private owners take care of their own lands. People don't
want to be controlled!"

Doolittle didn't go to those meetings, but he did read his own paper. "The
APA seemed like rich people keeping poor people down," he said.

The funny thing was that a lot of locals were also against the big housing
developments that were being planned. Most of them just wanted to be left
alone, and they wanted things to stay the same. Even more surprising—and,
to Doolittle, disappointing—was the fact that few Adirondackers said anything at all.

"Real estate people were more aware than other people," said Art Jubin, who owned several hundred acres adjacent to the ski center at Mount Van Hoevenberg. "I was an appraiser, so I would go around putting a market value on properties. I knew what zoning was, and I would take that into consideration. There were public hearings and it was in the papers, but people didn't pay attention. Ninety-eight percent of local people were not aware that any of this was happening."

It's a 150-mile drive from Albany to Saranac Lake, when the roads are open. Even in good weather, the drive up from Albany to many parts of the Adirondacks can take half a day if it includes county roads. The internet and cell phones did not exist in 1971, and many park residents did not have access to television or a daily newspaper. They were lucky if they could find an AM radio station to listen to, and that was only possible after dark.

Harold Jerry was right. In 1971, the park was "a meaningless entity." Locals thought of their territories as pie-shaped wedges that pointed toward Glens Falls, Plattsburgh, Watertown, or Utica-Rome, the cities where they did their shopping, and where their newspapers came from. Their loyalties were to their churches, volunteer fire departments, schools, and supervisors, whom they would call when they had any business with the government—and in the 1950s and 60s, they almost never did.

"I don't know how many times I've heard it," said Richard Booth, an early staff member of the APA who spent two years at the DEC and another nine as an APA commissioner. "People up there would say, 'Don't tell me I live in a park. I live in a town.'"

Most of the towns weren't doing well. In Saranac Lake, the dominant source of jobs had been rest homes for tuberculosis patients who came to heal in the cold, dry air. Penicillin destroyed that trade in the 1950s, and nothing had taken its place. Unemployment was extremely high in many parts of the park. In several counties, the population declined during the 1960s. People who lived in the park had to hustle just to make ends meet.

The idea that the government could keep you from doing anything you wanted on your own property was, to most Adirondackers, the same as a takeover by the Soviet Union, and about as likely. When North Country residents who lived near subsistence level talked about "planning," they meant making sure they had enough food, water, and firewood to get through the winter. It seemed unlikely that decisions made in a big city like Albany could have any real effect on their lives.

"If all you know is the Adirondacks, then the Forever Wild idea makes no sense," said George Davis. "We were telling people who had never left the park that we needed zoning to protect open space, and they were saying, 'Holy God, all I got is open space.' We faced people who had divorced themselves from the rest of the world."

Bill Doolittle sided with those people. He wrote an editorial on June 2 opposing the APA while endorsing all of the other bills. Then he went back to his business.

On May 23, 1971, at 2:25 a.m., residents of Blue Mountain Lake heard a loud explosive noise, like a thunderclap, which was followed by the sensation of their buildings shaking. Two earthquakes had been caused by slippage on nearby fault lines. Or perhaps they happened because Johnny Oakes had just decided to write the editorial that ran in the *New York Times* on Wednesday, May 26.

"How long does Governor Rockefeller plan to wait before letting his party leaders in the legislature know that he wants action on the bill to create a State Adirondack Park Agency?" Oakes wrote. "The session may be over before the end of the week . . . if the Governor sincerely wants to protect the Adirondack Park, his only course is to speak up strongly for passage of the bill now."

Peter A. A. Berle, a second-term assemblyman, Democrat of Manhattan, led the floor fight for the bill. "He was of the athletic type," said his colleague, Oliver Koeppel. "He had short crew-cut hair and looked like a tennis player, very vigorous. I remember he didn't use elevators; he always took the stairs. And he was also a bit brusque, very determined. Friendly, but not effusive."

Peter Berle was the son of Adolf Berle, a corporate lawyer and assistant secretary of state to Franklin Roosevelt. The younger Berle's chair in the assembly chamber was just two seats away from that of Glenn Harris and was separated by the aisle. Berle was also on the assembly's Environmental Conservation Committee, along with the lone Democrat who represented the Adirondacks, Dan Haley. Berle and Haley's committee assignments often put them in conflict with the Joint Legislative Committee on Environmental Management and Natural Resources, which was chaired by Republican Glenn Harris.

On Thursday, June 3, Berle met William Verner, a curator at the Adirondack Museum who was also (informally) Harold Hochschild's research assistant. Verner had driven to Albany with his wife, Abbie, and a secret weapon for Berle. It was a vest-pocket notebook crammed with facts, figures, and talking points in favor of the APA bill. Verner had done a great job of putting that together, according to Abbie. "After it was all over, both Berle and Haley said they wished they were as well prepared on every issue as they were for the Agency bill," she wrote to her friend Marge Lamy.

Berle and Haley began cruising the capitol, talking up the bill. They hammered on the point that the park's future was an issue of statewide importance, so Glenn Harris's objections should be overruled. Haley added that he was an Adirondack legislator, too, which irritated Harris immensely.

"I would meet with Peter Paine at the end of the day to trade lists as to who had the votes for what," said Berle. "We would meet at eleven o'clock at night at some fast food joint outside of Albany, so we wouldn't be observed." The news at those meetings got better and better. Legislators were hearing the same message from people in their districts that they heard from Berle. The assembly was coming around. In the senate, solid Democratic support combined with Rockefeller's Republican loyalists made passage certain, because Ron Stafford was keeping quiet.

With passage of the APA bill looking more likely, Glenn Harris went to his friend Perry Duryea to discuss amendments. Duryea took Harris's list to his weekly meeting with Rockefeller. "Nelson Rockefeller didn't have to agree to any amendments to get the bill passed, but Rockefeller gave him some anyway," said Michael Whiteman.

Duryea persuaded Rockefeller to increase the number of appointed members of the APA who are permanent residents of the park from three to four. Logging operations and agriculture would be exempt from APA review. The regional zoning plan had to be submitted to the legislature for approval by June 1, 1973, and there had to be public hearings before it was submitted.

Duryea did not get the change Harris wanted most, however. Harris wanted a large window of time between the day the law was passed and the day it took effect, so locals would have time to adjust. But Hochschild and the other TSC commissioners felt just as strongly that the park needed "injunctive relief." They wanted to freeze development. The law had to take effect immediately.

"Harold Hochschild and I were basically living in Albany at that point," said Peter Paine. "While we were having lunch one day, an aide to Ron Stafford came up to us and said that they had found a solution. All we had to do was agree to make the effective date of the bill September 1, 1971, instead of June 1.

"There was a provision in the interim legislation that said that the interim land use powers of the park agency shall not apply in any community that has land use controls or zoning and subdivision regulations. At that time, only a few places in the park had those laws. So Harold and I made a few calls and discovered that yes, printing presses all over the Adirondacks were cranking away. People were trying to get communities to quickly pass standard half-acre zoning laws. They would have put the top of Mount Marcy in half-acre zoning if it had been privately owned."

The governor was in a bad mood on Saturday, June 5, 1971. It was the end of a remarkably difficult legislative session. The budget fight had been terrible. And when things started up again after the recess, Nelson Rockefeller, who always described himself as a frustrated architect, found himself on the verge of losing another cherished project. He wanted to build an enormous bridge across Long Island Sound. The legislature had passed a law blocking the project as extravagant. Rockefeller had vetoed the bill, and now the legislature had gotten within a few votes of overriding Rockefeller's veto. A legislative override of a governor's veto is extremely rare and would be embarrassing to the governor, but this time it seemed likely.

Rockefeller met in Duryea's office with Stanley Steingut, the senate minority leader. Steingut wanted Rockefeller's promise that he would appoint Democrats as well as Republicans to the APA. Rockefeller readily gave that promise, and then he asked Steingut to help him override the veto. Steingut refused, citing the bridge's negative environmental effects. Rockefeller became enraged. He struck Steingut, digging his fingers into the minority leader's chest. Steingut said that the governor was "despicable" and stormed out of the room.

It wasn't any quieter in the ornate, crowded hallways lining the assembly chamber. "The opposition was there on Saturday in full force," Abbie Verner wrote, "including DeZalia, Plumadore, and Pappagallo or whatever his name is [Louis Papparazzo]. . . . At one point we all came together in a head-on collision in the Assembly Lobby with Glenn Harris, Andy Ryan, Paul Schaefer, Winnie LaRose, Dave Newhouse, Almy Coggeshall, Bob Geandreau, Bill, myself, and a bearded teacher who was there just to observe. Everyone started bellowing, and at one point I almost hit Plumadore over the head with my purse."

Perry Duryea was the grown-up in the room. The 1971 session was his tenth year in the assembly, and the third as majority leader. The sessions always ended with dozens of bills pushing for a vote as time ran out, and it was normal for things to get crazy, but this session was the worst he had seen. In addition to the bridge, Duryea was juggling a proposed airport in Newburgh, housing in New York City, a proposed site for a nuclear power plant, and the annual effort to outlaw the kosher slaughtering of meat. The APA was just another item on a long list.

Duryea also had to balance these bills against his own ambitions. He wanted to be governor, so he had to be careful not to alienate important blocs of voters, like urban environmentalists. So even though Duryea had agreed to push for his friend Glenn Harris's amendments weakening the APA, he might not have had his heart in it. Duryea's father, who had built the family's lobster-fishing business, had served as the state conservation commissioner for nine years. "Perry knew how important it was to retain the purity of water," said Whiteman, "because water pollution would destroy his family business."

Back in the assembly lobby, Abbie Verner decided to escalate. "I had taken a telephone poll in Long Lake the week before and had found quite a few people who were in favor of the Agency," she wrote. "I had typed it up, and Bill shoved it in the faces of Glenn Harris, Plumadore, and DeZalia. At that point DeZalia told me I was a liar, and Bill rushed around Glenn Harris (and believe me, you do have to go around Glenn as he is not a particularly small person) and I panicked, thinking Bill was going to punch DeZalia in the nose. He said, 'you call my wife a liar, do you?', and I wished that I could faint on command.

"But Plumadore relieved the whole situation for me by shouting, 'you people (meaning Bill) have a vociferous, well-organized group that can make all these telephone calls.' That remark amused me considerably, so I replied, 'yes he does, and here I am.' That was a highlight for me. I have always had a secret desire to be known for something, and I never suspected I would be called a 'vociferous, well-organized group.'"

Harry Albright arranged for a last-ditch meeting between Hochschild and Duryea to try to iron out their differences on the APA bill. The only time he could get the meeting was at the end of business on Sunday, June 6. It had been another rough day. Duryea had managed to keep the assembly from overriding Rockefeller's veto of the bill deauthorizing the Oyster Bay-Rye Bridge. But he did it by denying a roll-call vote when the override seemed certain to pass, and that had caused a near riot in the assembly chamber. Duryea was exhausted.

Three eyewitnesses to the meeting between Hochschild and Duryea agreed on the main points. First, it happened late at night. Albright claimed that the meeting happened at 2:30 a.m.; Whiteman and Paine said it was around midnight. The three men were there to support Hochschild, but they all agreed to keep quiet and let Harold handle Perry by himself. This is Peter Paine's version:

> Harold and I reported our finding about the zoning plans to Harry Albright, and he checked and found out that it was true. He got back to us and said that the governor wasn't buying the idea of pushing off the effective date, but that the governor also didn't want to tell Perry Duryea any more bad news. Harry said that Harold Hochschild had to do it. That is how we all found ourselves in the speaker's office in the middle of the night.
>
> Duryea was a big, tall, handsome man with a shock of silver hair, and he had three or four people with him. Harold was a very small, wrinkly guy sitting straight up in a chair in front of the speaker's desk. The speaker got on his feet and made an impassioned plea for us to consider this really modest change. He was getting unbearable heat from the upstate legislators. It wouldn't make any difference in the long run. He went on and on, and finally, he stopped.
>
> I remember this moment so clearly. Harold waited two beats and then said, "No. I would rather have no bill than that bill."
>
> Of course, Duryea knew that if the bill did not pass, the *New York Times* editorial page would immediately name the person who was responsible for the failure of this great scheme. I remember Perry's shoulders slumped, and he was just looking around. "Dammit," he said. "Okay, Mr. Hochschild. You win. Can anybody here draft this thing?"
>
> The change was very easy to make. So I introduced myself and offered to do it, and Duryea said, "You just fill in what you want." I wrote that the bill would take effect on July 1. Duryea showed it to Harold and said, "Is this all right with you, Mr. Hochschild?" Harold said yes. He showed it to Harry and asked if it was all right with the governor, and Harry said yes.
>
> Then Duryea gave the bill to one of his minions and said, "All right. Pass the fucking thing."

So now it's about one in the morning. As we're walking back to the car, Harold says, "I would like to be in New York City tomorrow morning. I have a meeting. Would you mind driving me down?" Well, I wasn't going to say no. When we got to the Thruway, Harold said, "I'm going to go to sleep. If I don't wake up at the George Washington Bridge tollbooths, please wake me."

It takes about two and a half hours to drive from Albany to New York City. Somehow, I got us to the George Washington Bridge at some ungodly hour. Harold woke up, just like that, at the tollbooths. He looked at me and smiled, and he said, "I rather liked the look on the face of the speaker when I told him no."

The APA law finally passed the assembly around 8 p.m. on June 7, 1971, by a vote of 123–24, and the senate on June 10, 22–14. Construction projects that began before September 1, 1971, would be exempt from agency oversight, but localities only had until July 1 to pass zoning laws tough enough to stand up to a legal challenge, and few were likely to do so. "We needed injunctive relief, and we got it," said Harry Albright. "That was a true miracle."

Rockefeller appointed Harold Jerry to a permanent slot on the State Public Service Commission, where he served for twenty-four years. Clarence Petty retired, taking Ferne on the first of several trips to Alaska. George Davis went back to family life and pursuit of a doctoral degree at Cornell.

The TSC commissioners also scattered. Harold Hochschild returned to Eagle Nest and his beloved wife, Mary. Hochschild knew that the next step would be an even bigger challenge than the one he had just faced. He was relieved that he didn't have to be the leader anymore. He was happy to pass the torch to Dick Lawrence and Peter Paine.

Chapter 8

# THE BIG MAP

George Davis remembered his first day at the Adirondack Park Agency in Ray Brook. "I got the key to the building from the fellow next door. There was absolutely nothing inside. But I had a strong feeling that I had to get going, so I went into town and bought two big cartons of toilet paper. It was practical for obvious reasons, but also because I could use one case for a desk and the other for a chair. I put a coffee pot and a phone on top of it. I was alone for a few weeks."

The APA opened for business in September 1971. It faced two enormous deadlines, one in six months and one in fifteen months, but it took Davis and his boss, Dick Lawrence, nine months just to hire the staff. The governor did them no favors. The agency was created in early June, but it took the governor three months to decide who its board members should be. The APA's budget was a fraction of what it needed. Emergency spending cuts that took effect a few weeks after Davis came to work left him with even less.

Davis was not easily deterred. "I put an ad in the paper," he said. "I actually asked for handouts to start up a state agency. And what do you know, we got them. Some of the donations were nice Adirondack-style furniture, and then I'd get a table here and a table there. But I was still alone. I hired a secretary, but I couldn't pay her.

"The DEC [Department of Environmental Conservation] folks told me that when they needed things for their offices, they gave the store a purchase order and it always worked. I had to get out into the field and start surveying, so I decided that I needed a new four-wheel-drive Jeep Wagoneer. I filled out a purchase order and bought one and took it out and got it all muddy. Shortly after that I got a phone call from Albany, telling me that purchase orders were only for $25 or less. They were terribly unhappy because the car cost $5,500, but of course I couldn't give it back. I didn't feel like I was getting a lot of sympathy from anywhere. But we worked it out."

The APA had enormous responsibilities. The law ordered it to "insure optimum overall conservation, protection, preservation, development, and use of the Park's unique scenic, historical, ecological, and natural features." During the two-year period when it was drafting the land use plans, the agency was also expected to write and enforce interim regulations, evaluate construction projects, and issue permits for a territory about the size of Connecticut. But it had been allotted only thirteen staff positions, and some of those folks didn't leave the office. It also didn't have any enforcement officers.

The APA's budget was so tight that Davis kept a wish list of small office supplies, ranging from a slide projector and screen ($175) to pencils and pens ($1), that he needed but couldn't afford. But all of these things were minor concerns to him. He was carrying on the work of the Temporary Study Commission (TSC). He was twenty-nine years old, and he was going to save the park.

The governor had sent eight bills recommended by the TSC to the legislature in May 1971. The APA bill was the only one that had passed. The others would be reintroduced in later legislative sessions. In addition to supporting the bills, the APA had until March 1972 to release a master plan for the management of 2.24 million acres of state-owned land. And another job loomed over everything else.

The Land Use and Development Plan had to be released by the end of 1972. It would set up a process for regulating all future development in the park's privately owned land. No one had ever done anything like it before.

All of these things had to be done at the same time. But Davis had a secret power: self-confidence. He was convinced that the APA could succeed.

"It was as if he could see the whole Adirondack Park in his head," said Richard Booth, who joined the APA in August 1972. "He was extremely bright, and he wanted you to know that. He seemed to remember every specific thing that had come out of all of those meetings and field trips. He had charisma that came from a great passion for what he was doing. He inspired that feeling in us."

Like his mentor, Harold Jerry, Davis was picky about his hires. "I worked out a relationship with our contact in the State Department of Civil Service," he said. The APA had to follow the state's hiring rules, but Davis also felt it essential for him to hire whomever he wanted. "Fortunately, the civil service guy happened to be a trout fisherman," Davis said. "So I arranged for him to get to the nicest trout fishing spots anyone could ask for, any time he wanted. And in return, he helped get approval for the positions I came up with. He would help me come up with a job title that had not been used somewhere else, so we wouldn't have to fit it into their existing rules. We could come up with our own job descriptions and pay grades. It worked out real well."

The people who worked for the early APA had multiple tasks with a nearly impossible timeline, and when they went out after work, they were regularly attacked just for holding their jobs. They had to work evenings and weekends and do whatever it took. "So we only hired people who were driven by their desire to protect the Adirondack Park," Davis said. "That was the baseline value we needed."

It was a start-up business, and a start-up will take employees with attitude if they deliver high performance. That was what the APA got with Davis. "I had a lot of difficulties with him," said Richard Persico, who became his supervisor in 1973. "We came from different directions. He was a visionary. He loved to be called that. I appreciated that we needed him, and I didn't want to tamper with his work. But I was on the team that had to get this thing done and turn it into a law that could pass. I had an entirely different focus than George did."

There was no fallback strategy if Davis's plan failed, and the pressure kept building to do something. The APA's interim powers expired on June 1, 1973, and if the land use plan did not pass the legislature, there would be almost no controls on the development of private land in the park starting on June 2. Davis was still scrounging for furniture when a former client of his unveiled detailed plans for a residential development on 18,388 acres north of Tupper

Lake. A few months later, another developer announced plans for something even bigger.

Environmental activists organized to stall the developments until the APA's land plan could become law. But for many months, no one knew what the plan was going to be except Davis. The APA's board didn't hire lawyers and staff to bring the plan to completion until summer 1972. The board didn't get their first good look at the plan until October, just a few weeks before they had to send it out for public hearings.

Most of the APA board members were delighted when they finally got to examine the staff's work, but a few of them were outraged, and the split made the early APA's decisions much more difficult. Pro or con, everyone struggled to come to terms with the radical measures they were about to propose.

On April 1, 1971, the day after George Davis's job at the TSC ended, he went back to Cornell's Department of Natural Resources. He reenrolled in the doctoral program, but he was not the same person who had arrived in Ithaca to begin graduate school two years earlier. For one thing, he had a grant from the Association for the Protection of the Adirondacks (AfPA) to help him pay the bills.

"There was kind of an amorphous group of people who decided that if there was going to be an Adirondack Park Agency, we had to start developing its methods right away," he said. "It became clear that once the agency was set up, the plan would have to be written quickly. Arthur Crocker stepped forward and agreed to pay for me to develop the methods, which was great, because I said, 'Hey, this could be my thesis.' So I went back to Ithaca and did the literature search, and that's when I really studied Ian McHarg."

Ian McHarg, professor of landscape architecture at the University of Pennsylvania, was a flamboyant Scotsman with a large, brushy mustache and a wild sense of humor. He was also a man of his time. He delivered his planning ideas with the style of an artist who had an agenda, celebrating the spiritual benefits of nature while making broad attacks on the profit motive. Davis didn't ever get to know McHarg personally, but he said that "his ideas played a very big role in the plan."

"We are the bullies of the earth," McHarg wrote in his autobiography: "strong, foul, coarse, greedy, careless, indifferent to others, laying waste as we proceed, leaving wounds, welts, lesions, suppurations on the earth body, increasingly engulfed by our own ordure and, finally, abysmally ignorant of the way the world works, crowing our superiority over all life."

This was more than just overblown rhetoric. It was also the rallying cry for a revolution. McHarg's *Design for Nature* (1969) outlined a method that measured the natural characteristics of an area and used those data to rate its capacity to "carry" buildings and other kinds of human activity. The idea behind "carrying capacity" was sustainability. The goal was to use measurement and mitigation to reduce the impact of human activity on the natural environment. This was also the goal of the National Environmental Policy Act, passed in January 1970, which required that an environmental impact statement be approved for large-scale federal contracts.

"Our basic premise was borrowed from McHarg," Davis said. "The land, if it's undeveloped, will tell you what it is best suited for."

Davis agreed with McHarg's poetic attacks on the uncontrolled exploitation of land, but he did not have the freedom of a tenured college professor. He was a graduate student whose wife, Joan, was home with children aged seven, three, and one. He needed to support them.

In addition to the AfPA grant, Davis also took two side jobs. One of them was really another grant. It came from Harold Hochschild, who was aware of Davis's value to the project, and who also took a fatherly interest in Davis's welfare. Hochschild hired Davis to write a forty-page pamphlet about Adirondack ecology for a general audience and paid him up front, although the pamphlet was not published until 1977.

The other job also helped move the thesis forward. But "I had some moral difficulties with it," Davis said. It was a contract with Louis Papparazzo, the developer who had bought those 18,388 acres in 1970. Papparazzo was an experienced town-builder who had completed projects in Connecticut, California, and elsewhere. He wanted to build four thousand to seven thousand homes in the town of Altamont, five miles north of the village of Tupper Lake. Papparazzo also said he wanted his development to be environmentally sound, so he found Davis and offered him a consulting contract.

"I did not think the Adirondacks were the right place for a big second-home project," said Davis, "but I also thought, in May 1971, that it was highly likely that this was going to get built. I tore my mind apart trying to decide what to do. I finally decided to do it on two conditions: first, that I would have total freedom to do a general survey that didn't get down to nitty-gritty details, and second, that I would be free to do whatever I wanted with the final report."

Davis's passion was protecting land that he thought should remain free of human impact. His thesis would compile data to show which Adirondack lands were suitable for development and which should remain undisturbed. So he went to the library and got government data on the topography and other characteristics of Papparazzo's property. Then he tramped through the property's boreal forests and wetlands, determining soil types and depths, counting birds and wildlife, poking around in bogs, and stopping to record especially beautiful views.

Next, Davis turned his data and field notes into a visualization. Back in 1971, before computers had sophisticated graphics software, this process usually started with a planimetric base map, which shows surface features but does not include elevation or other data. Davis overlaid the base map with sheets of clear polyethylene, which is also known by its trade name, Mylar. Each sheet had been prepared with Zipatone, a clingy plastic film that put a 20 percent screen on the Mylar, making it darker. The screens came in different colors that could be used to denote soil types, wetlands, steep slopes, and so on. Using an Exacto knife, Davis carefully cut the screens to denote areas with conditions that made them less suitable for development. When the Mylar sheets were overlaid, the areas with multiple 20 percent shades turned darker. Two screens (40 percent shading) meant that some limited development might be possible. Three or more meant proceed with extreme caution.

This kind of work involves making a lot of judgment calls—and in Davis's judgment, a lot of Papparazzo's land should remain undisturbed. In July 1971, he turned in a report urging the developer to reduce the number of units to no more than two thousand and leave more than one-third of the land untouched. Also, he added, please do not dam Windfall Brook to turn a bog into a recreational lake. It contains rare plants. Papparazzo paid Davis, but he never got back to him about the bog.

The Papparazzo contract was a test run of the method Davis would bring to the Adirondack Park Agency. After the legislature passed the APA law in early June, Davis knew that he would be asked to return. Harold Jerry and Harold Hochschild were pulling strings so that he, Richard Estes, and Neil Huber would be offered positions as soon as the agency's board chair was given permission to hire staff. But Davis didn't know when that invitation would arrive.

When the governor asked Jerry which members of the TSC should serve on the agency board, Jerry turned to Richard Estes and George Davis for advice. "We recommended Richard Lawrence, Peter Paine, and Fred O'Neal," said Davis. "We got two of them."

The interim law authorized the governor to appoint seven APA board members. It also named two high-ranking state officials who would either serve or delegate voting members. While a term on the APA lasted four years, three of the original commissioners were appointed for staggered terms of one, two, and three years. Also, the law required that four citizen members of the APA be full-time residents of the park.

Rockefeller spent several weeks unsuccessfully searching for a high-profile chairman before he asked Richard Lawrence to take the job. He trusted Lawrence, who had worked on the governor's campaigns in 1966 and 1970. Lawrence also ran in the same social circles as Rockefeller. He was that rare creature who lived in the North Country but had a Princeton pedigree and New York City connections. Those who knew Lawrence often used the same word to describe him: "aristocrat."

Lawrence was sixty-two in 1971, tall and thin, nearly bald, with close-set eyes and a fondness for self-deprecating humor. He was born and raised in New York City to a family with business and banking connections. His first wife had died in childbirth in 1945. His second wife, Elizabeth Hand Wadhams, came from a family that had cofounded the Essex County hamlet of Elizabethtown, a tiny place (population 1,200) where wealthy New Yorkers started building summer homes shortly after the railroad arrived in 1875.

Lawrence moved to Elizabethtown in 1946, riding the train 275 miles with his six-month-old daughter in his arms. He handed the baby to his new wife, and a few days later, he got back on the train. He rode that train round-trip once a week for twenty years as he commuted to his job in Manhattan. Although he was a weekend resident of Elizabethtown, Lawrence developed a reputation there for doing good works. He served on the boards of local schools, the state university in Plattsburgh, and the new community college in Saranac Lake. He also supported the "preservationist" wing of the Adirondack Mountain Club starting in the early 1960s.

Lawrence's style was to seek consensus. He used humor to defuse the tension in a meeting, so that people who disagreed could continue to work as colleagues. "A false issue has grown up—an issue that looks upon people and the environment as adversaries," he once said. "The implication is that if environment takes priority, people will somehow be deprived. That's nonsense. It's possible to have both." He was the kind of person who expected good behavior from the people he met, and he almost always received it.

He had another side. "He had steel," said Richard Booth. "It was impossible to intimidate Richard Lawrence." People who disagreed with Lawrence expressed this quality in different terms. "He didn't give a shit what the locals thought," said Bill Doolittle, owner of the *Adirondack Daily Enterprise*. "That was so obvious."

When Rockefeller called and asked Lawrence to be chair of the board of the APA, Lawrence said no. He was about to retire. He and Elizabeth already had two tickets booked on an ocean liner to Europe. "I talked to my wife about it," Lawrence recalled in 1998. "Liz knew me so well. She asked me, 'do you want it to go to someone else?' At that point my ego rose up and I said hell no, so I took it."

Lawrence agreed to work for Rockefeller, but he knew that his real master was the calendar. He had to produce an enormous amount of work in a short time. "We moved rapidly because we had to move rapidly," Lawrence said. "If we had succumbed to the syndrome of delay, I don't think the park would still be here. And in so doing, we stepped on toes."

The first ex officio member of the APA was the commissioner of the Department of Environmental Conservation (DEC), Henry Diamond. Three years earlier, Diamond had pitched the original idea of the TSC to Nelson Rockefeller. He had also served on the commission as Laurance Rockefeller's top environmental advisor, and he played a crucial role in passing the APA law. But with his DEC responsibilities, Diamond was usually too busy to attend APA meetings. He sent his first deputy commissioner, Ron Pedersen, who had been the other advisor in the room when Diamond proposed the TSC to the Rockefeller brothers.

The second ex officio member was Richard Wiebe, a long-time member of Rockefeller's inner circle. Rockefeller had just named Wiebe head of an office in the executive chamber.

The Office of Planning Services (OPS) was essential to the APA because it provided the agency with professional cartographers and Albany lawyers. Map making was important because the legal requirements for the land use plan were unusual. Most land use laws use text to describe the boundary lines of the area being regulated. But the Adirondack Park was far too big and complicated to use that technique. So the law called specifically for a map—what would become a big, complicated map—with explanatory text.

Wiebe had no personal interest in the Adirondacks, but he was an important APA board member for several reasons. He had worked closely with the governor since 1963, so he had a good sense of what Rockefeller would and wouldn't approve. He also took professional pride in doing his job well. "I didn't know a damned thing about the Adirondacks, but I went to those meetings and voted, you bet," he said.

Wiebe was to the early APA as Harry Albright was to the TSC. He was the governor's man, which usually made it unnecessary to bother the governor himself. And he was also regarded as the smartest guy in the room. "Remember, Rockefeller wanted to be president," said Dick Booth. "He paid from his own pocket to get extremely bright people to work for him. I'm sure that if Rockefeller had made it to the White House, Dick Wiebe would have been his chief of staff."

Rockefeller found it difficult to fill out the APA board. Different groups suggested lots of candidates to Harry Albright, who served as the nominating committee. The nominees held wildly divergent opinions. Many of them were not inclined to compromise. And four of the seven appointed members had to come from a pool of just 110,000 people who were full-time residents of the park.

In mid-July, the Essex County Board of Supervisors nominated Leo Friedman, an attorney and the town justice of Schroon. In their resolution, the Board said that Friedman had refrained from making personal attacks on members of the TSC "until he was first personally attacked." Hochschild wrote to Albright that Friedman "has probably done more than anyone in the Adirondacks to sabotage the work of the Commission."

Albright relied on the advice of people he knew and trusted. Harold Hochschild sent him seventeen names on June 29, including Richard Lawrence, Peter Paine, Fred O'Neal, and two others who had been opposed to the agency plan but were distinguished by their "university education," Hochschild said.

Albright shared a list of fifty names with Hochschild that included two who made the final cut. James Bird was a builder and resort owner from Raquette Lake who had been recommended by Senator Ron Stafford. Whitman

Daniels of Glens Falls was a retired public relations executive recommended by the state Republican Committee and several executives from mining and forestry companies, including the president of lumber company Finch Pruyn.

Later in the process, Hochschild recommended Mary Prime, a Lake Placid community leader and fourth-generation Adirondack native who he said was "civic minded and strong on conservation." He also sent along a resume and cover letter he had received from William Foley, an attorney who lived in Old Forge and was active on the Town of Webb's planning board. Foley was also a Democrat. This was important, because the law said that no more than four of the appointed members could come from a single political party.

Foley, Prime, Bird, and Lawrence filled the in-park seats on the original APA board. Peter Paine got one of the out-of-park seats, and the second went to Whit Daniels. The last seat almost went to Fred O'Neal, a Democrat, but Rockefeller needed to honor the promise he had made to Stanley Steingut on June 5. So he gave the seat to Joseph Tonelli, the president of United Paperworkers International Union. Like O'Neal, Tonelli served on the executive council of the national labor coalition, the American Federation of Labor and Congress of Industrial Organizations (AFL-CIO). Unlike him, Tonelli had no interest in or knowledge of the Adirondacks.

After Lawrence, the most important appointment was probably Peter Paine, who had never stopped working for the cause. Paine had spent weeks in Albany helping Peter Berle and Harold Hochschild push the APA bill through the legislature. And like Hochschild, Paine also stayed in touch with his contacts on the governor's staff as they considered APA board candidates.

The APA law also instructed the governor to seek the "advice and consent of the Senate" when making his appointments. He did this by checking his names with Senator Ron Stafford, the Republican from Plattsburgh whose district encompassed most of the park. Stafford had no objections to Rockefeller's choices and was enthusiastic about working with Dick Lawrence and Peter Paine. In fact, Paine stayed on the APA board for the next twenty-five years. He was reappointed seven times by five different governors. One reason for his lengthy service was the support of environmentalists. Another was his friendship with Stafford.

Paine practiced law on Wall Street and had several big commercial clients. One of them was the French car maker Peugeot, which made his movements in the North Country easy to track. People knew that if they saw a Peugeot parked among the pickup trucks and rusty American sedans in Warrensburg or Saranac Lake, they could bet that Peter Paine was in town.

Paine knew that the APA board would be a lot of work. It would take him away from his family and his commercial clients. But he had wealth to fall back on, and he was eager to take the assignment as a way of keeping the vision of the TSC alive. The board also gave Paine working relationships with the governor and other high state officials, and that was a plus for his legal career. Paine was singled out for praise in a *New York Times* editorial when word reached the paper that he had been appointed to the APA. He was promoted to partner shortly after the editorial ran.

As alumni of the TSC, Lawrence, Paine, and Davis knew each other well and agreed on what needed to be done. Davis turned to these two board members for advice and support, but he mostly worked alone. "I had no experience with local zoning laws in the park, because there weren't many," said Peter Paine. "And there were no similar commissions to model ourselves on." Was the APA board making things up as they went along? "I think that's fair to say, yes," Paine said.

Hochschild knew what his young friend had signed up for. When he found out that Paine had been given a board seat, he wrote a note:

> Dear Peter:
>
> Mary and I want you to know that in your hour of shock our thoughts are with you and particularly with Patty and the children. You have our heartfelt sympathy in the blow fate has so cruelly dealt you. Cursed by your law partners, reviled by your neighbors, shunned by your former friends, sued by countless Adirondack landowners—yours is a future indeed grim to contemplate.
>
> We are not going to desert you. When the need arises, you, Patty and the children will find shelter with us—but we would prefer you to arrive after dark.
>
> Yours, Harold.
>
> PS: Obviously some enemy of yours has been at work. I hope you catch him.

Hochschild originally thought it would be a mistake to appoint anyone from the TSC to the APA. He put that recommendation in the cover letter he submitted to the governor with the TSC's report. But Harold Jerry argued that it was essential to appoint people who had extensive knowledge of the TSC's vision, and Hochschild changed his mind. That was a fateful decision.

Robert Flacke, who succeeded Richard Lawrence as Chairman of the APA, said that it was a big mistake to allow veterans of the TSC to lead the original APA board and staff. The commission's job was to craft a long-term vision for the Adirondacks. The agency's job was to turn that vision into regulations, and then enforce them. The problem, according to Flacke and other critics, is that visionaries don't make good cops.

The governor couldn't give the Adirondacks his full attention. On September 10, 1971, the day he announced his appointments to the APA board, a riot at a maximum-security state prison 350 miles west of New York City had become a standoff. Rockefeller did not respond effectively. He let tensions escalate until Attica exploded into the bloodiest prison uprising in American history, with forty-three deaths and extreme violence that played out in newspapers and television coverage.

The tragedy in Attica polarized New York voters, who either demanded racial justice or law and order. Anger and recriminations over Attica followed Rockefeller for the rest of his life.

Rockefeller's usual response to a problem was to throw money at it, but in fall 1971, his power to do that was rapidly fading. Sharp increases in unemployment and inflation in 1970 and 1971 had cut growth in state tax revenues to a crawl. A budget shortfall developed and quickly became a fiscal crisis, exposing a web of hidden debt and off-budget financing that Rockefeller had used to build colleges, hospitals, a vast new state capitol complex, and dozens of other projects he couldn't wait to see.

As tax revenues remained low, the debt payments became more burdensome. By 1971, the state of New York's debt was nearly ten times higher than the average for all fifty states. Rockefeller searched for a way to keep his house of cards from collapsing, and his search became more desperate as the bad news kept coming.

But even during a budget crisis, a state job sounded good to George Davis. So he pushed. "By mid-August 1971, I knew that Dick Lawrence was going to be involved," he said. "I hadn't heard anything, so I called Dick and asked him, 'Where I should enroll my daughter in elementary school, Ithaca or Saranac Lake?' He hemmed and hawed and finally said I should move to Saranac Lake. The money came through a week or two later."

When Davis took the APA job in September 1971, he started earning three or four times more than he would have earned as a teaching assistant. The job also promised a staff. But his wife, Joan, would have preferred that he stay at Cornell and get his degree. The APA job was another temporary appointment. It was another big set of deadlines that would keep him away from home, and if the legislature didn't pass the plans, George would be out of a job again. Davis moved his family to Saranac Lake with the self-assurance only graduate students seem to have. He got almost no oversight from agency board members, except for Dick Lawrence.

The APA's office building is made of logs the Conservation Department salvaged from the Big Blowdown of November 1950. The DEC had recently vacated that building for a new headquarters next door. They had planned to burn down the log cabin until the APA moved in. Davis may have been sitting in a salvaged chair in front of his toilet-paper-box desk on the Monday morning in September when he read about his old client Louis Papparazzo in the *Daily Enterprise*.

Papparazzo had been the speaker at the chamber of commerce's annual banquet in the village of Tupper Lake on Saturday night. He had showed artist's renderings and painted a glowing word-picture of the housing development he wanted to build a few miles north of town. He called it "Ton-Da-Lay," a name he had invented. Before the dinner and dancing, the developer told about 150 community leaders that he planned about four thousand homes on seven thousand acres of his property. On the rest of it he would put ski slopes, stables and bridle paths, snowmobile and hiking trails, an eighteen-hole golf course, a campground, a marina, and even a museum of local history.

Papparazzo stressed that he was a long-term town-builder, not a cut-and-run lot-seller. He had done large-scale developments in Indiana, California, and his home state of Connecticut. He bought a home for himself in Tupper Lake and opened a sales office. He said he wanted to be a good neighbor and citizen.

Papparazzo and the man who had sold him the land—Hayward "Red" Plumadore, chair of the Franklin County Republican Party—had fought hard to try to stop the APA. But at the dinner, Papparazzo did not seem concerned that the agency might change his plans. The Town of Altamont had its own zoning plan, and the APA law stated that towns with preexisting plans would be exempt from the agency's interim regulations. All Papparazzo needed was water and sewer permits, which the town readily granted. It seemed like a done deal.

George Davis had been a consultant for Papparazzo, but he was not a fan of Ton-Da-Lay. The area Papparazzo had set aside for stables and an equestrian ring was, in fact, a bog. Homesites were planned to cover prime habitat for a rare bird, the spruce grouse. The proposed sewage system was inadequate. Papparazzo was selling dreams. Davis knew that the reality of Ton-Da-Lay was biting bugs and sticky mud. Yet in fall 1971, it seemed that there was not much he could do.

A good day for Davis was when he scored a bunch of surplus desks from a nearby state prison, or when the phones were installed. He also gave several public presentations about the APA at group meetings around the park. He occasionally met a supporter, but more often his comments were met with polite silence, sarcasm, or flat-out hostility.

The budget crisis in Albany stunted the APA. Even if the governor had remained interested in long-term planning for the Adirondacks, he no longer had any time for it. And as the fiscal crisis worsened, the APA's funds grew much tighter. The legislature had appropriated $250,000 for agency operations for the 1971–1972 fiscal year. But in the fall, the State Budget Department said that only $100,000 would be available through the end of the fiscal year on March 30. Davis would be able to hire only two or three people between September and April. He would have to beg for whatever other help he needed.

In mid-November, Lawrence asked Davis to describe the work facing them. Both men were trying to figure out the best ways to move forward on their stripped-down budget. Davis recommended that the APA develop close relationships with the eighty-six towns that are wholly or partially in the park, and especially the thirty-nine that had planning boards. The staff needed to collect data on "soil types, stability and effluent capacities, slopes, elevation, water resources, and unique physical features," as well as unique ecosystems, rare and endangered plants and animals, and important habitats such as deer wintering areas. They needed to determine existing land uses and survey travel corridors, historic sites, and wild rivers. They also had to write a master plan for 2.24 million acres of state land.

In mid-November 1971, the State Land Master Plan was due in a little over four months. The Land Use and Development Plan for private property needed to go out for public comment in a year. No wonder Davis was fighting an ulcer.

Davis loved to go out in the field in the APA's brand-new green Jeep Wagoneer, which he named "Julep." The car did not stay new-looking for long. When he wasn't too far away from a town, Davis could find a radio station which, for a few minutes at least, occasionally provided him with Marvin Gaye as a traveling partner. Gaye's song "Mercy Mercy Me (The Ecology)" was on heavy rotation in early fall 1971. "What about this overcrowded land?" Gaye sang. "How much more abuse from man can she stand?"

Driving through miles and miles of open space, Davis saw a critical need for protection because he saw the vast Adirondacks as a small piece of North America. "Regional planning doesn't make sense unless you broaden your horizons to think about the entire state, or even the northeastern United States," he said. "Then it makes a great deal of sense."

Americans remained fixated on environmental issues. Researchers had recently estimated that two-thirds of the country's lakes, rivers, and coastal waters had become unsafe for fishing or swimming. Untreated sewage was still being dumped into open water. In 1972, Congress overrode President Nixon's veto to pass the Clean Water Act, which had ambitious goals: to "restore and maintain the chemical, physical, and biological integrity of our nation's waters" by reaching "zero discharge of pollutants into navigable waters by 1985, and fishable and swimmable waters by 1983."

Saving the Adirondacks was a noble goal, worthy of sacrifice. Davis looked for staffers who agreed with that point of view. It was especially easy to sell the job to people who also thought that long, bushwhacking hikes in bad weather were fun. That was how Davis got his first employee.

Clarence Petty had returned from an extended trip to Alaska with his wife Ferne, only to discover that retirement didn't suit him. Davis lured Petty back into state employment by offering him a key position. Petty would be the wise elder, sharing his lifetime of experience with eager young staffers. Also, Davis offered him another multiyear tramp in the woods. This time, Petty would get to do it with a canoe on his head.

The idea of designating a river as "wild, scenic, or recreational" had been proposed by Laurance Rockefeller's Outdoor Recreation Resources Review Commission (ORRRC) in 1962, and the federal wild, scenic, and recreational rivers system had been established by Congress in 1968. Thirteen states had also passed rivers legislation when the TSC proposed that New York desig-nate its own statewide system in 1971.

In the 1960s, Adirondack rivers and streams were often posted with "No Trespassing" signs when they flowed through private land. Activists like Paul Jamieson, an English professor at St. Lawrence University, fought a lengthy court battle to establish the right of canoes and other small boats to use any waterway that was judged to be "navigable." Petty's job would be to lead a team to survey the rivers and streams of the Adirondack Park and find the navigable waterways that qualified as either wild, scenic, or recreational. These waterways would be added to proposed legislation starting in 1972 and continuing until all 1,500 miles had been surveyed.

"George Davis and I went down to Washington and interviewed the people who had established wild and scenic rivers on the federal level," Petty said. "We followed what the Forest Service had done. That was typical of the State Conservation Department. They often changed their policies about twenty years after the Forest Service did."

Davis used the same technique to attract Greenleaf Chase, a wildlife manager for the Conservation Department who lived in Saranac Lake and was a few years away from retirement. Chase, who was universally known as "Greenie," had an unmatched knowledge of the park's plant and animal com-munities. He had known Petty for decades, worked with Davis at the TSC, and possessed an exuberance toward the natural world that suited the intense job environment Davis was offering. "He would see something unusual out in the field and just light up," Davis said. "He would act like an eight-year-old boy."

Greenie did not go onto the APA's payroll until February 1972, but he was available earlier because he worked next door at the DEC's regional of-fice. When Davis had a question, he took it to Petty or Greenie, who usually knew the answer. If they didn't know, they knew where to look for it. The two older men served like faculty advisors to Davis as he collected data for a doctoral thesis that was destined to become law.

Davis had just installed surplus desks from the state prison when Anita Riner showed up in early October 1971 to inquire about a job. Anita was new in town. Her husband Robert had just started teaching drama at North Country Community College. She had two young children and was not par-ticularly eager to go back to work, but she had also worked for the planning department in Tacoma, Washington, and "I had an appreciation for environ-mental problems," she said.

The job sounded good, and Davis seemed interested. He says he became even more interested in Anita when she said, "I do *not* want a typewriter on my desk. I am *not* interested in being a secretary."

Anita Riner moved in next to Clarence Petty. On her first day, Davis brought her a copy of *Design with Nature* and told her to read it. Shortly afterward, he gave her a topographic map of the area around Saint Regis Mountain. Riner's job was to look carefully at areas of privately owned land on the map, mark the places where steep slopes or high altitudes made land less suitable for development, and then transfer the marked areas onto a Mylar sheet with Zipatone. She spent many, many hours doing that.

In mid-October, a professional planner joined the staff when Richard Estes, Davis's colleague from the TSC, came on loan from Richard Wiebe's Office of Planning Services. Estes had studied McHarg's theories and had actually met the man when he was pursuing a planning degree at the University of Pennsylvania. He helped Davis refine his adaptation of McHarg's ideas to a new kind of territory dominated by large working forests, wetlands, and isolated pockets of human settlement. But Estes's first job would be writing the interim regulations the agency needed to release ten weeks later. Estes's partner on that job was another TSC alumnus. Neil Huber had been hired by Frederick Sheffield's law firm, but the firm made him available to the APA as a consultant.

Around January 1, 1972, Dick Lawrence secured another $25,000 from Albany. That allowed Davis to hire Gary Duprey, who started on January 3. Duprey is a Saranac Lake native whose uncle, Horton Duprey, was well known for his knowledge of local history and his genius at repairing boat engines. This mattered because it meant that Gary was also well known in town.

Duprey often found himself working after hours because he had to defend the agency to people who wouldn't talk to outsiders "They'd say, 'Oh, how can you do this?'" Duprey said. "I'd try to tell them, 'Don't blame me, I'm just the messenger.' And there was one guy who gave me an awful hard time. We went nose to nose one night. In the end he just walked away. We didn't start swinging, but it didn't end pretty either.

"Dick Lawrence absolutely knew what it was like to be pounced on like that. Peter Paine did, too. One day Peter told me to remember a phrase, *Illegitimi non carborundum*, which translates as 'Don't let the bastards get you down.' I never forgot it."

Duprey had a college degree in environmental science and in 1970, he was working for a land surveying crew. He said that one of his clients, the local developer Frank Casier, was indirectly responsible for his decision to take a job at the APA.

"When I first heard about the APA, I didn't like the idea. None of us did," Duprey said. "Then we went out to survey some lots for a development of Casier's called Fish Creek Park. He told us what he wanted, but when we got out there, we found that the land was either boggy or bedrock. The lots he wanted were too small to handle septic tanks. We told him that, and he got mad.

"He said, 'You lay out those lots the way I told you to. I'm going to put them on the market and I guarantee you they will sell.' He said that his primary customers were retiring school teachers, and that they usually bought the lots sight unseen, so they wouldn't learn about the septic problems until later. I thought, this guy is unscrupulous. He wants to dump raw sewage into the lake. There has to be a better way to do land development around here."

Duprey's first job at the APA was riding in the passenger side of a state car while Clarence Petty drove at about twenty miles an hour, both of them intently looking out the windows. Whenever they saw an unobstructed view, also known as a "scenic vista," they stopped the car and marked its location on a map.

Recommendation no. 106 from the TSC states that "in highway planning, roadside appearance should receive as much emphasis as the roadbed." It adds that the state should assist town and county highway departments for "screening, scenic overlooks, and vista cutting." Duprey said he and a partner spent months slowly driving every road in the park to map the scenery. Sometimes it was Petty; other times it was Riner or Estes. "It was informal," he said. "Every morning George told you what needed to be done, and you did it."

In February 1972, Nelson Rockefeller awarded the APA's executive director job to Harry Daniels, a political ally and former Oneida County executive who had lost his reelection bid. Daniels mostly did administrative work and served as a liaison to APA board members, the public, and Albany officials. He had a passing knowledge of Ian McHarg because he had supervised the Oneida County planning department. But Daniels was also easy going. He didn't act like a boss. He gave Davis more time to work on the plan.

The APA map project was also fortunate to have a resource that had just become available. In 1967, the state contracted with Cornell University to produce aerial photographs that were taken at a consistent altitude, so that the images would match the scale of topographic maps produced by the US Geological Survey. These were the photos Davis and Harold Jerry had tried to get in time for the TSC's work. However, by the time of the APA, the photo survey had been completed and Cornell researcher Ron Shelton had developed a Land Use and Natural Resources Inventory (LUNR) classification system, showing 135 categories of land use that could be determined from the photographs.

Davis ordered a complete set of aerial photos of the park as soon as he arrived at the APA. He and the other staffers used them to make preliminary judgments about the different ways each acre was being used. LUNR gave the staff its first rough draft of the land use plan. But it also raised countless questions, and the only way to find the answers was to hit the road.

The park agency's board was also active in fall 1971. Members held nine meetings, several of which lasted two days. They went on several field trips, including an all-day, five-hundred-mile ride in a DEC helicopter that flew at low altitudes from Albany to Plattsburgh and back again. The flight log describes a large triangular route that took in three rivers, eight lakes, five mountains, three islands, and two wilderness areas before stopping for lunch at the Clinton County airport; then, after lunch, another river, eight lakes, two mountains, and two more wilderness areas were covered before landing back at the Warren County Airport at 3:15 p.m.

The staff and board were both looking at the Adirondacks from above and at a distance. That was surely how a lot of local residents felt about the APA's approach. And it didn't help the agency's image when Richard Lawrence decided that the initial meetings of the APA board would not be open to the public. Lawrence wanted board members to be able to talk freely while they discussed broad concepts and searched for points of agreement. But this was a public agency, and *Daily Enterprise* editor Bill Doolittle attacked the decision in his newspaper for its "monumental arrogance." He urged "every citizen to demand from their agency lords a public accounting at public meetings."

Richard Lawrence had lived in a small North Country town for twenty-four years, so he knew about the destructive power of rumors. But he was also following a tight schedule, and he couldn't release information before his board had agreed to it. The APA held a few press conferences in 1971, and they were able to send more staff to public meetings after Harry Daniels showed up in February. But for the most part, their plans took shape in private.

George Davis presented some general ideas for the Land Use and Development Plan at a board meeting on December 17, 1971. The staff would put overlays of 20 percent screens on fifty-eight planimetric maps that covered the entire park, with a scale of one inch representing about one mile (1:62,000). A screen would go onto the map in areas where the slope, soil, or another characteristic made it less suited to development. If an area got no screens, it meant that development there would have no significant environmental impact. Three screens meant "severe limitations." Four meant the area would be completely off limits to development.

Whether or not an area got a screen depended on several factors, including its capacity to filter wastewater, its susceptibility to erosion, its scenic qualities, and the presence of something rare or unique. Davis described the Cornell-developed technique that used the LUNR aerial photographs to infer twenty-four different types of soil, because soil surveys had not yet been completed for the Adirondacks, and four different slope categories, which could be calculated from the US Geological Survey topographic maps. All land with an elevation of 2,500 feet or more would automatically get a 40 percent screen. So would any land that was found to be habitat for rare plants and animals. Bogs, alpine areas, and forests that had never been logged would get 60 percent. And more subjective categories, such as scenic views and historic sites, could get screened, too.

The content of Davis's presentation seemed familiar to four of the nine APA board members. Dick Lawrence, Peter Paine, Ron Pedersen, and Dick Wiebe had already been introduced to McHarg's ideas through the TSC, so they knew what to expect. The plans also did not particularly alarm Joseph Tonelli, who was indifferent to any discussion of Ian McHarg.

Tonelli sped up and down the Northway in a chauffeured car to get to the APA meetings. He always had somewhere else he needed to be, so he usually had his eye on the door. He was there to protect one thing—union jobs, especially if they were in the paper industry—and he made it clear from the beginning that his support for the plan depended on excluding forest land from the regulations. If he got that, Tonelli would go along with whatever the chair recommended. So Dick Lawrence made sure he got it.

"I think Tonelli did the governor a favor by serving on the APA," said the APA's general counsel, Bill Kissel. "He was always in a hurry. He came to meetings, but you knew you were inconveniencing him. He had a chauffeur, Babe, who looked like he came right off the set of a Mafia movie. All the staffers were sure that Babe was packing heat under his suit coat." They were probably correct. In 1978, Tonelli pled guilty to embezzling $360,000 from his union and was sentenced to three years in prison.

"Joe and Babe had a routine," Kissel said. "Babe would never come into the meeting room. He would stand at the door. And at some point he would say, kind of gangster-style out of the corner of his mouth, 'Five minutes, Joe.' Dick Lawrence knew then that if he had a motion and he needed Joe's vote, it was time to vote, because Joe always voted with Dick Lawrence."

Mary Prime was the opposite of Joe Tonelli. She was beyond reproach. Prime was unfailingly sweet and positive in her personal dealings, and she was active in charities that served Lake Placid. She was also well known for her support of regional zoning in the Adirondacks. She was a calming presence who kept disagreements from getting out of hand. "She was such a delightful lady," Davis said. She also liked Davis, and she was concerned about him. She could see that he was under great pressure, and she worried about his health.

In addition to often being the only woman in a boardroom, Prime was also comfortable in a barroom. A lot of park residents half a century ago didn't mess around when it was time to get a drink, and Prime didn't either. "After meetings we'd go to the bar at Howard Johnson's in Lake Placid," remembered staffer Bill Curran. "Mary would get a double bourbon, neat, with a glass of water. She'd down both of them, boom, boom. That was it."

When George Davis sketched out his plan on December 17, 1971, it raised the eyebrows of three board members who were concerned about the effect it would have on small businesses and local economies. "Whit" Daniels had retained a small contract representing a group of upstate businesses. The minutes reflect the fact that he was a consistent advocate for low-income families. Jim Bird agreed with the overall principles of environmental protection, but he had also spent decades doing construction in the park. He often pointed out things the other commissioners hadn't considered. "Jim was a wonderful guy," Kissel said. "He was really smart, in a practical sort of way. He was like a lawyer on a backhoe."

Kissel and other staffers had a lot less affection for Bill Foley. They remember his slovenly appearance and abrasive style of cross-examination. "He was against almost everything we did from day one," Kissel said. "He was not friendly, not a constructive presence. Sometimes he would ask good, pointed legal questions, but he was always attacking."

After Davis finished his presentation on December 17, the agency board started to argue about it, with Foley, Bird, and Daniels squaring off against the majority. Lawrence finally told Davis to work with DEC and OPS staff to smooth out as many rough edges as he could. The board had to move on to their main focus for fall 1971, which was drafting the interim rules and regulations that would be used in towns that did not already have zoning plans.

Staff members Estes and Huber had given their first draft of the interim regulations to the board back in October. It took more than two months for the board to approve them. This would be their first show of authority. They knew it was going to be unpopular, and they didn't even have any maps yet.

The regulations were published in North Country papers in mid-January 1972. They excluded many kinds of projects: anything built by the state on state lands, anything having to do with agriculture or forest management (thanks, Mr. Tonelli), improvements on existing homes, and developments of less than five acres that also had fewer than five lots.

The proposed regulations suggested that developers consult with the agency's staff before beginning a project, to get specific recommendations and preliminary approval. But the approval process was complex. Developers had to provide information on three dozen aspects of their land; this included a twelve-point site description, their plans for sewage and pollution abatement, and the answers to five questions about financing. There would be a public hearing, and the full agency board was required to vote on each permit application. People who went ahead without permission could be fined $500 a day or jailed.

For most builders, the biggest problem with the interim regulations was that the agency gave itself ninety days to study a project application. That was also about the length of the prime building season in the North Country. Most builders saw the regulations as a big wad of red tape where none had existed before.

The board considered about ninety project applications in 1972, and it approved most of them. But the APA also had no way of knowing how many builders went ahead without telling them. The rules did not apply to the majority of park residents, many of whom remained unaware of their existence. It was a 140-mile drive from APA headquarters in Ray Brook to the far southwestern edge of the park. Neighbors didn't usually report violations, and the APA also couldn't spare any staff to pursue the violations it did know about. As 1972 wore on, a lot of locals formed the impression that the APA wasn't for real.

But Louis Papparazzo and other developers kept moving forward. And on March 6, 1972, a new player emerged. A large Tucson-based corporation announced that it had paid $2.3 million to buy 24,300 acres at the northern edge of the park. The corporation planned to carve the land into ten thousand homesites. The site was in the Town of Colton (population 1,200), which did not have zoning. That threat was real.

Chapter 9

# The Nature Business

Robert Kafin knew his bet had paid off when he and his law partner, Ed Needleman, were invited to a meeting at Harold Hochschild's Great Camp in October 1971. Kafin had been talking to Ted Hullar from the Sierra Club, David Newhouse from the Adirondack Mountain Club (ADK), and Courtney Jones, a philanthropist from the Lake Champlain town of Westport. Paul Schaefer, who had ties to dozens of organizations, was also in the group.

"Courtney had the idea that this loose federation of environmentalists needed a central core," Kafin said. "He was important because he knew some of the fancier people, like Arthur Crocker. The Sierra Club's Atlantic chapter was energetic, but it needed to become more organized. The president of the ADK didn't want anything to do with environmental activism, but he let Newhouse organize through their Conservation Committee.

"So we sat around a table at Eagle Nest with all these great Adirondack people. They proposed to pool their resources and hire us as kind of a clearinghouse. We called it the Adirondack Project." The checks came from the Sierra Club Legal Defense Fund, and the lawyers' job was to represent

the clients and keep them informed. "We organized for all the public hearings, and we sent out a newsletter reporting on what happened and what was
coming up," Kafin said. The firm of Kafin & Needleman sent out at least
fourteen newsletters in the next year with news, gossip, and rumors about
goings-on in Albany and Ray Brook.

Environmental law was new in the early 1970s, and many of its clients came
from the environmental movement. The report produced by the Temporary
Study Commission (TSC) persuaded Kafin that there might be work for an
environmental law firm in the Adirondacks. He was right. Six months after
they hung out their shingle in Glens Falls as Kafin & Needleman, the two men
started playing a central role in the campaign to regulate land development in
the park. The Adirondack Project gave them a lot more billable hours, too.

Lawyers, donors, and grassroots activists joined forces to "save" the Adirondacks in 1972. They coordinated marketing, lobbying, and lawyering to
multiply their force as they pursued the same goal. The environmentalists
wanted strict regulations on the use of every acre of the Adirondack Park.
The matter was urgent, they said. Town and county governments were ill-
equipped to handle the challenge. The new rules had to be written by the
state legislature and enforced by state officials.

To locals, it felt like another invasion from outsiders and an assault on privileges they had taken for granted. But it was really the beginning of something new. Nonprofit organizations, staffed by professionals and supported
by fundraising, were going into the business of protecting nature.

"The measure of the power of a public interest group is not how loud it
trumpets," Kafin said in their job proposal, "but how persuasive it can be
with policymakers and how ably it assists the staff." Their job, he said, was
to pay attention to "the actual rules and regulations which will govern the
future of the park."

Kafin smiled as he recalled his early 1970s career shift. He spoke clearly and
carefully, as one might expect from a powerful lawyer. But the younger self
he described had not always taken the safe route.

He grew up in an inner suburb of Philadelphia, the son of schoolteach-
ers. He graduated from Harvard Law School in 1966 and got a job doing
securities law at Proskauer Rose, a prominent New York City law firm. The
money was very good, but Kafin was like a lot of young lawyers in the 1960s.
He wanted to work in the public interest.

"Environmentalism was a hobby that I did after work," he said. He had trouble keeping his hobby under control, as he kept coming up with clever ideas and pushing to make them real. "I don't just join things," he added.

The Kafin family lived near Carl Schurz Park, where the mayor's residence, Gracie Mansion, is located. Kafin is not a large person—he is about five four and 135 pounds—but he is fierce. "The park was a horrible mess," he said. "Broken benches with no paint, scraggly vegetation, litter. We got together with other young parents and decided we were going to clean it up. We created the Schurz Park Conservancy, which today is a substantial organization, but in the beginning the city wouldn't support us. So here's what we did. We went and bought our own paint and paintbrushes and flowers, and on the day of the cleanup we persuaded Mary Lindsay, the wife of the mayor, to join us. That broke the ice."

Kafin also became president of a New York City–based group called Citizens for Clean Air. He began attending lunch meetings organized by a friend, William Hoppen, who was an early practitioner of environmental law. "Bill would invite all these hippie, Earth Day types to get together, and that's how I got to know the Sierra Club, Friends of the Earth, and another group called Environmental Action. Those lunch meetings eventually became the Environmental Planning Lobby, which today is called Environmental Advocates." Kafin also kept up with new legal groups like the Environmental Defense Fund (formed on Long Island in 1967), the Environmental Law Institute (1969), and the Natural Resources Defense Council (1970).

Like so many New Yorkers of the professional classes, Kafin learned what was going on in the Adirondacks by reading the *New York Times*. But he didn't know much. "The Adirondacks was a place to go on weekends," he said. In February 1971, the Kafins spent one of those weekends in a house on Lake George with the Needlemans. Kafin was twenty-nine, with a wife and children ages four and one.

"We were sitting in a warm comfortable room, looking at Pilot Knob Mountain. It was absolutely beautiful," he said. "Someone said, 'Wouldn't this be a great place to live?' and I said that was the dumbest thing I ever heard. But I kept thinking about it."

Kafin remembered two documents that changed his mind about moving upstate. One was the TSC's report, with its recommendation for an Adirondack Park Agency (APA). The second was *The Greening of America*, an ode to countercultural values and natural living by Charles Reich, a Yale Law

School professor who had climbed all but one of the Adirondack High Peaks as a teenager.

Reich wrote that the street protests and unconventional life choices of young people in the late 1960s marked the beginning of "Consciousness III," a new age marked by peace, understanding, and a nonviolent sense of cooperation, with "a renewed relationship of man to himself, to other men, to society, to nature, and to the land." His starry-eyed prose didn't impress all the reviewers—one of them said that "he writes like a Madison Avenue public relations officer who has been given the hippy account"—but the book sold two million copies.

Reich's message resonated with Kafin and others who found financial goals alone to be insufficient. Reich told his readers that social change began with changes in personal behavior, and they took that to heart. Moving to the Adirondacks also seemed like it might work as a business proposition, although Kafin and Needleman might have been the only ones who thought that. "Our families were terribly concerned," he said. "They thought we had lost our minds."

Kafin saw that the National Environmental Policy Act (NEPA) and other new federal laws were broadly written and not widely understood, especially by law firms north of Albany. The Adirondack Pack Agency Act added a big new state law to that pile. These laws could be used to shape or stop development. They would also generate plenty of legal work, because challenges would inevitably end up in court. So in April 1971, Kafin & Needleman rented an office in Glens Falls.

Just before he left, Kafin told a few friends in the city about the move. One was David Sive, who was generally acknowledged as the founder and leader of environmental law, even though he was just forty-eight years old. Sive, who happened to be organizing the Sierra Club Legal Defense Fund at the moment he received Kafin's letter, wished his young friend well.

The contrast between the Upper East Side of Manhattan and the small city of Glens Falls was stark. Kafin & Needleman took whatever work they could find. They represented inmates at the Warren County Jail because the county paid $10 an hour, or $15 for those who actually visited the jail. Some of their clients paid them in firewood or chickens. After a few months, they started getting jobs that paid more.

Kafin was hired as a part-time aide to State Senator Roy Goodman, a moderate Republican who had been his representative when Kafin lived on the Upper East Side. "He was one of seven New York City Republicans who maintained the Republican Party's control of the senate, and he needed to have a good record on the environment," Kafin said. "He hired me to advise on environmental issues, and eventually I ended up doing everything for him. I was his Swiss Army knife. He was a terrific mentor."

The new job was demanding. On Albany workdays, Kafin would leave home at 7 a.m. and get back home at midnight. "At the end of the legislative session I would be working two full-time jobs," he said. But his children were growing up in a small town close to nature, far away from the crowds and grit of New York City. And then the environmental jobs started coming along.

In November 1971, a few weeks after the meeting at Harold Hochschild's house, Kafin & Needleman won an important decision for a county planning board in the northern Catskills. They blocked the route of a high-tension power line that was planned to bisect a scenic area by arguing that the Federal Power Authority had not complied with the requirements NEPA had set. The case eventually made its way to the US Supreme Court, and people started noticing them. But money was still very tight.

"We put in thousands of hours on that case and were paid for a small fraction of that time," Kafin said. "When we went to the hearings in Washington, DC, we slept on someone's floor."

The Adirondack Project was a big break because it paid steadily, and also because it established Kafin & Needleman as the people to talk to if you wanted to block a development in the Adirondacks. The possibilities seemed endless. Among the developers who had big things planned for the park in April 1971 was Boise Cascade, which had purchased 3,248 acres in the northeast corner of the park near Lyon Mountain, intending to develop the property for retirement and summer homes.

At Loon Lake, eighteen miles northeast of Saranac Lake, an industrial designer from Queens named Tony D'Elia led a group that had purchased an old resort and 3,500 acres. He hoped to build one thousand homes there. Around that same time, the International Paper Company sold seven hundred acres in the central Adirondacks to a subdivider. And a Toronto developer planned to turn the boggy North Branch of the Moose River into five thousand lakeside lots on a ten-thousand-acre tract north of Old Forge.

A *New York Times* real estate reporter wrote of the Moose River project, "All that is needed here is to replace the remains of the broken old dam . . .

with a good new earth dam, rip out the alders, and scrape the bottom of the bog. One week of the spring runoff, they contend, will turn the little valley into a brand-new lake." Paul Schaefer, who had spent a decade fighting to keep the Moose River undammed, thought that was a terrible idea.

Local officials in North Country towns did not have the time or the background to evaluate big projects like these. "I got involved in planning because of a hot dog stand," said John Collins, cofounder of the planning board for the Town of Indian Lake.

> In 1968, I was running a lodge that had a restaurant, and one morning we noticed that a hot dog stand was parked next to our public beach. We lived on Blue Mountain Lake, where everybody placed a high value on the beauty and the quiet. The hot dog stand seemed out of place, and it was also cutting into our lunch business, but there was no rule against it. So I went with another guy to the town supervisor to complain, and he said, "Great. I just got some money from Governor Rockefeller for community planning. You two are now on the planning board."
>
> We immediately faced a proposal for a three-hundred-lot subdivision. It was going to increase the number of homes in our community by almost half, and the planning board was absolutely unprepared for it. We had no background in planning. We had no background in law. All we had was the money that the governor had handed out to the towns, which was good, and a gentleman from the State Department who was there to help with local planning named Roger Swanson. He was most helpful.
>
> We ended up approving nearly three hundred lots. We didn't know that we could ask them to settle for two hundred, or demand that they invest more in community services. We did improve things a bit, but we were raw. That experience made me aware that somebody better know these things.

The Adirondack Park had 107 local governments in the early 1970s. Forty-one of them had planning boards, but only nineteen had master plans and only sixteen had subdivision regulations or building codes. Few towns were equipped to evaluate large-scale road, water, and sewer proposals. Before 1971, local government land use regulation in the park meant restricting the locations of mobile homes (thirty-four towns regulated them) and junked cars (regulated in forty-five towns), but not much else.

When the APA announced its interim regulations in January 1972, two unwritten rules immediately took effect. The first is a rule land developers use, which states that it is far more difficult to stop a project once earth moving starts. Developers were eager to break ground before the APA's permanent rules went into effect in mid-1973. But the developers were challenged by the second rule, which states that every action has an equal and opposite reaction. The APA's interim regulations also sent neighboring landowners and "extreme conservationists" looking for lawyers who could stop the developments.

Kafin & Needleman stood out from other North Country law firms. They were creative and aggressive. "We were bomb throwers," Kafin said. "When you oppose a development, part of your goal is to gum up the works until you can figure out how to proceed. We were never accused of any breach of legal ethics, but we played hardball. We had no money, so we did things that more genteel lawyers might consider undignified.

"We would go into hearings and make what everybody regarded as outlandish motions, but the judge would have to deal with them because we had done our research. We would say that the law required A and B and C, and it hadn't been done. The judge might give us the back of his hand, but we persisted in a very strong manner. Nobody was going to push us around. We just didn't give up."

The Adirondack Park Agency was formed at the end of a decade of growing affluence for the middle class. In 1971, it was easy to make a profit by buying land in a picturesque rural area, subdividing it into smaller lots, and selling those lots to people who dreamed of owning a vacation home. Developers had transformed several southern Vermont villages almost overnight in this way. Many longtime residents of Vermont hated the side effects.

Concerns about traffic congestion, water pollution, and higher taxes drove the Vermont state legislature to pass Act 250 in 1970. The law divided the state into nine regions and required developers to get approval from a citizens' board before they could proceed. But the law was full of loopholes and the advisory boards didn't have the expertise needed to evaluate big projects, so the problem persisted.

It takes about two hours to drive from Boston to southern Vermont. It's a three-and-one-half-hour drive from Boston or New York City to Glens Falls, and five hours to Tupper Lake. Vacation-home salesmen prowled these cities and others, looking for credulous buyers who had discretionary income and a dream. What mattered to the salesmen was the sale. Police, fire, schools, and other municipal services were someone else's problem.

The Horizon Corporation was one of the biggest players in this market, with sales of about $100 million in 1971. It had subdivided large tracts in New Mexico, Colorado, North Carolina, and Michigan. One of its biggest markets was American soldiers stationed in Europe. According to a 1971 series in the independent military paper *Stars and Stripes*, the company raised $12 million a year by hiring soldiers to sell lots to other soldiers, sight unseen.

Horizon's sales tactics were later judged to be fraudulent. But in 1971, nobody knew that they were dishonest. Locals only knew that the company had deep pockets. Horizon bought 24,345 acres of foothills and forests in the Town of Colton, northwest of Cranberry Lake, instantly becoming the fourteenth-largest landowner in the Adirondacks. They paid $100 an acre for the land. It seemed like a bargain to them, although it was well above local market rates. The 1,200 full-time residents of Colton had a hard time finding good jobs, and most of them were delighted by the prospect of wealthy neighbors and higher pay.

St. Lawrence County is larger than Rhode Island or Delaware. Its southern third is inside the Blue Line, but almost all of the county's 110,000 residents live in Ogdensburg, Massena, and small towns scattered along the Saint Lawrence River on its northern border. Horizon outlined its plans at a chicken dinner hosted by the St. Lawrence County Chamber of Commerce in Canton, the county seat, in April 1972. Sid Nelson, Horizon's suave cofounder and president, and four others promised a "biseasonal community" on six thousand to nine thousand lots, with an eventual population of twenty-one thousand to thirty-six thousand. They said their new community would have an eighteen-hole golf course, a ski area, an Olympic-sized swimming pool, motels, shops, and three lakes they would create by damming Deerskin Creek and the Grass River.

Franklin Little, owner of the daily *Ogdensburg Journal*, was completely sold. "St. Lawrence County needs new investment, new people, new jobs, and Horizon Development could eventually mean the investment of $100 to $150 million in this county," he wrote. Horizon and its homeowners "would provide new employment" and "pay tens of thousands of dollars in new taxes." And when the developers were finished, "a great many more people could enjoy that area developed by Horizon than can now when it is a heavily posted, impenetrable wasteland and closed to the public."

Local officials throughout the county shared Little's enthusiasm. But when Peter Van de Water heard about the proposed development, "my bullshit antenna went right up," he said. "There was no way that this could be good."

Van de Water was an administrator at St. Lawrence University in Canton, a private school with about 2,400 students. St. Lawrence was the first college in New York State to admit women, in 1856. In the early 1970s, St. Lawrence, Clarkson University in Potsdam, and state university campuses in both places were more liberal outposts in a solidly conservative region. Canton and Potsdam were at least twenty miles from the land Horizon had purchased, but both towns would be transformed by a development that size.

"There were about eight or ten people who had the same reaction I did," Van de Water said. "We started to meet, and before I knew it, I was elected president of Citizens to Save the Adirondack Park."

The new group was mostly concerned about the environmental impacts. "They were going to dam up the Grass River and make golf courses in the mountains and do a lot of other things that didn't make a lot of sense to us," Van de Water said. The group's strategy was to delay Horizon until the park agency's Land Use and Development Plan could go into effect. Citizens was a local community group, so its members wrote letters, made calls, and staffed information booths at barbecues, parades, and field days. But they quickly became the focal point of public concern throughout the entire Northeast.

The publicity came quickly. In May 1972, the *New York Times* published a long article about the Horizon project that quoted former Secretary of the Interior Stewart Udall, who said, "If the large-scale land speculators are allowed to invade the Adirondack Park, this could mean the gradual dismemberment and degradation of one of the nation's finest conservation reserves. This invasion should be fought by all conservationists who know and love the Adirondack country." Then the most popular news source in the country, *The CBS Evening News*, broadcast a report that was sympathetic to the group. Citizens' paid membership swelled to 2,600, although Van de Water estimated that only about 200 of them lived in St. Lawrence County.

The money allowed Citizens to hire David Sive and Peter Berle, the two best-known environmental lawyers in the country. Sive's brilliant, unconventional arguments had stalled two enormous construction projects in the lower Hudson River, and he had a reputation as a giant-killer. "Lawyers often say that an expert is somebody who has done something once," Sive said, "and in the environmental cases, there weren't many people in the early days who had done an environmental case even once. So I became an expert." Berle was the state assembly member who led support for the APA in the legislature.

The lawyers didn't do much except lend their names, but that was enough. "We hired Sive and Berle mostly to scare the bejeezus out of [Horizon President] Sid Nelson," Van de Water said. "I think it made a difference."

Citizens was also fortunate that Horizon was not particularly smart. When the short 1972 construction season began, the company did not rush to start earth moving. In fact, Horizon never went to the APA for preliminary project approval. They might have been scared off by Peter Paine, who said in June 1972 that the project was "a make or break issue for the park agency." Horizon poses questions "that are basic to the agency's existence," Paine said. If their original plans got the go-ahead, he added, "we might as well kiss the agency goodbye."

Citizens had a privileged relationship with the park agency. "We worked hand in glove with them," Van de Water said. "George Davis slipped us information on the side. We knew we were helping to set them up." And the benefits flowed both ways. In August, APA Executive Director Harry Daniels showed the park agency's board members a box containing letters he had received about the Horizon project. He reported that 1,052 of the letters expressed opposition to the project. Only three were in favor of it.

Horizon might have been a "make or break" project for the APA, but the Ton-Da-Lay development was a greater challenge.

When construction season started in 1972, Louis Papparazzo thought that he already had the permits he needed to start building. He was also more sensitive than most developers to environmental concerns. His family-owned company had drawn national attention for building large clustered-housing projects that left a lot of open space. Ton-Da-Lay would be built on only about one-third of the property Papparazzo owned, and the lots were sold with covenants that restricted home sizes, placements, and construction materials.

The APA law passed in 1971 said that towns with preexisting zoning laws would be exempt from the agency's interim regulations, which expired on June 1, 1973. The Town of Altamont, where Ton-Da-Lay was located, had those laws. The town had also issued water and sewer permits to the development. But Ton-Da-Lay's opponents saw a small opening. The development required a centralized water and sewer system, and those required the approval of the State Health Department.

"Historically, the Health Department had approved water and sewer systems based on narrow engineering and public health criteria," Kafin said.

"If you could prove that there was enough water there to serve your territory, and that you treated the water so that it wasn't a public health problem, and you had engineers to get pumps and pipes right, you could get your permit. Likewise with wastewater. All you had to do is to demonstrate that you had a good sewer engineer who knew how to do it."

In April 1970, the newly established Department of Environmental Conservation (DEC) absorbed the sections of the State Health Department that approved water and sewer plants. The DEC's first commissioner, Henry Diamond, made it clear that he intended to review permit applications using a much higher standard. Diamond told Boise Cascade executives that he would do a thorough review of their Lyon Mountain project. Shortly after they got Diamond's letter, Boise Cascade cancelled that project.

In October 1972, Diamond announced that a similarly thorough hearing would be held for Ton-Da-Lay, beginning December 5. He also signaled that he expected the matter to end up in court. "We are going to look beyond the immediate fruits of this water system permit and see what's going on here environmentally," he said. "We raised the statute and the general powers of the department to include these things. Now somebody else might read it another way, and that's what the courts are for."

Bob Kafin said that the hearing was his idea. "I wish I had been this creative my whole life," he said. "As part of the Adirondack Project, we went to John Hanna, who was counsel for Diamond, and pointed out that the DEC statute said that a water system had to be justified by 'public necessity.' We said, 'Look, the department cannot determine whether or not this system is a public necessity without an environmental impact statement and a hearing on the overall impact of the project.'" Hanna and the DEC were "listening and cooperating," he said.

"A lot of what we were trying to do in those days at DEC was pretty fuzzy," said first deputy commissioner Ron Pedersen. "Strong public opinion wanted this or that done, and nobody knew how to do it. But there was broad language in the statute about water supply. We thought that it might give us a handle." Kafin & Needleman's November 13 newsletter was informed by Kafin's meetings with Hanna and other DEC officials. It gave specific instructions to letter writers about timing, content, and where to donate funds.

"So now we needed to gear up for a sophisticated, scientifically backed environmental hearing," Kafin said. "That required us to hire engineers and ecologists and landscape architects. Environmental groups were not used to spending that kind of money." Fortunately, the Ton-Da-Lay site adjoined three large estates whose owners agreed to pay for Kafin & Needleman's services: Bay Pond, owned by William Rockefeller; Brandon Park, owned by members of the DuPont family; and the Kildare Club, owned by the wealthy Friedman family.

This was going to be an entirely new kind of hearing. "The developer expected that it would be a 'notice and comment' hearing, where you show up and make speeches and it lasts a couple of days," Kafin said. "But we knew that the Ton-Da-Lay hearing was going to be much more formal. It would be conducted like a trial, with sworn testimony and cross-examination. It would go on for months."

The hearing was held at the DEC's offices in Ray Brook. "We tried our best to present evidence on every single aspect of environmental quality that would be affected by this development," Kafin said. "The developer didn't know what hit him, and neither did his lawyer. The hearing transcript runs into thousands of pages."

Kafin brought to the hearing Philip Hoff, governor of Vermont from 1963 to 1969, who said that the benefits of second-home developments in his state had not been worth the costs. Then he brought in disgruntled residents of Heritage Village, a development Papparazzo had built in Connecticut, who said that the developer had not kept his promises. And he produced a parade of scientists and engineers that went on and on. The hearings continued into spring 1973.

During the hearing, the scientists repeated what George Davis had told Papparazzo in his environmental report a year earlier. The Ton-Da-Lay site included many wetlands and fragile ecological areas. One of these is Spring Pond Bog, a five-hundred-acre peatland where 130 species of birds have been spotted, including spruce grouse, short-eared owl, and other species that are endangered in New York. Botanists testified that the site was also home to rare northern bog plants and unique species, like the carnivorous pitcher plant, leather leaf, bog laurel, and Labrador tea. It turned out that there was an awful lot to say against Ton-Da-Lay.

Papparazzo and local officials gradually realized that they had been drawn into a quagmire. As the hearing dragged on, their anger boiled over. David Vanderwalker, a member of the Franklin County Board of Supervisors, said that if the DEC deprived the county of the economic benefits of Ton-Da-Lay, "we may see one of the biggest bonfires in history." He was bringing up the local folklore referencing an incident in 1908, when hunters and trappers set fire to William Rockefeller Jr.'s Bay Pond estate to protest the way he had denied them access to his property. Now Vanderwalker was threatening to burn down the woods again, this time to protest actions funded by Rockefeller's great-grandson.

"The hearing officer was an older lawyer and was very smart," said Richard Booth. "One day near the beginning, he decided to let the public come and speak, probably so they could blow off steam. The rules were like a city council meeting, with no cross-examination, no swearing in, and a three-minute limit for each speaker.

"A lot of people showed up, and as the day went on, a pattern developed. An environmentalist would speak against Ton-Da-Lay, and at the end there would be applause. Then a local official would speak in favor, and there would be silence. It was pretty much fifty-fifty.

"After lunch, another environmental person sat down to applause, and then a young man sitting in back raised his hand. He asked the hearing officer, 'May we boo if we don't support what a speaker says?' The older lawyer says, 'Yes, absolutely, just keep it orderly.'

"The next speaker was George Nagle, an ordained minister from Saranac Lake who was opposed to Ton-Da-Lay. He stood up and gave an impassioned sermon about why turning down Ton-Da-Lay was necessary. He said it represented the opposite of what God is talking about in the Bible, and he read some scripture to back up his points. Then he sat down. Solid applause. Who is going to boo the guy who's quoting Scripture?

"Also, there was no booing for the rest of the day. This was the only time I ever witnessed divine intervention."

Kafin's objective was to "gum up the works" until the APA's plan for private land could be passed. The strategy worked. The park agency's draft of the Land Use and Development Plan, released for public comment on December 21, said that big projects like Papparazzo's would have to be approved by the APA after all. The draft plan also indicated that Papparazzo might get approval for about one-tenth as many lots as he wanted.

Ton-Da-Lay became an early case study in the environmental activists' playbook. The play is to delay, add complexity, and drive up the price until the numbers don't work anymore and the developer pulls out. The teams are made up of organizers, lobbyists, and litigators. Lawyers are often the managers.

The environmental movement was also growing in another direction in the early 1970s. The new branch was just as committed to the cause as the antipollution and anti-development groups were, but it was far quieter, and in the beginning, very few people understood how important it would become.

Some lawyers are attack dogs, like Kafin & Needleman. Others are guard dogs, like David Sive and Peter Berle. And other lawyers are big dogs. They try not to attract attention, and the public is often unaware of what they do. But they have power and influence, and when they want something to happen, it almost always does.

Arthur V. Savage was that kind of lawyer. He was a member of the Hand family of Elizabethtown; Richard Lawrence's wife was his cousin. He was also the only grandson of Augustus Noble Hand (1869–1954), a pillar of American jurisprudence who served on the federal district court and second circuit court of appeals with his more famous cousin, Learned Hand (1872–1961). Augustus wrote or concurred in the decisions that legalized condoms, allowed James Joyce's *Ulysses* to be published in the United States, codified the rules for conscientious objection to military service, and reorganized the film industry, among many others.

Arthur Savage was a graduate of Phillips Exeter Academy, Princeton University, and Harvard Law School, but he was also a rare creature in another way. He was a lifelong environmental activist from an old-money family who loved to laugh and didn't take himself very seriously. He was fun to be around, and his many friends were happy to see him whenever he dropped by.

Savage practiced law in New York City, but he spent nearly every summer of his life in Elizabethtown, and he devoted much of his professional life to protecting the Adirondacks. He was a founding trustee of the Adirondack Museum and served on its board for forty-nine years. When Harold and Mary Hochschild rewrote their wills, they named Savage as legal guardian of their only child.

At different points in his career, Savage served as president of the Association for the Protection of the Adirondacks and cofounder of the Adirondack Council. He was on the board of the APA for eight years, and on the board of the state university's College of Environmental Science and Forestry for nineteen. But the most consequential thing Savage did might have been cofounding the Adirondack Chapter of The Nature Conservancy (TNC).

TSC recommendation no. 181 states that "an Adirondack Nature Conservancy to encourage gifts in the Adirondack Park should be established by private interests." It was the last recommendation on their long list, but it was far from an afterthought. The commissioners knew of several large parcels of private land in the Adirondacks whose owners might be interested in selling or donating to the state. They had drawn up a much longer list of private lands that they thought should be added to the forest preserve if they ever became available. But the state's ability to buy land depended on funding, and state funds were often scarce. It could take months or years for the state to get the money together to close on a land deal, and sellers were not always willing to wait.

The Temporary Study Commission envisioned a private group like TNC serving a crucial role as an honest broker. The nonprofit could focus on desirable pieces of land and establish long-term relationships with the state and landowners. When opportunities arose, it could act quickly to buy and hold the properties until the state got its money together.

"Paul Schaefer called me to see if I would help get a chapter of The Nature Conservancy started in the Adirondacks," Savage said. "He wouldn't give up, and the third or fourth time he called I finally agreed to do it. But I thought it would make more sense if I had a co-chair who was a full-time resident of the park." Savage persuaded a relative, Wayne Byrne, the owner of a hardware store in Plattsburgh, to join him.

Savage and Byrne's connections allowed them to quickly put together a thirty-five-person board with diverse backgrounds. The members included many of the usual suspects, such as Arthur Crocker, Courtney Jones, Robert Kafin, David Newhouse, Clarence Petty, and Paul Schaefer. But it also included natural science experts, wealthy camp owners not otherwise involved in environmental politics, and North Country business leaders. It was easy to attract nonactivists because the cause was not controversial. The state government was not directly involved, and few could object to the goal of connecting a willing buyer with a willing seller.

The Nature Conservancy, based in Alexandria, Virginia, was a small organization in 1970. It had about thirty thousand members, but they were dispersed in chapters all over the United States that were focused on acquiring and maintaining local nature preserves. In 1967, the conservancy purchased Mason Neck, a small peninsula on the lower Potomac River, and resold the land to the state of Virginia as a park. Pat Noonan, a young lawyer in their national office, thought he saw a similar opportunity in the Adirondacks.

Noonan, who became president of TNC in 1973, liked to refer to his organization as "the real estate wing of the environmental movement." He stayed away from politics and focused on deals. He usually wore a suit to work, because his days were full of meetings with bankers, business executives, and wealthy landowners. As the years went by, Noonan amassed an impressive list of business executives who were on his side. They might be too buttoned down to support confrontational groups like the Sierra Club, but they also believed in wilderness protection, and they could do a lot for the cause.

Noonan approached Crandall Melvin, a Syracuse lawyer whose family owned Camp Santanoni, a 12,446-acre preserve just south of the huge, undeveloped section of the forest preserve known as the High Peaks. Santanoni contained several beautiful lakes, the southern end of the marsh known as Duck Hole, and architecturally distinguished camp buildings from the late nineteenth century. Noonan knew that the family had approached the State Conservation Department in 1957, offering to sell, but the state had no money to buy the preserve. He hoped that TNC might do a bigger version of the Mason Neck deal, this time with New York State, so it could add Santanoni to the forest preserve. But the property had been appraised at $1.7 million, a price far too high for the conservancy or the state to pay.

Then things took an unexpected and tragic turn. On July 10, 1971, eight-year-old Douglas Legg, Crandall Melvin's grandson, walked away from the main building at Santanoni and vanished into the woods. The search for him became one of the largest manhunts in Adirondacks history. Hundreds of volunteers combed the woods for over a month, but the boy's body was never recovered. His fate remains unknown.

After Douglas disappeared, Crandall Melvin never wanted to go back to Santanoni. In the fall, he dropped the family's price to $1 million, after he and Noonan agreed to a deal sweetener called a "bargain sale." Since the appraised value of the land was $1.7 million, federal tax laws would allow the family to claim the extra $700,000 as a donation, which would significantly reduce their income taxes. Bargain sales are one of several incentives TNC uses to encourage conservation-minded landowners to turn their property into parkland.

One million dollars was still an extremely ambitious goal for TNC in 1971. But the new Adirondack chapter had access to wealth and connections. Arthur Savage and other board members started making calls, and things began to move.

One call paid off. The federal Department of the Interior's Land and Water Conservation Fund had been set up in 1965 on the recommendation of Laurance Rockefeller's Outdoor Recreation Resources Review Commission. It offered an $875,000 grant toward the purchase of Santanoni, with one condition: a local planning agency had to sponsor the grant.

Savage called on Winifred "Winnie" LaRose, a real estate agent in Lake George who had been president of the local historical society. LaRose was a supporter of regional planning, and she had joined the board of TNC's Adirondack chapter eagerly. She was also a forceful person. As one admirer put it, "Winnie was like a cross between Lyndon Johnson and Golda Meir," the prime minister of Israel.

LaRose put the deal in front of the Lake George Commission and got them to agree to sponsor the Santanoni grant, with one condition: the architecturally significant Great Camp buildings had to be protected. The condition irritated hard core wilderness advocates, because the Santanoni parcel could not be added to the adjacent High Peaks Wilderness Area if it contained buildings and roads. Peter Paine, Ted Hullar, and others had hoped to burn the buildings. But they needed the money to make the deal happen, so they compromised.

The Nature Conservancy still needed to raise $125,000, but all they could come up with was $50,000. Then another old friend came forward. Harold Hochschild understood how important the deal was, and he also trusted Arthur Savage. But Hochschild was also aware of how controversial his TSC recommendations had become, so he asked that his donation be made anonymously. Hochschild's $75,000 closed the deal. The Nature Conservancy signed an option to purchase Santanoni at the end of November and transferred the property to the state a few months later.

The Santanoni deal was a turning point for TNC. For the first twenty years of its existence, the group's focus had been on identifying the habitat of endangered plant and animal species and acquiring small preserves to protect them. But the Santanoni property was about as large as the island of Manhattan. It was the organization's first foray into what they now call "landscape-level" conservation projects that protect entire ecosystems.

Santanoni was also a public relations coup for the new chapter. Press reports describing the Santanoni deal announced that the chapter and a partner organization, Trout Unlimited, had launched a $500,000 fundraising campaign for future land acquisition in the Adirondacks. Savage and Byrne were confident that they could find that kind of money. They had already secured enough pledges to hire their first staff member.

Tim Barnett was a recovering ski bum in 1971. He had been drawn into skiing and mountain climbing after he got out of the Army in 1962. He did earn a bachelor's degree in English from the University of Colorado at Boulder in 1965, mostly because it didn't interfere much with his outdoor interests. He drifted back east to his family's home in Westport, then found work in New York City. There he met and fell in love with Claire Lillis, a research reporter at *Time.* Tim liked Claire, he said, because she was so much smarter than he was.

"I took her for a date on the Staten Island Ferry," Barnett said. "I wooed her with hot dogs."

Barnett is a big, friendly fellow. He had long hair in those days, and he liked nice clothes and fine liquor. He was also very good at sales. He married Claire in 1966. He sold ski equipment for a while, and then he got a job at WPIX-TV, Channel 11 in New York City, selling local ads. The money was good, but his clients—ambulance-chasing lawyers, used car salesmen, and furniture stores—were less than inspiring. Claire didn't like her job either, and in 1971, the Barnetts found out they were expecting. They were both ready for a change.

They visited Tim's parents in Westport on Columbus Day weekend, and Barnett ran into a friend of a friend. "Once in a while I would go on a boat ride with a couple of my rich friends from Westport to Essex, to a restaurant called The Old Dock," he said. "We would drink a lot, and every so often we would stand up, open the side door, and jump into Lake Champlain fully dressed, just because it was fun.

"So we went to The Old Dock on Columbus Day, and then we got back in the boat to go to a higher-class place on the Vermont side called Basin Harbor. On the ride over I started talking to Courtney Jones, who I had just met. When we got to Basin Harbor, we noticed that they had a heated swimming pool, so this time we took off all our clothes before we jumped in. We were in the pool, naked, when a guard came out with a state trooper. The guard asked, 'Are you going to arrest them?' And the state trooper said, 'No, they're from out of state. Go home, you guys.' So we got away.

"Now we're on the way back home across the lake. Courtney said, 'Why don't you move up here?' And I said, 'What would I do?' And he said, 'I'm on the board of a small conservation group. We're going to hire an executive director. You'd be perfect.'"

Barnett met Winnie LaRose, chair of the local TNC chapter's recruitment committee, at the Howard Johnson's hotel in Lake George for his job interview. "I left Claire in a strange parking lot with a three-month-old baby because Winnie said we needed to talk in her office," he said. "She did all the talking for two hours, and then she reported to everybody that I was brilliant." The chapter offered Barnett "starvation wages" and a spare room with a desk in Lake George. He reported for work in spring 1972.

"We printed up a brochure and mailed it to anybody who had anything to do with Santanoni," he said. "We just bumbled along." Barnett also negotiated small land deals for the next six years, adding 5,685 more acres to the forest preserve. The breakthrough came in 1978, when two easements secured the development rights to much of the land that was adjacent to Ton-Da-Lay.

Barnett's sales skills took off when he believed in what he was selling. Under his leadership, TNC protected 99,473 acres of forest preserve land by the end of 1980, another 89,168 acres by 1990, and another 14,076 acres by 1997, when Barnett's career was cut short by a serious injury. In 2020, Barnett looked back in wonder. The Adirondack chapter of TNC has protected nearly 600,000 acres inside the Blue Line, and other branches of the organization have protected 119,000,000 acres worldwide. TNC is a global organization with roughly one million members. As one of WPIX's steady advertisers, the New York State Lottery, used to say, "Hey, you never know."

Tim Barnett said that he didn't go to Ray Brook often, and he had almost no contact with the APA in those early years. Maybe that's why he had such a good time. Most of the original APA staffers remember the early 1970s with pride, but few of them say that their jobs were fun. They remember the pressure.

On June 17, 1972, the heat was building on the staff and board of the APA, and especially on their star lawyer. "I don't sleep nights, to be honest with you," Peter Paine told a reporter for the *Watertown Daily Times*. The APA "is a responsibility I don't think any nine men should have, and yet the reason we have it is because no one else has been willing to assume it, or they have assumed it badly. It is not an easy thing to live with, I can assure you. It's about all I do.

"My law practice has gone pretty well to hell," Paine continued. "My family life has ceased to exist. I think the job can be done. I think we are on the verge of a reasonable success. But it's going to be a close squeaker."

Chapter 10

# The Big Push

Peter S. Paine was a partner at Cleary Gottlieb, an international law firm with offices on an upper floor of a skyscraper in downtown Manhattan. Richard Booth says that the view of New York Harbor made him feel as if he were "standing at the steering wheel of the world."

Paine charged hundreds of dollars per hour to represent banks and big businesses. But he spent much of the first half of 1972 ignoring these clients while putting in long hours as a board member of the Adirondack Park Agency. Paine had a lot of responsibilities. The governor had sent eight Adirondack bills to the legislature in 1971 after receiving the report of the Temporary Study Commission (TSC), but only one of them, the APA Act, had become law. Four of the remaining bills were reintroduced to the legislature in January 1972. Paine acted as a liaison between the APA, his fellow TSC alumni, and state legislators to move those four bills along.

While the bills were important to the TSC's vision of the Adirondacks, the APA's main job was drafting two land use plans. The State Land Master Plan, which was due by June 1, 1972, ordered specific, permanent changes in the management of the Adirondack Forest Preserve. It did not require the approval of the legislature, but it did need the signature of the governor, and Nelson Rockefeller would not sign the state land plan without the blessing of the Department of Environmental Conservation (DEC) Commissioner Henry Diamond. The second land use plan was much more elaborate, and it was also the one Paine had said would be "a close squeaker." The Land Use and Development Plan aimed to prevent inappropriate development on 3.45 million acres of private property inside the Adirondack Park. It was the environmental movement's only hope of stopping several huge housing developments that were proposed inside the Blue Line. The APA was required to collect comments on a draft version of the plan in the fall and deliver the final version to the legislature in January 1973.

George Davis had been gathering data for the Land Use and Development Plan since September 1971, and he had put in long hours. But budget cuts had slowed him down. The plan was a massive amount of work, and the staff was not fully hired until summer 1972, when the deadline for submitting the plan to the public for comment was just a few months away. Seventy-hour weeks and all-nighters became the norm for many APA staffers as Davis struggled to keep the process on track. "One of the first things we got was a beer refrigerator, and I kept it full of beer," said Davis. "Beer did it."

As the workdays stretched into evenings, the executive director and at least one board member showed their support for the staff by bringing them six-packs. Staffers drank beer on breaks, mostly in the office but sometimes at roadside bars. They cracked beers in the car on the long drives that ended most days of fieldwork. At least once, two staffers drank beer for breakfast. All of this was illegal and would be considered grounds for termination today, but this was 1972. The rules for state jobs were looser, and the Adirondacks were a different place.

The Land Use and Development Plan had a good shot at becoming law, because almost everyone hated the thought of big vacation-home developments like Horizon and Ton-Da-Lay blotching the park. Most full-time residents of the park did not like the idea of the APA either, but a lot of them were either not paying attention or were equally alarmed by the prospect of big second-home developments. They kept quiet as the Land Use and Development Plan took shape, even if they hated the concept of giving up local control.

As the two plans moved along, environmental groups across the state continued to push their representatives to stop the big developments and "save" the Adirondacks. William Verner, a pro-APA activist, put it this way: "If these big developments hadn't come along, we would have had to create them."

Bill Kissel arrived for work at Cleary Gottlieb in mid-April 1972. Kissel was twenty-nine and had been hired as the APA's chief counsel. He doesn't recall the grand view from the office windows. "We weren't allowed to look out the window," he said. "We were grinding away, working late into the night."

Kissel remembered Peter Paine sitting in his office and banging on a pale green Olivetti Studio 44 manual typewriter. The Studio 44 is portable, but it is also unusually large and sturdy. "He had secretaries, but he didn't use them much," Kissel said. "He loved that typewriter." Paine's typewriter had been pushing the Forever Wilders' agenda for years. When Kissel arrived, it had just finished helping Paine shepherd four leftover TSC bills through the legislature.

The first bill was the Environmental Quality Bond Act. Governor Rockefeller asked the legislature to propose $1.15 billion in new state bonds for voter approval in November. About $44 million of that was earmarked for land purchases in the Adirondack Forest Preserve. That was only about one-third as much as the TSC had asked for, but it was a lot better than nothing.

Paine and other APA board members kept tabs on the bond act as it moved through the legislature, making sure the $44 million was not cut. When the governor signed the bill on May 31, sending it on to the voters in November, Paine relaxed a bit. New York State voters had never rejected a bond issue aimed at buying land or improving the environment.

The second bill was the Wild, Scenic, and Recreational Rivers Act. Temporary Study Commission recommendation no. 88 proposed a New York State rivers system, and the bill designated the first 172 miles of it along fifteen rivers in the Adirondacks. George Davis and Clarence Petty used their TSC fieldwork to identify sections of the Hudson, Cold, Opalescent, Indian, and Sacandaga Rivers that qualified as "wild," along with one section of West Canada Creek. Seven other sections of Adirondack rivers were designated as "scenic." But there are about 1,500 miles of rivers inside the Blue Line, and many of them would be eligible for protection. Once the law passed, an APA field crew would be sent to survey every single mile.

The third law came from Arthur Savage. "I was up at Blue Mountain Lake with the Hochschilds for a weekend when he was the chairman of the Temporary Study Commission," Savage said. "I had recently realized that there was nothing in the world preventing the legislature of New York State from amending the boundaries of the Adirondack Park with a simple yes-or-no vote. I told him that I felt this was a real problem, and he agreed, so I submitted a paper and testified at a commission hearing to suggest what I thought should be done about it."

The TSC submitted a bill that would require a constitutional amendment to diminish the park's boundaries. "The legislature didn't go for that," said Savage, "but they did accept a bill requiring two successively elected sessions of the legislature to vote before diminishing the acreage of the park. That is my central contribution to the constitutional law of New York."

Finally, Paine helped write a 1972 bill that expanded the size of the park by about 250,000 acres. The TSC had found that 161,174 acres of forest preserve land were entirely outside the Blue Line, and that more than 90 percent of those acres were submerged. New York's legislature had drawn the park boundary to follow the Vermont state line, which is halfway across Lake Champlain. The lakebed was important because it allowed the park to claim four small islands in New York waters. The submerged acres were outside the Blue Line because the towns of Willsboro, Essex, and Westport, which bordered the lake, were not in the park.

The TSC looked at previous additions to the park to determine the legislature's intent. "It was apparent that the Adirondack Park should include forested land in the mountains and the foothills, but not the flat lands on the edges of the mountains," Paine said. "When the Blue Line was originally drawn in 1891, a lot of land in the Champlain Valley and along the northern edge was farms. But the farms were abandoned in the twentieth century, and the forests grew back."

Paine and the other commissioners also felt it was important for the park boundary to be unbroken, because this would make it easier for the state to preserve the integrity of its ecosystems. The commission also identified 12,806 acres of forest preserve land in isolated parcels that were outside of the Blue Line. These parcels could be absorbed if the park's boundary was expanded slightly to the north and southwest. The park could also claim jurisdiction over fifty additional miles of Lake Champlain shoreline if Willsboro, Essex, and Westport were included.

"I remember flying with Dick Lawrence and Bill Cowles, who was the Vermont co-chairman of the Lake Champlain Committee," Paine said. "Bill had a Helio Courier plane that could fly very low and very slow. We hung about five hundred feet over Clinton, Franklin, and St. Lawrence counties. Dick was in the copilot's seat, Bill was flying, and I was sitting behind Dick. Dick had a map open on his lap. We drew a line on the map as we flew, trying to approximate the extent of the forested land."

They did not get all the land they wanted. The three towns did not object to being included, but the DEC balked at adding a parcel south of Malone because it was actively logged. Also, well-connected friends of Senator Ron Stafford used their influence to exclude apple orchards along the northern edge. But Stafford did give his blessing to include Valcour Island, a 968-acre parcel just south of Plattsburgh, and Garden Island just to its south. The islands contain a large great blue heron rookery, and they were also the site of an early naval battle in the Revolutionary War.

"The State Parks Commission hired an architect in 1970 to develop Valcour Island into a recreational park, with ball fields and a marina," Paine said. "I remember them talking about digging an artificial feeding pond with coin-operated vending machines that would dispense corn so people could feed the ducks. Wayne Byrne led a group of local people who were outraged by this idea. They came to the Temporary Study Commission and persuaded us to recommend that the Blue Line should be extended to include Valcour Island."

Paine worked for a corporate law firm, so he had not spent much time drafting legislation. He relied on another lawyer, Richard Persico, who worked for Richard Wiebe's Office of Planning Services. Persico was present at most of the APA's meetings, and "he was a superb bill drafter," said Paine. Persico would be appointed executive director of the APA in 1973.

Few park residents or business organizations objected to these four bills, and they were approved without a lot of controversy. The bills mostly regulated state-owned land. Also, the location of the Blue Line wasn't that important to private landowners at the time the bills passed. In 1972, there were not a lot of rules restricting how privately owned land inside the park could be used. One year later, all of that would change.

The State Land Master Plan was mostly a creation of the Temporary Study Commission, and the TSC had been informed by more than a decade of background work. New York State's Joint Legislative Committee on Natural Resources had charted roadless areas and documented their conditions in the 1950s and early 1960s. The report of Laurance Rockefeller's Outdoor Recreation Resources Review Commission was issued in 1962. And when the federal Wilderness Act passed in 1964, it established a legal definition of "wilderness" that the TSC used almost verbatim. "Completing the State Land Master Plan was a natural evolution of thinking about public land management," Paine said. "It wasn't rocket science."

Getting the plan ready for state officials was a lot of work, however. "George Davis brought down his draft of the State Land Master Plan in April," Paine said. "It was poetry, but it was also completely useless. He explained the whole philosophy of wilderness, but we couldn't use it. Our job was to draft a regulatory document that would force the Department of Environmental Conservation to do X, Y, and Z. George's version, beautiful as it was, would not have done any of that." Paine rewrote the entire thing.

The draft of the master plan was released for public comment in May. It separated the forest preserve into four categories. Half of it (1.15 million acres, or 50.5 percent) would be managed as "wild forest," and would allow cars, motorboats, and snowmobiles to use specified roads and waterways. Forty-five percent (1 million acres) would be set aside in fifteen "wilderness" areas and the Saint Regis Canoe Area, which would be managed as a wilderness, following a stricter version of federal standards. Three percent (75,670 acres) of the forest preserve would be in sixteen "primitive areas," which were like wilderness areas, but smaller.

The final 1.5 percent of state land was a grab bag. Most of it was designated as "intensive use," including large campgrounds, boat launches, ski areas, parkways, and visitor centers. The plan also created a small number of "special management areas" to protect endangered species; acknowledged the creation of wild, scenic, and recreational river corridors; and allowed separate regulations for major travel corridors.

Harold Jerry's idea, carried forward by George Davis, was that the standards for wild forest lands would be roughly similar to the way the Conservation Department had interpreted the Forever Wild clause prior to 1972. The rules for wilderness and primitive areas would be stricter.

David Sive, who supported the state land plan, contacted David Newhouse to reassure him that this zoning scheme was a step forward for their cause. "Conservationists are now at the zenith of their political power," he wrote.

"Every politician is a conservationist." Weakening the Forever Wild clause was "a political impossibility," Sive continued. "Snowmobiles, garbage, motor scooters, motor boats, and many other activities—all [permitted] within the [current] Forever Wild restrictions—are the threats." Sive told Newhouse that the moment had come to minimize those threats and maximize wilderness.

In their report to Watson Pomeroy's legislative committee in 1961, Clarence Petty and Neil Stout had found twelve areas, totaling 801,000 acres, that would qualify as wilderness. The TSC proposed adding 170,000 acres to that total by removing a few existing structures. "If we saw a ranger cabin surrounded by fifty thousand acres of pristine land, we recommended burning the cabin down to get more wilderness," George Davis said. "We wanted removal unless it created a huge problem, because we wanted to maximize wilderness." The plan included a list of cabins, fire towers, and roads that were slated for removal.

The APA held public hearings on the State Land Master Plan in mid-May 1972 in Ray Brook, Lake George, Old Forge, Rochester, and New York City. Outside of the park, almost all of the speakers supported strong wilderness protection. Many at the Rochester hearing said that the protections were not strong enough, although a lot of activists also wanted existing structures to remain. "We proposed taking down some fire towers that were no longer useful," said Richard Lawrence. "This caused more objections than the actual state plan itself."

Inside the park, almost everyone just shrugged. "People on the Indian Lake planning board felt that what happened on state land was the state's business," said John Collins. The APA proposed to eliminate a few miles of snowmobile trails from wilderness areas, but it was careful to replace those with an equivalent amount of snowmobile trails in wild forest areas.

One aspect of the plan did cause hard feelings among several hundred key people. They had been enthusiastic defenders of the Forever Wild clause, but the new rules that arrived with the State Lands Master Plan turned them against the APA.

In 1917, the Conservation Department began allowing individuals to build wooden platforms with wooden sides, covered with canvas, and leave them up at choice spots in the forest preserve if they renewed an annual lease. By the early 1970s there were about six hundred of these "tent platforms." Two-thirds of them were on Lower Saranac Lake and the smaller lakes of the Saint Regis Canoe Area. The annual lease cost $25.

"Mom and dad had seven boys, and we all lived in the area," said Don Hickey, who owned a grocery store in the western Adirondack village of Star Lake in the 1960s. The family leased a tent platform site on the Bog River, where they would gather every summer. It had plywood walls, a tin roof, a propane stove, furniture, and a garbage pit. Some of these things were illegal, but everyone knew that the Conservation Department rangers did not enforce the rules. The Hickeys loved that place. "We knew that area better than the APA ever did," Hickey said. But in 1971, the DEC announced that it was ending the annual leases.

The state constitution clearly prohibits the government from making gifts, and lawyers at the APA and DEC pointed out that the leases were probably unconstitutional. But the lease holders had been using those sites for generations. Ending the leases meant taking something precious away from their families. The cabins were located in fabulously beautiful places, and many of their leaseholders could not afford to rent anything similar on the open market.

The tent platform tenants hired a lawyer and organized a lobbying effort, but the DEC stood firm. Tent platforms were a "nonconforming use" of the forest preserve, and they all had to be removed by December 31, 1975. And in September 1971, as he proclaimed that he was ending tent platform leases, DEC Commissioner Henry Diamond also announced that he had created a new Division of Law Enforcement. He planned to hire additional officers and give them advanced training to enforce pollution and solid waste laws, as well as the new rules for the forest preserve.

An old relationship had changed. State forest rangers who had been seen as neighbors were now much more likely to play the role of cops. "We were told that some of the strongest local supporters for protecting the Adirondacks ended up feeling that the state of New York had done them wrong," Booth said.

Talking about it forty-five years later, Don Hickey still got angry, and he didn't bother to make any distinction between the DEC and the APA. "We got off on the wrong foot with those state bureaucrats, and it went downhill from there," he said. "I think they are the stupidest people in the world."

The hardest thing about the State Land Master Plan wasn't writing it or turning it into law. It was getting state forest rangers to accept it.

In 1972–1973, the budget of the APA was equal to about one-half of 1 percent of the budget of the DEC. The APA did have the power of the governor behind it. It also had the support of DEC Commissioner Henry Diamond, who had served on the TSC.

Diamond was so enthusiastic about the proposed Environmental Quality Bond Act that he rode a bicycle across New York State in summer 1972, stopping in small towns to talk about how important it was for voters to pass the referendum. "I thought it was a dumb idea," said his first deputy commissioner, Ron Pedersen. "But he did get a lot of good publicity."

Henry Diamond was skilled at public relations. But inside the DEC, he struggled with what a management consultant would call "legacy issues." The DEC had been created by combining the two-thousand-employee Department of Conservation with five hundred employees from the Health Department. It had been a shotgun marriage. Both groups had become accustomed to doing things their own way. Diamond was distracted by their infighting.

The Conservation Department's Division of Lands and Forests had managed the forest preserve for decades, and their responsibilities did not change much when Conservation became DEC. Two regional directors ran park operations in the eastern and western halves of the Adirondacks. They had always done their work with little supervision from Albany. "They treated the land like they owned it," said George Davis.

When your office is hundreds of miles away from the State Capitol building, you can get away with stuff. Peter Paine remembered a time when he and his wife hiked to Duck Hole, a scenic lake in the High Peaks Wilderness ten miles away from a gate that blocked a fire road. "I mentioned our plans to [Regional Director] Bill Petty, and he invited us to stay in the ranger's cabin there," Paine said. "It was very comfortable. The ranger and his wife welcomed us and showed us to our bunk beds. The bathtub was robin's egg blue. And there was a phone line, so I was able to call my office in Paris with my credit card.

"We arrived on Friday, the day before the opening of deer season. After we showed up, six or eight DEC jeeps came down the fire road, full of rangers and their friends. The next morning, one of them shot a nice eight-pointer not far from the cabin, and I helped him drag it into his jeep. Then at the end of the day on Saturday, two guys from [the hamlet of] Peru staggered into the camp on foot, dragging their deer carry cart. I thought to myself, something is wrong here. This should not be the private hunting ground for DEC rangers just because they can legally drive their jeeps here and the public can't."

Many Conservation Department alumni were not happy when the APA delivered the draft of the State Land Master Plan to them in mid-May. Vic Glider, director of the Division of Lands and Forests, wouldn't even talk to the APA. "He'd say, 'Keep me away from those goddamn people,'" according to Norman Van Valkenburgh, a DEC employee who reported to Glider.

Glider and others did everything they could to derail the master plan. "I moderated a meeting where the APA folks and the DEC folks argued their cases," said Ron Pedersen. "The rangers were very unhappy that their truck trails, these well-maintained gravel roads that they had worked hard for years to keep in good shape for fire protection and safety, were being abandoned. Fire towers were another thing. The transition to using aircraft for fire surveillance had just started, and some people did not believe that aircraft could do a good job."

On March 23, 1972, Kafin & Needleman's private report to environmental leaders said that the DEC and the APA were at an impasse, that there had not been any communication between the two agencies for several weeks, and that Dick Lawrence and Henry Diamond were about to meet to try to get the process moving again. The negotiations that followed were not friendly. Kissel said he noticed the tension as soon as he arrived in April.

Paine would come back to his office from negotiations with the DEC, hand the text revisions to Kissel for fine-tuning, then send them to Albany and repeat the process. "The back and forth between Peter Paine and the DEC got to be pretty heavy duty," said APA board member Dick Wiebe. Eventually they reached a compromise. The DEC would draw up detailed "unit plans" for each wilderness, wild forest, and primitive area, based on the master plan's guidelines. This was a significant concession, because the DEC said it could not fulfill the State Land Master Plan's mandates for an area until its unit plan was written, and some of those unit plans took decades to complete.

"We kept the essence, but they watered it down," said Paine. The DEC launched a "hard rear-guard action" that lingered until Peter Berle became DEC commissioner in 1976, Paine said, and traces of it remained during the twenty-five years he was an APA board member.

"I'm not saying their approach was wrong," Paine added. "It was a different approach, based on the decades they had spent serving hunters and anglers. It was typical of that time. The APA wanted something different."

Governor Rockefeller signed the State Land Master Plan on July 26. Despite the fighting inside Albany, it was politically an easy thing to do. The governor received 684 letters about the Adirondacks in 1972, and all of them were in favor of protecting it in its natural state.

Task forces don't get a lot of respect. They examine complex problems and recommend solutions, and then they are blamed when the problems are not solved. But the Temporary Study Commission was a spectacular success. A very high proportion of its recommendations were adopted, and in 2021, many of the policy changes it proposed are taken for granted. The one recommendation they didn't get just proves how far-sighted the TSC was.

It was recommendation no. 11, which said, "A statute should be enacted to clarify the authority of the state to acquire scenic easements and the validity of such easements once acquired." A New York law aimed at this goal finally passed in 1983. In 2021, state-owned easements protect more than three-quarters of a million acres of private land in the Adirondacks. Across the United States, easement laws like New York's enable the protection of nearly forty-four thousand square miles, an area the size of Pennsylvania. The New York statute was part of a major change in land use law that swept the country in the 1980s. But in 1971, the conservation easement's time had not yet come.

The state did want to acquire more land for the forest preserve. Norman Van Valkenburgh ran the Conservation Department's Bureau of Land Acquisition in the 1960s, and part of his work was to maintain a list of land parcels the state should buy when funds became available. But there was a lot of land, and there were almost never any funds. Acquiring the development rights to land through an easement, while still allowing the land to remain in private hands, might let the state accomplish its goals for less money.

The TSC proposed two bills in 1971. The first would establish a new category of easement called a "conservation restriction" that allowed the state to permanently acquire the development rights to land without owning it outright. The second bill said that the taxable value of development rights acquired by the state would no longer be assigned to the landowner. Instead, the state would continue to make up the tax revenues lost to localities. That sounds simple now, but in 1971, it was a lot for the legal community to handle.

"Judges were suspicious of easements because they interfered with the free transfer of land, and land was the most valuable economic asset," said Dick Booth. "They were particularly hostile to 'negative engross' easements that permanently extinguished part of the land's economic value, which is what a conservation easement does."

Towns feared the loss of tax revenue, despite the second proposed law. Old-timers at the DEC were also suspicious. "The DEC didn't believe in conservation easements," George Davis said. "They insisted that any easement would have to allow the public to use the property, and the landowners we were talking to balked at that."

The situation changed in the mid-1990s, when the state reached agreements with timber companies to protect thousands of acres of privately owned forest while permitting limited public access. But in 1971 and 1972, the public just couldn't accept the idea. The easement bills ran into trouble at a December 1971 public hearing in Plattsburgh. Although easements are voluntary agreements between sellers and buyers, speakers at the hearing said they were opposed to the proposed laws because they didn't want to make it any easier for governments to condemn private land. Andrew Ryan, the assembly representative from Plattsburgh, who should have known better, said, "Anyone could come in and condemn it and pay whatever they wanted, and the homeowner would have nothing to say."

Ryan pointed to a recent action by the State Department of Transportation (DOT) that he said "kind of hit the easement idea over the head." The DOT had used strong-arm tactics against James Merrithew, who owned land near the Northway interchange in Chestertown. The state told Merrithew it was putting deed restrictions on his land, paid him a small fraction of the land's value, and left him holding title to a field that he could never sell to a developer. Merrithew sued, and in 1971 the court of claims awarded him the full value of the land.

The Merrithew case allowed Ryan and others to lump easements into a popular narrative in the North Country, which portrayed the state's proposals as land grabs. The APA and their supporters tried again to pass the easement bills in 1972. The governor introduced the bills but did not support them. And in 1972, Nelson Rockefeller's support—or lack thereof—for Adirondack bills worked the same way oxygen works on fire.

On April 1, 1972, a new fiscal year began, and the APA's budget jumped to $300,000. Bill Kissel reported to his temporary assignment in New York City on April 15. Kissel had applied to work at the APA after seeing Peter Paine at a conference early in 1972. It was one of the first-ever conferences on environmental law, and Paine gave a presentation describing the APA. "He was very much Peter Paine that day," said Kissel.

After Paine finished his peroration, he mentioned that the APA was hiring. Kissel was bored by his job at a Rochester firm, so he did not hesitate. He was a native of Watertown and had spent lots of time hiking and fishing in the park. While a student at Syracuse University Law School, he had written a journal article on the working definition of "forever wild" that had been used by the TSC. Paine had admired the paper, and Kissel was quickly hired.

The budget increase also allowed George Davis to finally snag another key person. Davis had met Gary Randorf when they were both enrolled at Cornell. Like Davis, Randorf had spent several years in the labor force before he went to graduate school. Like Davis, he was married and looking for work in the field of natural resources. And like Davis, he loved wild land and was passionate about the need to protect it. But there was one big difference between Randorf and Davis.

"I was not at all interested in George's job offer at first," Randorf said. "I loved being in Ithaca, and my wife also loved the area, so we had decided to stay after I graduated and look for jobs in town. George kept calling me once a month to ask me up for an interview. I kept saying, 'No, it's too cold up there, too many snowmobiles, it's mud and redneck country, I'm going to look for a job here.'"

Davis kept calling. "He was a force to be reckoned with," Randorf said. "He had vision and determination." But Randorf only accepted the APA job eight months later because he couldn't find a suitable position in Ithaca. He showed up for work in Ray Brook in the spring.

"When I walked into the APA offices for the very first time, I saw this tall, thin guy, wiry, with a lock of gray hair," Gary said. "He had on a green shirt, green trousers, and he was always smiling. I knew immediately that this was Greenleaf Chase, the famous Adirondack naturalist.

"On the second or third morning, George sent me out with Greenie to look at property on Upper Saranac Lake that was proposed for a development called Bungalow Bay. On the way, Greenie stopped at a little store to buy some lunch and came back with a big brown paper bag. We left our car and started walking into the property. We had walked no more than a hundred yards when he opened up the bag and turned to me and said, 'Would you care for an ale? We won't drink a lot, but I've found that one beer loosens up the right-hand side of the brain. We'll be a little more creative.' So we had a beer.

"The first thing we did that morning was take out our binoculars and do a bird count, because the spring migrants were coming back and birds were flitting through the bushes everywhere. We did that for an hour or two, and then we ate lunch sitting near the shoreline of Upper Saranac Lake. There was no one else around. It was a beautiful day, with the waves gently breaking on the shore. They were forming bubbles that looked like gems. All the concerns I had about the Adirondacks just melted away.

"I said, 'Greenie, what have I done to deserve being placed in this paradise, getting paid to do this kind of work?' He said, 'You're just the right guy for it.'"

The work wasn't always easy. The days began early, and Davis followed the rules he had learned from his mentor, Harold Jerry, who insisted that fieldwork had to be based on eyewitness evidence. But after the evidence was collected, it had to be written down. Randorf noticed the pattern immediately. The DEC offices next door would empty out promptly at 5 p.m., and the lights in the APA's log cabin would stay on.

Anita Riner was one of George Davis's first hires, and the two were married a few years later. "We were all very highly motivated and dedicated to the project," Anita said "We also believed in George's leadership, and we would have done whatever was needed to finish the project. It was a marvelous group."

"I hate to use the term, because it has become so overused, but we were pursuing sustainable development," George Davis added. "We were developing a process to prove that sustainable development can work."

The workplace offered a high sense of purpose, immersion in natural beauty, and regular happy hours to shore up team spirit. The research and fieldwork kept accumulating more and more data, and that gave Davis the same thrill of discovery he had experienced when he was a boy roaming the backcountry of Tug Hill.

When doing research, he said, "You can look at things that maybe are not politically acceptable at that moment. But you can decide on things that ought to be done, and suggest them, and let the politicians worry about when the proper political time might be."

The proper political time was January 1973, when the law required that the APA submit the Land Use and Development Plan to the state legislature. But as spring turned into summer in 1972, there were still literally mountains of fieldwork to do.

Henry Diamond said he was too busy at the DEC to go to APA meetings, but that might have been an excuse. Diamond also knew from the beginning that the APA had an impossible job. "This will be a Solomon-like operation," he said in September 1971. "The 'Forever Wild' people are going to want to stop everything and the developers will want to keep eating away."

"Solomonic" is defined as "being marked by notable wisdom, reasonableness, or discretion, especially under trying circumstances." The APA board struggled to reach that level. It circulated a questionnaire to town offices in the park in the summer of 1972, asking local officials to project their need for water and their total population in 1990. Few local officials were able to answer the questions. Their nonparticipation was one of several chronic problems the board faced.

Another problem was town governments trying to sneak by the APA. The agency's interim regulations exempted communities that had passed zoning ordinances and subdivision controls before July 1, 1971. After the law passed on June 9, about one dozen communities hastily adopted land use controls. Some of them had been working on their ordinances for years. Others took a standard suburban-style half-acre zoning ordinance and wrote their town's name on it. A Kafin & Needleman newsletter suggested several possible ways to challenge the legality of the "hurry-up laws," but it also reported that the APA board had decided not to challenge them unless a large development tried to exempt itself under the protection of one of these laws. The lawyer-activists said that the APA board had enough on its plate already.

The board also struggled with crossed signals from Albany. The APA's interim rules and regulations were not always in sync with existing rules from the DEC and the State Health Department. This created confusion and obstacles, especially for larger development proposals. The board asked Bill Kissel to work on an agreement with the two state agencies that would allow one permit application to satisfy all the different regulations, but progress on that was very slow. In the meantime, confused contractors couldn't get straight answers.

The board's biggest problem was internal. It was split, with five APA members solidly in favor of regional zoning, one whose support was conditional, and three who were skeptical of the idea. Dick Lawrence, Peter Paine, and Mary

Prime were strongly in favor. The *ex officio* members, Pedersen and Wiebe, would carry out the wishes of the governor. And Lawrence could reliably get a sixth vote as long as he stuck to the deal he had made with board member Joe Tonelli, head of the paperworkers' union. Lawrence knew that Tonelli would vote with him as long as the APA went easy on timber and paper companies.

As a union boss in the early 1970s, Tonelli was not overly concerned with the finer points of good government. "We were hanging around outside of a board meeting in Lake George with Babe, his driver, who always had this suspicious bulge under his jacket," Dick Booth said. "Babe mentioned that Mr. Tonelli was due in New York City at 5 p.m., and it was already well into the afternoon. I said to Babe that Mr. Tonelli was going to be late. Babe didn't seem worried. He said, 'It will be fine. Every state trooper in New York knows who rides in this car.'"

The first skeptic on the board, Jim Bird, emerged as a spokesman for the unique problems faced by small businesses inside the Blue Line. "He was always upbeat and helpful, and he pointed out weaknesses and omissions because he had local experience the staff didn't have," said Bill Kissel. "Poor Jim must have held his tongue so many times, listening to all these young know-it-all planners and lawyers."

Whitman Daniels was also skeptical. His emphasis was on protecting jobs, but several observers said that he was also confused by the details of land use planning. "It's fortunate that we didn't have to depend on him for calculus," said Bill Curran, who joined the staff in July. "Whit had a very high opinion of himself," said Peter Paine, "but he wasn't particularly helpful. Near the end, Dick Lawrence wouldn't even speak to him."

Kissel and Paine agree that the most difficult board member was Bill Foley, who assigned himself the role of cross-examiner and tried to discredit and slow down the proceedings whenever he could. In September, Foley asked that the meetings be transcribed by a stenographer, and several of them were. The transcripts show long, tortuous discussions of small points, with Foley bringing up hypothetical cases and dismissing the responses with sarcasm.

Peter Paine was the one who usually took Foley's bait. "There are few people with as nimble a mind as Peter," said Curran, "but he can also be the most pompous person on the face of the earth." Art Jubin, the Lake Placid business owner, called him "Peter Paine in the ass."

Bill Curran was in the first year of his first job out of graduate school when he heard about the APA. He had taken a position at the St. Lawrence

County Planning Department, but the job in Ray Brook paid more and also seemed more interesting. As a graduate student, Curran had used Ian McHarg's ideas to measure the carrying capacity of agricultural land in southern New Jersey. Unlike George Davis, Curran had used the overlay system to produce materials that satisfied a professor and a client. He got to Ray Brook on July 10, and it didn't take him long to see the weak points in the APA's data.

"George did a fairly good job, but he could quickly overwhelm you because he was so motivated and enthusiastic," Curran said. The main problem, he said, was that Davis moved too quickly. He didn't always leave a record showing how he had reached a decision, and he sometimes jumped to conclusions. "I had lived my whole life around bullshitters. I knew when I was being given a load," Curran said.

During Curran's second week on the job, he and Davis got on a bus with board members to take a field trip to southern Vermont. They went to see second-home developments and talk to local officials about the problems associated with them. During the ride, Curran asked Davis specific questions and was frustrated by Davis's evasive answers.

"I finally told him to stop squeezing me," Curran said. "I didn't need it. Tell the truth, for Christ's sake. He was playing to Mary Prime and Dick Lawrence, trying to get things past them, but they weren't going to be in the office defending these surveys. Poor slobs like us were going to have to do that. I wanted to know the facts, because I knew that eventually we were going to have to stand up and defend them.

"George did a wonderful job on what he had to do. I'm proud of the work we did together. But it was just a lot. George had a lot of clinkers."

Richard Booth arrived in Ray Brook for his first day at work on August 1, 1972, a few days after taking the bar exam. He was twenty-five and fired up to save the park. Booth, a native of Plattsburgh, had spent many summers at Camp Chingachgook on Lake George, as a camper and a counselor. At the APA, his first job out of law school, Booth quickly learned the difference between theory and practice.

"The deadline for submitting the Land Use and Development Plan to the legislature was at the end of the year, so I thought they would be almost ready to send it out for public comment when I arrived," he said. "But nothing had been written. They hadn't even started."

Booth found his desk and started writing. That afternoon his new boss, Bill Kissel, told him that the two of them had to drive to Old Forge, ninety miles away, for a public hearing that night on the proposed regulations. Booth told his wife he'd be late, and the two men did not get back to Ray Brook until 1:30 a.m. As they got back to their own cars, Kissel told Booth to be back in the office promptly at 8:30 a.m. They had to keep working on the report.

The pace was just as relentless among the field workers. Bill Curran said he and Dick Estes were responsible for finishing the surveys in five counties (Franklin, St. Lawrence, Lewis, Clinton, and Washington). George Davis was responsible for the other six counties, in consultation with Clarence Petty and Greenie Chase. Most of the survey work was done from roads, without much hiking. The most important thing about the surveys was to determine the existing uses of the land.

"Basically, we got into the car to check the things we had found on the maps and in the data," Curran said. "Some of the things we checked were very easy, like agricultural land. But there were things where you could just go on endlessly, like scenic views. How long does the view last? Where do you see it? We had to set limits."

Curran often did field-checking days with Gary Duprey, the Saranac Lake native George Davis had hired in February 1972. "We would get into the office at 7 a.m., come back at 5 p.m., go home for dinner, and then come back and work until 10 or 11," Duprey said. Many days began and ended with long drives in bad weather through areas so remote that you couldn't tune in a radio station. Several staffers say that the APA always got the worst cars from the motor pool they shared with DEC. "One of the cars had floorboards that had rusted through," said Duprey. "You had to be careful not to let the maps fall off the seat, because they would get wet."

"One day I ran into a roadblock just up the road from the office," said Gary Randorf. "State troopers were checking inspections. The trooper walked up to my car, put his hand on the roof, and said, 'What the heck are you driving here? I've seen much better cars in the dump. You've got bald tires, no inspection sticker, and one of the headlights is aimed up into the sky. Nobody should be driving this car.' I told him I needed to get somewhere, and that was the car the motor pool gave me. I got a ticket anyway."

As the work hours grew longer, the beer refrigerator in the back room became more important. The staff followed unwritten rules about its use. Gary Duprey said that it was not acceptable to drink a beer at your desk, except in the evenings. You could have one after you returned from field-work, or if you were taking a cigarette break out back. If the beer started running low, Harry Daniels would go out and get more.

Davis and others said the intensity and the beer were absolutely neces-sary, given the massive amount of work and the limited time they had to do it. No one was paid overtime, and Davis estimated that the average staffer was working fifty-five to sixty hours a week. The beer refrigerator contrib-uted to the sense of camaraderie that allowed the staff to work quickly. "You couldn't get loaded at work," said Duprey. "There was too much to do."

There was a cost, however. Several staffers were drinking and smoking heavily, and families were being ignored. But as long as a person kept work-ing, no one brought it up. And everybody kept working.

Davis was the boss, the coach, and the star player on the team. "He had to go out into the field, but he also had to check everyone else's work," Bill Kissel said. "Somehow he did it. He was a twenty-four-hour whirlwind. He was totally dedicated, and I never saw him complain.

"Sometimes he would do crazy things. One day Harry Daniels had all the papers for an agency mailing lined up on a table in the lobby that was about thirty feet long. George came in, let out a whoop, ran up to the table, and did a belly flop. The papers went all over. He said, 'I'm sorry, Harry, you've got to do it all over again.' He was just letting off steam. He was a crazy guy, but you couldn't fire him."

"George would just go off," said Curran. "He'd run around all silly and nonsense, and that's when we'd call him the Tug Hill goat farmer."

Davis kept working as summer turned to fall and meetings between the APA board and local people grew more heated. He tried to deflect the pres-sure with jokes. On September 20, driving north out of Speculator, he passed the gate to Harold Jerry's camp at Dug Mountain and left his old boss and mentor a note, which Jerry found and kept.

Sept. 20, 1972

To Whom It May Concern:

   All private lands beyond this point have been officially inspected and clas-sified by the Adirondack Park Agency. Effective October 1, 1972, these lands shall be used only for industrial purposes. Paving of the access road shall com-mence next week so as to have the site ready by October 1. All paving ex-penses will be borne by the industrial site landowner.

Any questions pertaining to the order may be directed to the APA headquarters in Ray Brook. Questions must be submitted by September 19, 1972
to be considered part of the official record.

Cordially,

The Adirondack Park Agency

PS: Article 27 of the Executive Law declares the paving of your access road
to be subject to Agency project review. We are anxiously awaiting your project application, which may also be obtained from Agency headquarters so long
as requested under separate cover from other correspondence. This form subject to a ninety-day cooling-off period must be approved by the Agency prior
to your commencing your project next week.

The day that stood out in Davis's mind was October 23, when the staff
had to finish the map of the southern half of Hamilton County. "The agency
was meeting in Lake George to approve the maps the next morning, but we
still had things we needed to check," he said. "Anita and I left at 4:30 in the
morning and drove ninety miles to Speculator. We got there at 6:15 and had
breakfast. When it was light enough to see, we started field checking.

"We did our checking without stopping for lunch or dinner until it got
dark, which was about 7:30 at night. We called the office, and they were all
still there. I told them we had just finished field checking, and we had fifteen changes that had to be made on the map we were presenting tomorrow. Then we stopped for dinner. By the time we got back to the office in
Ray Brook, it was just after midnight. All eight of the professional staff were
still there, plus Don Smith, the janitor, who I guess was there just because
he felt left out. They were sitting there waiting for us.

"We fell into the office and gave them the stuff, and Don Smith got our
beer. It was that total dedication that made the whole thing fall into place.
A few hours later, we drove the maps ninety miles to the APA meeting. We
presented them to the board at 10 a.m."

The deadline and the workload made it difficult for the staff to meet professional planning standards. "Documentation is spotty at best," wrote Roger
Wells, a planner and landscape architect who was hired to evaluate the quality of the maps in the late 1970s. "Without documentation, how does anyone
effectively challenge the validity, accuracy, or appropriateness of the Plan?"

Richard Estes and Bill Curran, the professional planners on the staff, didn't
have the time or the influence to force changes in the procedures set up by

Davis. Estes's family lived in Albany, so he drove home every weekend while Davis stayed in the office. One Sunday afternoon, Bill Kissel came in to get something and found Davis alone at his desk, coloring in a map with a crayon. Davis was either working from memory or taking an educated guess, and Kissel didn't stop to ask which it was. His job was to turn the map into text.

The Land Use and Development Plan specifies how much development can take place on private land in the Adirondack Park, based on a list of "development considerations." It also sets rules for lakefront development and the siting of industrial and commercial areas, among other things. The APA board started to consider the "how much" question in September 1972. They kept arguing about it until their final vote in March 1973.

On October 5, during a meeting that was transcribed, Dick Estes presented an outline of a plan that separated private land into six categories and set the maximum density of buildings allowed in each category. He apologized at the outset because the outline was handwritten. "Obviously a good deal of refinement remains to be done," he said.

The most restrictive category, "resource management," allowed ten buildings per square mile, or one for every sixty-four acres. The second-most-restrictive category, "rural use," allowed fifty buildings per square mile, or one for every 12.8 acres. The least restrictive category was "hamlet," or the park's historic commercial centers, where the agency would have little or no jurisdiction.

This was a step away from what George Davis wanted. He thought that only one residence should be allowed on each parcel in resource management areas, even though some of the parcels were thousands of acres in size. Davis was sticking with the wishes of Harold Jerry, who said from the beginning of the TSC that allowing any development to happen in the backcountry would lead to "death by a thousand cuts."

Several APA board members immediately focused on the most restrictive category. "There's a good chance that some areas are already above these density limits," said Whit Daniels. "Are we telling the town they can't have any more buildings?" Yes, Estes said, but only in the areas specified by the maps. The board had not seen the maps yet. The three skeptics, Daniels, Foley, and Bird, were taken aback by this news. They asked questions about the density limits for several hours, and as time went on, they repeatedly asked why Adirondack towns were being held to a different standard.

Peter Paine replied that a different standard was appropriate because the Adirondack Park is more than a collection of ordinary towns. "We are dealing with a special resource," he said, adding that the legislation would describe how and why the park required different rules.

A fourth board member wasn't buying this. "We must be fair, and we must be uniform," said Joe Tonelli. If people get the impression that the plan isn't fair, he added, "the staff will be put through the wringer."

"No matter what we come up with, we will be put through the wringer," Kissel replied.

Jim Bird said that the variety and volume of data was going to be too much for board members to digest, and that they would have to trust the staff. That was fine with Mary Prime. "If this was left up to the individual towns, we would not have good planning," she said, as the October 5 meeting drew to a close. "These people don't know anything about planning. We have been put in a position to lead them. We have the responsibility of deciding what will be good for the next generations."

The staff finally showed their maps to the board on October 16 and 24, revealing that they were placing the vast majority of private land into the two most restrictive categories. On the twenty-fourth—the meeting when the all-nighter southern Hamilton County map was presented—only a few days remained before the maps had to go to the printer so they could be distributed for public comment. That day began with the board showing the maps to sympathetic local leaders, including Waddington Town Supervisor Joel "Bud" Howard, Wayne Byrne of The Nature Conservancy, and syndicated columnist Bill Roden.

After getting the gist of the maps, Howard told the board that town officials in the Adirondacks would never take action on zoning unless the state forced them to. Referring to the APA, he said, "Hired killers have an advantage. They can move in, do the job, and get right out."

"I don't see how it can be otherwise," said Bill Roden. His town had elected a planning board, he said, but they had been unable to pass a zoning ordinance. "We had one hearing, and it was a disaster," he said. "I suspect that a lot of towns will say in the end, 'Let the agency do it.'"

The board began showing the preliminary county maps to local officials after the October 24 meeting. In 1981, Lawrence remembered that most of their interactions were friendly, and that a lot of town supervisors seemed to support what the APA was proposing.

The political winds continued to blow in favor of the APA. On November 3, voters across the state approved the Environmental Quality Bond Act by an almost two-to-one margin, and Lawrence reported that state legislative leaders had agreed to delay the deadline for submitting the Land Use and Development Plan until February 1973. That wasn't good enough for some APA board members, however.

On November 17, at the beginning of a two-day meeting intended to review and approve the draft plan for public comment, Whit Daniels hijacked the proceedings. He said that the park agency, "as it emerges from this plan, is a bureaucratic monster which dictates to local governments." That was not what he had in mind, he said, and he could not support the plan as it was currently written. Daniels proposed that the board request a one-year extension so it could seek a more balanced approach.

Foley and Bird agreed with Daniels, and Foley made a motion to request the one-year delay. The board spent the morning arguing over whether or not to go forward. Most members felt that they should review the plan in detail before deciding whether or not to seek a delay. Foley eventually withdrew his motion, but things didn't get any easier as the board struggled through each line of the plan.

At the end of the two days, Richard Wiebe said he agreed with Daniels's characterization of the plan as a bureaucratic monster. "We must try to figure out where the dividing line is between local interest and concern and state interest and concern," he said. He suggested that subdivisions of fewer than five dwellings be made exempt from APA jurisdiction. "I don't want to see the plan go down," Wiebe said. "We must start somewhere, and half a loaf may be better than none."

Tonelli and Paine praised Wiebe's suggestion, and the board agreed to meet again on December 1 and 2 to look at a revised version. They struggled through those two days and then decided to meet again on December 7, the last possible day before the text had to be sent to the printer. After another long day of tense discussions, this time about the minimum number of feet that buildings had to be set back from lakeshores and what boathouses should look like, the board finally voted to release the plan to the public. Foley voted no. Daniels and Bird voted yes, but both men made it clear that they still had serious reservations about the plan.

By this time, the Horizon Corporation's huge second-home development was running into financial trouble. On December 5, Kafin & Needleman began introducing evidence against Louis Papparazzo's Ton-Da-Lay project at a public hearing held on their terms. The unveiling of the Land Use and Development Plan was imminent. It was a terrible time to be a developer in the Adirondacks. But Tony D'Elia, the developer of Loon Lake Estates, wasn't stopping. He loved what he was doing, and he believed that the law should allow him to do whatever he wanted with his private property. He was all in.

Chapter 11

# Cashing the Chips

The Adirondack Park Land Use and Development Plan ruined Tony D'Elia's Christmas. The draft version was released on Thursday, December 21, 1972, just as Saranac Lake was enjoying a nice preholiday snowfall. It wasn't too cold that day. The overnight lows were about zero Fahrenheit, and the highs got to within a few degrees of freezing. People rushed around doing last-minute errands before buttoning themselves into their homes. The flurries were just heavy enough to whiten the old snow and make the Christmas lights twinkle.

D'Elia went to the press briefing in Ray Brook and took home a copy of the draft to read. He didn't understand exactly what the plan would mean for Loon Lake Estates, the vacation-home development where he had invested his life's savings, but he knew it wasn't good. He tried to put it out of his mind so he could pay attention to his two teenaged daughters at Christmas, but he couldn't shake a bad feeling. He spent the weekend writing.

When things reopened on Tuesday, D'Elia took his essay to Harrietstown Town Supervisor Ray LaRose, who he knew was no fan of the Adirondack

Park Agency. LaRose took D'Elia's response to the local copy shop, printed up several thousand copies of it, and started handing them out after New Year's Day. Melinda Hadley got her copy a few days later.

Hadley had graduated from Plattsburgh State University in June 1971. She and her husband had moved into her family's drafty old farmhouse in Sugarbush, a windswept collection of about a dozen homes on Route 3, with her parents living next door. Hadley is a fourth-generation Adirondack native. "That part is complicated," she said. "If you were born here but your parents were not, it isn't as good. You aren't a real native unless your grandparents were born here."

That afternoon in early January, Hadley was pregnant with her first child and highly focused on her grocery list. But the flyer's headline caught her attention. "THIS COULD AFFECT YOU," it began.

> The Adirondack Park Agency has released its preliminary plan, controlling the use of all the privately-owned land within the Blue Line . . .
>
> Many will agree that a master plan for the private lands within the Park is needed. But the APA's density use restrictions and limited growth proposals are shocking in their severity, and clearly confiscatory, as there are no arrangements for compensation for loss of use, which is certainly unconstitutional.
>
> If you are interested at all in your rights in private property, in the future economy of the area, if you want to keep your children from moving out of the area to get a job, read this criticism of the Agency's land use proposals. You will then be in a better position to make your views known to the APA Commissioners at the public hearing on January 20th in the High School.

Hadley took the flyer home and showed it to her mother. They had heard of Tony D'Elia, and they were suspicious of him. "He was an Italian guy from New York City, and he seemed to have all this money," she said. "We wondered whether he was from the Mafia." But when Hadley and her mother read the pamphlet, they realized that they agreed with him.

Hadley remembers two things that really set her mother off about the APA: the Rockefeller connection, and the tone the agency adopted toward local people. "They were coming from outside and telling us what we could and couldn't do," she said. The family would not be affected by the law. They owned two houses on their land, and they did not have plans to develop or subdivide it. Even if they did do that, it seemed that they would probably be exempt from the proposed regulations. But that wasn't the point.

Hadley and her family did not have much, and D'Elia was telling them that the Rockefellers wanted to grab what little they had. The whole idea of the APA felt like an insult.

The hearing in Saranac Lake was "crazy," Hadley said. About eight hundred people came out on a snowy Saturday afternoon and stayed late into the evening. "That was the beginning of the rebellion," she said. Hadley and D'Elia would end up fighting the APA together for the next eighteen years.

The staff and board members of the APA didn't have much time to think about local resistance, however. For Peter Paine, Dick Lawrence, and George Davis, passing the Land Use and Development Plan was the culmination of five years of focused effort. For Paul Schaefer, Clarence Petty, and hundreds of others across the state, it was a goal they had been striving after for twenty years. They weren't going to let a few North Country rednecks stop them now. The Battle of the Blue Line had begun.

The APA reopened old wounds among locals who had been cultivating their resentment for generations. Every year they saw the gaps of education and income that separated them from the tourists and the summer people, and it reminded them of what they didn't have. Grandparents and parents passed the attitude down to their children. Adirondackers have always been ignored and dismissed, they said. Now the APA wants to rob us, too.

Hadley's father was a carpenter who didn't get involved in politics, but her mother, Shirley Delano Ryan, more than made up for it. The Delano family had produced two presidents: Calvin Coolidge and Franklin Delano Roosevelt, who, Hadley was quick to add, fired her grandfather from his job at the Canadian border crossing because he was a Republican.

Shirley Ryan was far from wealthy but she was extremely proud of her heritage. She also hated the Rockefellers, whom she liked to refer to as "new-money trash." She was an enthusiastic believer in the conspiracy theories of folks like Emanuel Mann Josephson, who wrote that the Rockefellers ran a secret international cabal that was intent on establishing a tyrannical world government.

Growing up in the 1960s, Hadley rode the school bus to and from Saranac Lake every day. It was a one-way trip of eighteen miles on a cold, often snowy highway, shuttling between a small-town school and an eighty-acre lot that bordered the Adirondack Forest Preserve, where bears were far more common than police. The Delano-Ryans enjoyed a quiet life, close to nature and far from the wars, protests, and all the other events that were turning the world upside down. That started to change when the APA set up shop, although Hadley wasn't aware of the changes before she saw D'Elia's flyer.

Tony D'Elia was forty-nine years old in 1969. He had been an industrial designer in New York City for twenty-five years, but he was tired of it. Like Robert Kafin, D'Elia yearned to get closer to nature. He wanted to escape from the city and lead an authentic life.

D'Elia had a friendly relationship with George H. Bookbinder, a promoter and international investor in New York City. Bookbinder owned a summer home on Loon Lake, northwest of Saranac Lake and a few miles west of Sugarbush. Loon Lake had been a fashionable resort at the turn of the century, with a five-hundred-room hotel, a direct rail link to New York City, one of the first golf courses in the Adirondacks, and socially prominent guests. But the hotel burned in 1956, leaving the golf course and a cluster of about two dozen distinguished old homes, one of which was Bookbinder's. One spring weekend, he invited D'Elia to visit.

"I fell in love with it at first sight," D'Elia wrote. "There was a sweet dignity about it, even though it was shabby and run down. And nature's beauty was everywhere."

D'Elia came to the shore of Loon Lake and surprised a flock of Canada geese. "They rose into the sky, forming their great V-shaped flight formation," he wrote. "They headed northward to their breeding grounds. I thought as I watched them, every year . . . every spring and every autumn . . . I'll be here waiting for you."

D'Elia was creative, talented, and ambitious. He held several patents. He invented and sold everything from cotton candy machines to hand-painted coffee mugs. "He was a hustler," said his daughter, Barbara D'Elia O'Connell. And D'Elia was also an idealist. He was a member of the Sierra Club, and he taught an economics course at the Henry George School in Manhattan, a small institution devoted to the idea that all taxes—federal, state, and local—should be replaced by a single tax based on the value of land. This was not a typical background for a land developer, and D'Elia did not have much real estate experience, but he did have a powerful vision.

D'Elia went back home, cashed in his life's savings, and persuaded several friends to invest with him. He signed up his neighbors, the Nargellis, who owned Baskin-Robbins ice-cream shops on Long Island. George Bookbinder put in some money, too. The closing happened on May 1, 1970.

"Loon Lake was mine!" D'Elia wrote. Well, not quite. Loon Lake was mortgaged.

Loon Lake Estates, Inc. got off to a promising start. The APA awarded D'Elia provisional permit no. 1 in March 1972, which gave him permission to sell twenty-three lots. In September, he told APA staffer Dick Estes that those lots had doubled in value. Shortly afterward, the APA board visited Loon Lake. In November, they approved the sale of another thirty-eight lots.

"The APA wanted Tony to succeed," Bill Kissel said," because we wanted to show that we were not antidevelopment. I thought we were working well together."

D'Elia started putting in roads and planning for a central water and sewer system. He wanted to put nine hundred to a thousand lots on 940 acres of the property, with the remainder held for the common use of owners. But the whole thing started to unravel on that Thursday before Christmas.

The draft version of the Land Use and Development Plan designated the historic part of Loon Lake a "rural hamlet." Dense development there was theoretically possible, but much of that land already had houses on it. The land D'Elia owned was mostly in the low-intensity use category, which permitted a maximum of 150 buildings per square mile. That meant perhaps 800 units might be allowed on his 3,500 acres. But there was also a thicket of other regulations, and things got particularly complicated around lakeshores.

It was clear to D'Elia that if the Land Use and Development Plan passed, the APA was going to give Loon Lake Estates a thrashing. He had no way of knowing whether or not he would be able to meet his financial targets once the agency was done with him. The best outcome for him would be if the whole thing just went away.

Journalists use the term "news dump" when an unpopular announcement is scheduled for a time when people are less likely to pay attention to what's on television. The Thursday afternoon before a long Christmas weekend is an excellent time for a news dump. The APA's press briefing of December 21, 1972 was alarming, although different people were alarmed by different things.

At the briefing, Gary Randorf showed slides he had taken of junked cars along beautiful country roads, motel signs that blocked the view of mountains, and raw sewage that Randorf said was oozing out of an overflowing septic tank and draining onto a neighbor's property. The agency wanted to sound the alarm about pollution and ugliness overwhelming the park.

Board chair Richard Lawrence emphasized that the agency's mission was to enhance the quality of life for local people. Three-quarters of the land in the park is owned by nonresidents, he said. Villages and hamlets would be almost entirely exempt from these regulations. And since 1971, the APA had approved about one hundred development permits under the interim rules, "many with Agency-proposed modifications which have benefitted both the developer and the environment of the Park," according to its press release. "To date, no project has been rejected."

Lawrence asked that town officials submit comments and requests for revisions by January 10, 1973. He also announced fifteen public hearings, one for each county in the park and three more in Buffalo, Rochester, and New York City, between January 8 and January 20. A lot of people didn't hear those announcements. The APA dropped off copies of the draft plan at town offices and mailed them by request, but distribution was not as easy in those pre-internet days. Some people who wanted copies could not get them, and many copies sat unread. Most local people who did pay attention to the draft plan were indeed alarmed, but what alarmed them was the plan itself.

The plan had three parts. The first part divided the park's private land into six categories, each allowing progressively less development. The second part described how the regulations on these six categories would be implemented, and the third was a grab-bag of topics like billboard regulations and tax policies.

The plan also placed development proposals into three categories. The largest proposals were "regional" projects, and the APA would be highly involved in vetting and approving them. Somewhat smaller developments were identified as "special use." The agency would have authority over them, too, but the approval process would be simpler. And the draft plan said that the agency would have little involvement in projects the regulations put in the third category, known as "permissible use."

The first category of land, "hamlets," could be "urban" or "rural." Urban hamlets like Saranac Lake, population 5,200, "will serve as the major service and growth centers," the plan said. Rural hamlets like Inlet, population 300, should remain "small, concentrated communities." No growth limits were proposed for urban hamlets, but rural hamlets would be limited to 1,280 living units per square mile, or 1 per half acre. Also, the totals were cumulative. If one square mile of a rural hamlet had 128 structures, each with 10 living units, that part would be considered fully developed.

Most of the land in the second category, "moderate intensity," is located next to hamlets. This category is intended for single-family homes, recreational parks, beaches, and agriculture. The draft proposal limits development in this category to 400 buildings per square mile. Only projects with 74 units or less are categorized as "permissible use" in the draft plan, and only as long as they avoid a list of other nonconforming uses. If you wanted to put a commercial building of more than 3,750 square feet in a moderate intensity zone, for example, you couldn't do it without the blessing of the APA.

The third category, "low intensity," included areas like Star Lake in the western Adirondacks, and the acreage Tony D'Elia owned around the rural hamlet of Loon Lake. Land in this category could have no more than 150 structures per square mile. Permissible use developments could have a maximum of 34 units. Also, fewer types of projects would escape the agency's scrutiny in the low intensity category. Proposed ski areas, sawmills, and mines would automatically be judged as regional projects, for example.

The fourth category, "rural use," was the Adirondack backcountry. It had "fairly stringent development constraints," according to the draft plan. The list of allowable uses was shorter than the list for low intensity and moderate intensity areas. No more than 65 structures were allowed per square mile. That translated into one for every 9.8 acres of land, although houses could be clustered; landowners could build two adjacent houses in an area zoned rural use as long as they owned 19.6 acres, and so on. The areas around Long Lake, Lake Marian, and Fern Lake were all rural use.

Land uses in the fifth category, "resource management," were the most restricted by the draft plan. In these areas, "the need to protect, manage and enhance forest, agricultural, recreational and open space resources is of paramount importance." Any single-family home in a resource management area would be considered a "special use" project. The maximum number of buildings per square mile was ten, or one for every 64 acres. The only "permissible" uses were tree farms, hunting and fishing clubs, agriculture, and game preserves.

The sixth category, "industrial use," was for areas where mining, sawmills, manufacturing, and other commercial activities would be "encouraged." However, any industrial use project would be considered under "regional use" standards, to protect the park's ecosystems.

And that wasn't all. Septic tank drainage fields had to be at least 100 feet from shorelines. The minimum width of lakeshore lots ranged from 50 feet (in hamlets) to 300 feet (in resource management). Buildings had to be set back 50 feet from the mean high water mark in hamlets, and 125 feet in resource management areas. And the details went much further. The rules also regulated landowners' abilities to trim vegetation on lakeshores, for example.

The biggest shocker was the map that revealed the allocation of the different categories. The APA proposed to put most of the private land in the park (53 percent, or 1.9 million acres) in resource management, the most restrictive category. Another 32 percent (1.2 million acres) was rural use, and 10 percent (360,000 acres) was low intensity. That only left about 200,000 acres where a mainstream 1970s-style single-family home development like Loon Lake Estates might be possible, if all the other rules were met.

Parts two and three of the draft Land Use and Development Plan proposed a way for the APA to assist town planning boards as they drafted local zoning laws that met these standards. The basic idea was that once the localities had met the APA's standards, the agency would relinquish jurisdiction over all but the biggest projects. Until the towns did that, however, the APA would be the enforcer.

The draft plan would have seemed reasonable for the Long Island shore, the hills around San Francisco, or another region where open space is part of a metropolitan area. But Adirondack towns are deeply rural places where zoning laws were almost unknown in 1973. These strict, complex rules were being imposed by people from "away." To many locals, it felt like an invasion.

Copies of the most detailed version of the APA map were posted at each county courthouse in the North Country. People who went to those offices had to digest complex schemes describing boundaries that they had never seen before. They were often confused by the boundary lines, which sometimes cut through the middle of their land, indicating that the permitted density would be higher in one part of their property than in another. People wanted to know why this was so. They wanted to know if it meant they would no longer be allowed to do as they pleased on their own land. The answers were not easy to find.

The map came from a new world, one in which ecosystems and carrying capacity dictated the extent and location of economic activity. "The land must be regarded just like water or air," said Richard Grover, planning director for St. Lawrence County, at a conference in 1972. "Everyone owns it, and everyone has a certain interest in it, and the right to alter for any purpose must be rejected. . . . What's obviously needed is a land ethic, an ethic involving stewardship of the land, as opposed to ownership of the land."

That view made no sense to someone whose property rights had never been questioned. People in the park's towns did not know what to do with the maps, but they sure didn't like them. Franklin Little, publisher of the *Ogdensburg Journal*, wrote that "in the good old days, people like Grover were banished from their home states and if they ever came back were arrested and put in a dungeon."

Page 1 of the *New York Times* on Tuesday, January 9, 1973, carried a chatty interview with President Nixon marking his sixtieth birthday. Nixon had just been reelected by a huge margin, carrying forty-nine of the fifty states, and a poll released around that time found that 68 percent of Americans approved of the job he was doing as president. On page 26, a small story summarized the opening of the trial of five men arrested during an attempt to burglarize the headquarters of the Democratic National Committee, which was in a Washington, DC, office complex called the Watergate.

An even smaller story, on page 42, reported that two hundred people had braved subzero temperatures in Saratoga Springs to appear at the first public hearing for the draft Land Use and Development Plan. "You're going too far, too fast," said Earl Edwards, supervisor of the Saratoga County Town of Providence. Like many of the speakers, he urged the APA board to delay action on the plan for a year so local people could learn more about it and the specifics could be adjusted.

Most of the speakers in Saratoga Springs agreed with Edwards or opposed the plan altogether. The plan was endorsed by a few speakers, such as Vincent Schaefer, who identified himself as "a landowner in Warren County." Like his younger brother Paul, Vincent Schaefer had been an activist for decades. He could have identified himself as a member of a half dozen environmental organizations. But he had been asked not to.

Schaefer's instructions came from an eight-page mailing sent to environmental groups by the activist law firm Kafin & Needleman on January 1, 1973. Titled "Instructions for Testifying on the Private Land Use and Development Plan: Not for Publication," it began, "If you own land inside Adirondack Park, say so. THIS IS VERY IMPORTANT." The memo also asked land-owning activists to state the number of acres they owned and how their land would be classified in the big map. "Do *not* recite your memberships in conservation organizations," it continued. "These organizations will speak loudly and clearly for themselves. The Park Agency wants to hear a variety of views and will not listen well to a string of individuals all announcing their conservation organization memberships" (emphasis in the original).

An analysis of the hearings found that about 5,800 people attended, 473 submitted comments, and seventy-three hours of live testimony were taken over the twelve days. In the public hearings in Buffalo and Rochester, 87 percent of the testimony was in favor of the APA's plan. The analysis did not include the New York City hearing, where nearly 100 percent of that testimony was in favor. In 1970, those three metropolitan areas contained more than 70 percent of the state's population.

Comments in the Adirondack counties were mixed. A little more than one-third (36 percent) were in favor, 41 percent were either against the plan or for a one-year delay, and 23 percent did not make their positions clear. But there were big differences by county, depending on local activity.

Many speakers were pro-APA at the January 10 hearing in St. Lawrence County because Canton, the county seat, was the hometown of Citizens to Save the Adirondack Park, the group that had formed to fight the huge second-home development proposed by the Horizon Corporation. But the next day, in the Lewis County hamlet of Star Lake, almost nobody was in favor. "In Lewis County and Old Forge (Herkimer County), I think I might have been the only one there in favor," said Samuel Sage, a Sierra Club activist who had roots in Lake Placid. "Old Forge was the hometown of Bill Foley, who was just awful." In Star Lake, Sage was shouted down when he said that float planes had a major impact on wilderness and should be better regulated.

The last four hearings were the most contentious, perhaps because they were in counties that contained some of the more remote sections of the park. Hamilton, for example, is the only county in the state that was entirely within the Blue Line in 1973. Its population was about 4,700, and locals liked to boast that their county did not have any stoplights. But the county's hearing in Indian Lake had symbolic importance, because these were "real Adirondackers." If they objected loudly enough, and the media noticed, maybe the state legislature would pay attention.

Shortly before the Indian Lake hearing began, a state helicopter containing Assemblyman Glenn Harris and Senator Mary Ann Krupsak, who represented Hamilton County, and Senator Ron Stafford, who did not, landed in a field outside the high school auditorium. Harris, who had just been appointed majority whip and was therefore fourth in the assembly's pecking order, was the second speaker, followed by the senators. He talked about a bill he had introduced that morning to delay consideration of the land use plan for a year so people could study it more thoroughly. Then he and the senators (who didn't say much) got back in the helicopter and flew back to Albany to fight for the "delay bill." A small group of Indian Lakers stood by in awe as the chopper lifted off. It was a high point in Harris's career.

The Indian Lake hearing took a dinner break and continued into the evening. The testimony was mixed; some speakers opposed the plan, some criticized specific parts of it, and some thought it didn't go far enough. Phil Terrie, a curator at the Adirondack Museum who would go on to a long career as a historian of the park, argued that no buildings of any kind should be allowed in resource management areas, that the size of the Indian Lake hamlet should be enlarged, and that the wilderness acreage in the state plan was not sufficient. "The question," he said, "is whether or not wilderness itself is worth saving."

As the hearing dragged on, John Hosley stood silently in back of the room, wearing a Native American-style feathered headdress. Hosley owned Hoss's Country Store in Long Lake. He sold groceries, snacks, and souvenirs, so he knew how to stop traffic. When it was his turn to speak, he read from a text. "Although the Park to you and your agency [is] looked upon as a National Resource, to those of us who live and work here, it represents our dreams, our heartaches, our heritage, in fact it represents our whole lives," he said. "And when you bring your huge bearaucracy [*sic*] to our doorsteps and regulate away our constitutional rights, stripping us of our hard-earned heritage, I think it is only human for us as a minority to demand our rights as have the Negroes, the Indians, and various other minority groups of America." To Hosley, a white man, this was a civil rights issue.

"I feel that this plan represents the greatest land grab since the Indians had theirs stolen by the Federal Government," he said. "In the event this plan is enacted into law without substantial changes from its present format, my last request is that I be notified as soon as possible where the reservation for the Adirondack Indian will be located."

Hosley brought the house down. "The hearings were fun for local people," said John Collins, who was chair of Indian Lake's planning board. "These were tiny little towns, with not a lot going on. Suddenly there were hundreds of people and reporters and microphones and high emotion. It was the best show in town."

The hearings in Lake George (Warren County) and Elizabethtown (Essex County) on January 18 and 19 were similar, with long, occasionally impassioned speeches mixing with droning prepared statements and regular interruptions from the gallery. After the Elizabethtown hearing, Dick Lawrence invited the APA staff to come over to his house for a small celebration. They were almost done.

"Lawrence was magnificent," said Dick Booth. "These were difficult sessions, and no matter what happened, he stayed absolutely cool. He kept things from getting out of hand because no one ever got to him. The only time I ever saw him get mad was when a reporter in Plattsburgh said something nasty about the agency staff. Lawrence just turned to ice. He told the reporter that he would not tolerate any attacks on such a hard-working, dedicated group. We all loved him."

The last hearing, in Saranac Lake, was a doozy. There was standing room only in the auditorium of the old high school, which had been built in the 1920s for much smaller crowds. Seventy people signed up to speak. The hearing started at 2:30 p.m. and went on until 10:30 p.m., with no break. Almost everyone who spoke was dead set against the agency's existence. James Ellis, chair of Franklin County Republican Party, said that the plan did not have "one human element" and presented a petition in favor of the delay bill that had 1,600 signatures. There was a lot of shouting and a lot of cheering. "It was hostile," said Peter Paine.

The vehemence in Saranac Lake came from several sources. Most of the tenants of tent platforms, who had recently been told that their long-term leases would not be renewed, lived nearby. Also, Tony D'Elia's flyer had an impact. And so did Bill Doolittle, the owner of the *Adirondack Daily Enterprise*, who had become a vocal opponent of the APA. Ten days before the hearing, Doolittle had published an exposé after a reporter got a copy of Kafin & Needleman's instructional memo of January 1. He wrote that the memo proved that the hearing would be a sham.

Doolittle highlighted the section of the memo that read, "The plan brims with rhetoric about the role of local government. This is because the Agency's legislative mandate requires it and because of the politics of the situation. In an ideal world, it would also make a great deal of sense. Unfortunately, we do not live in an ideal world, and realistically speaking, the plan's discussion of the roles and responsibilities of local governments should not be considered as anything more than a potentially pretty picture."

The next day, Doolittle said in an editorial that the plan's proposal to gradually transfer more responsibility to local governments as they develop their own zoning plans "has been included as an attempt to trick us mountain rubes into believing that we will have a role in our own growth destiny, when in fact we will not if the APA's private land use plan becomes law as it is currently written."

"Saranac Lake was definitely the most hostile crowd," said Richard Lawrence. "It took a lot of effort to keep the lid from blowing off the hall. The town police were terrified that they were going to have a riot."

One of the few pro-APA speakers in Saranac Lake was Ted Hullar, chair of the Atlantic Chapter of the Sierra Club. "I had a text that was strongly in favor of the APA," Hullar said. "The atmosphere in the room was really strong. The crowd would drown me out, booing and hissing and shouting me down. So every time they acted up, I stopped and remained completely silent until Dick Lawrence calmed everybody down.

"After I finished, as I was walking up the aisle to the back of the room, some guy told me he was going to shoot out my tires, or maybe take his knife to my throat. It was ugly, but there wasn't any other way. We were resolute. I had to say what I said."

Lawrence used a trick to keep things under control. "I was on a stage, so I was above and facing the audience. There was a long list of people who had signed up to talk, and everyone had that list. Now, these folks were mostly not used to public speaking. They were sitting out there in the audience, getting nervous while waiting their turn. When their turn came, I made them come up on the stage so they could address the audience instead of looking at me. Most of them cut their comments short because they wanted to get the hell off that stage."

The Saranac hearing did produce one change in the law. "After many hours, late in the evening, I noticed a man in the audience who had been listening but hadn't said anything," Lawrence said. "I asked him if he had any concerns, and he said, 'Yes. I want to know, will I be allowed to pass my land down to my children?' I told him that of course he could, but I also realized that we had made no provision for that in the draft version he had read. So we wrote that into the plan, to make sure it was clear to everyone that your children could inherit your land.

"I think the only reason we succeeded was a lack of media coverage of those hearings," Lawrence said. "The newspapers didn't follow the hearings across the park, so people in one area did not know that there had been a lot of protest in other areas. If the word had gotten around and the opponents had come together, we would not have had a chance. But no reporters followed us. We were terribly lucky."

Driving home after the Saranac Lake hearing, Richard Lawrence pulled over to help Peter Paine, whose Peugeot had spun out on the ice and was stuck in a ditch. Lawrence, who had a Jeep, got out his winch, pulled Paine's car back onto the road, and tried to calm him down. "Don't worry about the locals," Paine remembered Lawrence saying. "It's good for the animals to exercise their vocal cords."

Massive, sudden shifts in public opinion don't happen every day, but they do occur. As the Watergate scandal unfolded on the front pages of newspapers in spring 1973, President Nixon's approval rating plunged. By the end of the year, only about 25 percent of Americans approved of the job he was doing as president, and 38 percent thought he should be removed from office.

The Watergate scandal was about conspiracy, disregard for the law, and hiding the truth. Nixon's defenders made things worse for the president by circulating false stories about how the Central Intelligence Agency, the Pentagon, or other Washington institutions were conspiring to do him in. The lies contaminated the truth. Many Americans reacted with disgust and concluded that all governments were rotten. Some of those conversations happened in the diners and church basements of small North Country towns. Nelson Rockefeller was acting like a king, people said. Maybe it was time for a rebellion.

The state legislature was in session, so the clock was running on the APA. Perry Duryea, leader of the state assembly, said that the revised land use plan had to be on his desk at the end of the first week of March. And hundreds of requests for revisions had come in.

The biggest landowners in the park were timber companies. The APA had put most of their land in the resource management and rural use categories. Although the agency had placed almost no restrictions on timber-cutting, the companies still had a lot to lose if they ever planned to sell their land for house lots.

The timber companies worked quietly, secure in the knowledge of their political power. On January 26, lawyers for lumber company Finch Pruyn submitted a preliminary response to the land use plan. The company's memo made three points that would be repeated again and again as the APA struggled to establish itself. Finch Pruyn said it could sue on the grounds that the land use plan was an unconstitutional "taking" of private property rights without compensation, that the plan interfered with the rights of local government, and that the plan was a denial of due process.

Finch Pruyn's lawyers threatened to tie the plan up in court for years, and perhaps kill it, unless the APA made a long list of changes. So the agency did. The APA accepted Finch Pruyn's demands for twenty-one different changes to the maps, which pushed the maximum number of buildings allowed on the company's lands from 1,042 to 7,276.

Developers were not as calm. Louis Papparazzo, whose plan for Ton-Da-Lay clearly would not meet the standards in the agency's draft plan, sent a statement to *New York Times* reporter David Bird that said, "The first reading of the Agency's plan leaves one with the feeling that this proposal is about as American or Democratic as a red flag or a swastika . . . the Agency appears to have read its mandate as an order to establish a six-million-acre feudal state complete with a serf class."

The Horizon Corporation was more businesslike. On January 22, staffers announced that the company was suspending its Adirondack operations. A few months later, the company's CEO and top managers were charged with fraud and resigned. Horizon never recovered, but the weakened company did manage to sue the APA as a test of the "taking of private property" issue. Horizon's lawsuit would become important to the APA story a few years later.

The most successful local developer, Frank Casier, adapted to reality. The APA had ruled that four of his projects were exempt from review because they had been approved before the agency law went into effect, and this gave Casier a few more lots to sell. He changed his ads to say that with the coming of the APA law, "land is getting scarce" inside the Blue Line. "He disagreed vehemently with us," said Bill Kissel. "But when we met with him he was always businesslike and cordial."

Casier said he always thought that the plans of Ton-Da-Lay and Horizon were unrealistic. He worked on a smaller scale, and he was cagey. When he saw the APA coming, he started moving more of his investments into South Florida.

After the public hearings ended, hundreds of revisions came in from towns and local landowners. The revision requests ensured that the punishing workload at the APA offices in Ray Brook would continue.

According to Richard Lawrence, the meetings with local officials were far less contentious than the public hearings. "We would go over the plan with them in considerable detail," he remembered at a conference in 1981. "We would show them the map. We would talk to them about what was about to happen and what their reaction would be. With rare exceptions, we had very substantial acceptance . . . [but] at a public hearing later that evening, these very same gentlemen would stand up and condemn the whole business completely out of hand. That is a political fact of life, and a very strange phenomenon."

Anita Riner Davis remembered that many of the revision requests translated into more road trips for the staff. The stress was taking a toll, especially on George Davis. Other staffers remember him becoming hollow-eyed and edgy, taking pills to stay awake. He became angry and sad when the board made changes to the plan.

Although Davis tried to maintain a high-energy, enthusiastic demeanor, his close friend Lyn Jerry said that she thought it was a mask. Davis's behavior never became so erratic that he couldn't do his job, but something wasn't right. "I don't think that anyone realized at the time that George was bipolar, including George," said APA outreach director Dick Beamish. In those days, all anyone saw was George's high-energy exterior. The depression emerged later.

Glenn Harris's proposal to delay consideration of the land use plan for a year seemed reasonable to many legislators, and the traditional deference to home rule made it likely that the delay bill would pass the legislature. But it didn't stand a chance with the governor, and the APA board knew it. The main reason Rockefeller insisted on action in 1973, according to Dick Beamish, was that 1973 had no statewide elections. If calls for home rule became a statewide electoral issue during an election year, Beamish said, "it could be fatal."

Nelson Rockefeller might also have sensed that his power was fading in New York. And he also had his eye on the National Land Use Policy Act, a federal bill designed to encourage "developments of regional benefit." Rockefeller still wanted to be president. He wanted the Adirondack land use plan to pass before the federal law did because it would further enhance his reputation as an innovator.

The APA had hired Dick Beamish in October 1972 to do outreach. Beamish was a public relations professional. He had also been a volunteer leader of citizen opposition to a Louis Papparazzo development proposal outside of Amherst, Massachusetts. He came to the Adirondacks to join the fight to save the earth, but he said that during his first few months at the APA, he mostly answered phone messages.

Public relations inside the Blue Line was an orphan at the APA, Beamish said, mostly because Dick Lawrence didn't believe that explaining the plan to park residents would do any good. Most of the time, Beamish functioned more like an in-house political consultant.

The opposition started to organize. Despite his cordial mask, Frank Casier was so angered by the APA that he had trouble controlling his emotions. Bill Doolittle used to send his son, Will, over to play with Casier's son, David. "Frank had a huge amount of anger about the APA," said Will, who became a columnist for the *Glens Falls Post-Star*. "He would get so mad that he would just start shaking."

Casier and Tony D'Elia helped organize a group of local officials to coordinate opposition to the land use plan. They sent delegations to Albany, opened a news bureau to distribute material statewide, and coordinated local action. Opposing the APA was practically a civic duty in the area around Saranac, Placid, and Tupper Lakes. The Kiwanis and Lions Clubs, a group of school district administrators, the economic development–oriented Adirondack Park Association, chambers of commerce, and the Veterans of Foreign Wars all passed resolutions asking for the delay bill. The American History class at Saranac Lake High School even wrote anti-APA letters to Senator Ron Stafford.

On January 30, APA board member Jim Bird broke ranks and publicly endorsed the delay bill. He warned people to get their comments in soon anyway, because the plan would definitely be submitted in early March. Dick Lawrence knew that losing Bird's support would be a big problem. It seemed likely that Whit Daniels and Bill Foley would vote against the Land Use and Development Plan, and the governor had told Lawrence that he wouldn't support the plan unless the board vote in favor of it was at least seven to two. More compromises were necessary.

Back in November, Dick Wiebe had proposed that the board exempt subdivisions of fewer than five units in most cases. On December 7, just before the board sent the draft plan to the printer, they had also voted to increase the maximum allowable density in rural use areas from 50 to 64 buildings per square mile. There wasn't any research behind these numbers. Dick Wiebe proposed them at the end of a long, difficult day, Peter Paine moved to accept them, and they were quickly voted in.

The board's post-hearing meetings, on January 31 and February 14–15, 1973, were dominated by more discussion of the density numbers. Wiebe suggested that development proposals be separated into two categories. Larger projects would be "category A," and the APA would remain involved in their review. Smaller "category B" projects would be left to towns that had approved local zoning laws, and those towns could make their decisions without agency involvement. The distinction between "rural" and "urban" hamlets would be eliminated. Wiebe said that the APA's job was not to make the park perfect by correcting past mistakes. He said that the agency's proper role was "to keep things from getting any worse."

George Davis wasn't happy with the way things were going. On January 6, he wrote a memo addressed to "APA files" to put his objections on the record. "The very fact that we use a number [of buildings per square mile] opens the door for the number to be changed in the political arena," he wrote. "I consider it essential that the number ten [buildings per square mile] never be raised, and I feel that we would be on just as firm ground, if not firmer, should we say no building in the resource management area with two [minor] exceptions."

The board voted on the land use plan at a meeting in Albany on March 3. Someone asked where the current version of the map was—the one that contained all the revisions—and Dick Lawrence replied, "right now there is only one map, and George has that map in his car." Davis had brought the map down to give to the Office of Planning Services to be printed. He reported that the staff had received eight hundred requests for changes and had approved five hundred of them so far.

The board discussed distribution and printing matters at that meeting, as well as the likelihood that the agency would face multiple court challenges if the law passed. After the lunch break, they began moving toward the final vote. One by one, the commissioners stood up to thank their colleagues, especially Dick Lawrence. Even Bill Foley said something nice.

Henry Diamond attended that meeting. "I think it would be appropriate here to tell you about an experience I had," he said. "One night in 1967 I was with a rather shy guy, not really in public life very much. I went with him to make a speech in Warrensburg to a very hostile audience. That man was Laurance Rockefeller." The APA's Land Use and Development Plan was a "direct lineal descendent" of Laurance Rockefeller's national park proposal, Diamond said. If the national park proposal had not come out, he said, "this would not be happening here today."

"The whole thing has been rather like a blacksmith's shop," said Whit Daniels. "If ever a document was forged with heat and pounding, this certainly is the one."

The vote was seven in favor, with Foley opposed and Bird abstaining. Peter Paine said that he got Whit Daniels's vote by promising him the bill would include $250,000 for local assistance. It was a very small gesture that somehow took care of Daniels's objections, according to Paine.

Bird explained his abstention in a letter to Lawrence. The final version of the plan was "a vast improvement" over the preliminary version, he said. But the map was still full of errors and unfair judgements. It would take many months to sort them out, and Bird could not endorse it in its current form. So he abstained "with the earnest hope that the inequities still inherent in the map and Plan will receive attention and corrective action."

After the March 3 vote, the focus shifted to passing the Land Use and Development Plan in the state legislature. The drama unfolded in Albany, which is the Broadway of political theater. In Act One, Peter Berle, the trim, athletic thirty-six-year-old leader of the pro-APA forces in the state assembly, challenged Glenn Harris, sponsor of the delay bill, who was fifty-four and overweight, to a thirty-two-mile cross-country ski race that was scheduled to take place on the frozen surface of Lake George. "The first side to run out of wind or become incoherent will concede to the other side," he said.

Peter Paine put his job and family on hold and decamped to the state capitol again. He and Richard Persico, counsel to the New York State Office of Planning Services, started drafting the law that would ratify the Land Use and Development Plan, with assistance from Nelson Rockefeller's legal staff. Rockefeller asked Senator Bernard Smith, who represented the center part of Long Island, to sponsor the land use plan bill in the senate. Smith delegated a lot of the details to a young aide named Michael Silverman, who kept thorough notes as the bill took shape.

Delivering the actual plan to the legislature wasn't as easy as it sounds. Dick Lawrence was served with court papers during the lunch break at the board's March 3 meeting. Robert Purdy, supervisor of the Town of Keene, filed a request for an injunction with support from the ad hoc group of local officials and business owners that included Tony D'Elia and Frank Casier. A state supreme court justice scheduled a hearing for Monday in Plattsburgh, 160 miles north of Albany. The complaint claimed that the APA had not fulfilled its legislative mandate to consult with local officials.

George Davis said that on Monday, March 5, Harry Daniels put the master copy of the land use plan into his car and drove two-and-a-half hours to Albany, as promised. Daniels was stopped on the steps of the state capitol by a court officer because the hearing in Plattsburgh had not finished yet. So he drove the plan back to Ray Brook, which gave the staff a bit more time to proofread it. The next morning, the judge lifted the injunction and Harry Daniels drove back to Albany. This time he was followed by Bill Kissel, who had the master copy of the plan in his briefcase.

Kissel went to Dick Persico's office to do some last-minute work on the draft legislation. Kissel said that they wrapped everything up around 11 p.m. on Tuesday and decided to celebrate at a nearby bar. The master copy went back into Kissel's briefcase. And later that night, somewhere in Albany, Kissel's briefcase disappeared, never to be seen again.

But wait. Just before Kissel took his briefcase out for a drink, Dick Persico insisted that they take an extra half an hour to make a photocopy of the final version and leave it in the office for safekeeping. Photocopy machines were slower and more expensive in 1973, but Persico's office happened to have one. "Persico was instrumental to the plan for many reasons," said Kissel. "One was that he saved the only copy of the final version."

The APA staff threw a party on Tuesday night and slept in the next day. The next morning, "I'm in my office, and things are moving slow," said Dick Booth. "Gary Randorf comes in and says, 'Dick, there's a problem with the document we have just sent to Albany.' As Gary and I are speaking, the state printing office is setting the document in type to run off two thousand copies the next day.

"So I say, 'What's the problem?' 'It's the single existing vacant lot rule,' Gary says. We had written an exemption so a person who owned an existing lot could still build a single house on it. Fitting this idea into all the other rules was fairly complex, and several lawyers had worked on the language. So Gary reads it to me and says, this clause says the opposite of what you want it to say. I said no, it doesn't. You're not a lawyer, Gary, and here's our reasoning.

"Now Gary is maybe the nicest guy I ever met, and I was being very patient and reasonable with him, and we went back and forth five or six times, and then it struck me. I finally got it. Oh my God, I thought, Gary is right. Now it's maybe noon. I immediately called Dick Persico and went through the same thing with him. Once he got it, Persico called the print shop. Dick says that he literally stopped the presses so that Gary's small, very important change could be made."

Booth, who became a professor of City and Regional Planning at Cornell University, tells that story to his students every year. "I'm not trying to encourage them to go to law school," he said. "I want to show them that people who aren't lawyers should be able to think about the law. Gary was a smart guy. He could read and he could think, and that saved us a load of trouble."

At the next APA board meeting on March 16, Dick Estes asked if the staff could stop entering corrections on the Zipatone version of the big map, now that the printed version had arrived. Yes, Dick Lawrence said. Finally, the staff could get some rest. They needed it. Gary Randorf says that whenever he finally went home and undressed in those days, he would find little pieces of Zipatone stuck to his skin.

The two-thousand-copy printing of the plan and the big map was supplemented by another edition of twelve thousand more copies that was circulated to the public. Once Adirondack landowners started to check the revised version, a lot of opposition based on specific provisions in the map went away. The Lake Champlain Committee wrote to the governor to say that it had been greatly improved, and they were happy to endorse it. John Stock, the manager of twenty-eight thousand acres of timber at Litchfield Park, said the same thing. Stock said there were still a lot of problems in the Adirondacks, but on balance, the plan was a big step forward.

Dick Beamish took the map on a tour of newspaper offices around the state. "I was like Paul Revere," he said. "My message was, 'Beware, the developers are coming.' It was highly successful. I would call Dick Lawrence from different parts of the state, and Dick was always fascinated by what was going on. I remember him saying, 'Where the hell are ya now?' I would say, 'I'm down in Long Island. They love us in Long Island!'"

Beamish was a state employee, but he freely assisted environmental organizations as they coordinated their lobbying for the land use plan. He wrote a long pro-APA letter that was published in an Albany newspaper under the byline of Fred Hackett, president of the Adirondack Mountain Club. He worked with Ted Hullar to send a mailing to eight thousand Sierra Club members throughout the northeastern United States, urging them to call their legislators. The letter was signed by Sierra Club national director Michael McCloskey, but the copy in Dick Lawrence's papers has a handwritten note saying that Beamish wrote it.

Harris's forces made their move on March 22. The delay bill passed the assembly 86–41, with 14 "yes" votes from Democrats. Under Harris's bill, the APA could continue to review projects using the interim rules, but projects that were already in the works, such as Ton-Da-Lay and Loon Lake, would be allowed to go ahead. On March 27, the delay bill passed the Senate 33–22, with 5 Democrats voting "yes" and only 7 Republicans voting "no." That meant 26 Republicans voted contrary to the governor's wishes.

Then a month went by as the two sides played a game of legislative chicken. Senator Ron Stafford made the first move by pulling a procedural trick. After the New York State Legislature sends a bill to the governor, the governor has ten days to decide whether or not to veto it. Rockefeller had already indicated that he would veto the delay bill so he could introduce his bill approving the land use plan. Stafford's trick was to pass the delay bill but not send it to the executive chamber, thereby preventing the process from moving forward. Stafford's intent was to bring the governor to the negotiating table as the clock kept ticking on the legislative session.

But the governor did not have to be forced to negotiate. According to his counsel, Michael Whiteman, Rockefeller enjoyed it. "Nelson Rockefeller was a consummate negotiator because he always knew what his client's interests were," Whiteman said. "He always pursued his interests very hard, but he always kept in mind that the other guy had interests too, and he had to send the other guy home with something in his arms and his head held high. Rockefeller knew that if you shamed the other guy—if you stripped him of everything, if you really licked him—he would be after you for the rest of his life to get revenge. But if you made sure that he got to claim a few victories, you could accomplish a lot."

Rockefeller made the next move when Program Bill no. 39, the Land Use and Development Plan, was submitted to the legislature on April 4. Then he started getting his ducks in a row.

Both sides watched closely as public debate unfolded over the next several weeks. Senator Stafford's files are full of letters from constituents. The anti-APA letters outnumber the letters in favor, but there's an interesting pattern. The stationery used for letters opposing the APA isn't nearly as nice. "This property was paid for with very hard work, and I do not intend to let Gov. Rockefeller or his straw bosses tell me what I can and cannot do with it," wrote Claude Schene of Vermontville. "There are only about two hundred of us here, but we will fight TYRANNY in any way we can" (emphasis in the original).

Other letters were more pointed, and one of them even threatened the traditional Adirondack practice of revenge arson. "If the bill passes, don't come up," wrote H. Tennyson Baldwin of Chestertown. "It will probably be a very smoky summer."

The pro-APA letters in Stafford's files are weighted toward handwritten notes on printed letterheads, and several of them call the senator by his first name. "Ev and I (and most of your friends) were very happy about Gov. Rockefeller's veto on the APA delay and urge you to let it stand," wrote Mrs. Evalon Merritt, the wife of Plattsburgh's school superintendent. "This region, so precious, cannot stand delayed protection. We're in danger from within far more than from Commies in Vietnam or wherever."

The governor vetoed the delay bill on Friday, April 27, a signal that negotiations could begin. Harris and Stafford and their aides started meeting with Whiteman, Persico, Paine, and others the following Wednesday and kept going more or less around the clock until the evening of Monday, May 7. Bernard Smith's aide, Michael Silverman, kept a record of the changes.

Among the most important changes were increasing the size of the APA board from nine to eleven by adding another in-park seat (bringing that total to five) and the commissioner of commerce or his or her deputy. The governor's team accepted Glenn Harris's proposal that a local government review board be created for "advising and assisting the APA in carrying out its functions," with one member from each of the twelve counties that contained land in the Adirondack Park. State aid to municipalities was increased from $150,000 to $250,000, fulfilling Paine's promise to Daniels. Thresholds for the more intensively scrutinized "category A" projects were raised. And the State Board of Equalization and Assessment was ordered to study the impact of the plan on the local tax base. The list went on and on, adding up to about two hundred specific changes in the bill.

The most consequential changes were to minimum shoreline widths and setbacks in the low intensity, rural use, and resource management categories. A last-minute loosening of the rules—from a minimum lot width of 200 feet to 125 feet in low intensity areas, for example—had a powerful impact on the character of privately owned land on lakeshores. Peter Paine would not accept them. As the session on Sunday turned into an all-nighter, he remembered arguing so forcefully that he was eventually asked to leave the room.

On Tuesday, May 8, the negotiators announced that they had reached compromises that would allow the bill to move to a vote. "I am convinced that if I had not introduced the 'delay bill' and obtained the tremendous support of the legislature, the governor's office would not have been willing to negotiate any changes in the final bill," Glenn Harris said. "Nearly two hundred changes were agreed upon and virtually every page of the original bill was amended." Harris said he was still opposed to the bill because it was a violation of home rule, but he was happy with the concessions.

"That was good politics," said Michael Whiteman. "I got something, and I can go home to my constituents and tell them how much I got, even if in my heart I know it's a mess of pottage."

Wiebe and Persico both said they were surprised at how easy the negotiations were. "Peter Paine came down on me like thunder for weakening the shoreline restrictions, but I had to do it," Dick Persico said. Shorelines are where the money is.

"We can live with these compromises," said Dick Lawrence. He accepted them because the percentage of private land allocated to the different categories did not change. Resource management and the next-most restrictive category, rural use, claimed 85 percent of the park's private land in the bill approved by the legislature.

Environmental groups unleashed a final, well-coordinated blitz as the vote approached. But they had already won, and Glenn Harris knew it. During the debate on the floor of the assembly, he said, "If we were out to get the Horizons and the Ton-Da-Lays of the Adirondacks we should have been honest and said so! This 107-page bill is going to hurt all the little guys I represent more than anyone, and they're struggling already to earn a living.

This plan doesn't bring a ray of hope to an already economically depressed area. It places a knife in the heart of it."

The compromise bill passed the assembly on May 14, 117–12. It passed the senate, 52–3, a few days later. Interim controls would remain in effect until the law took effect on August 1. Back in the park, the initial reaction was mixed. Several members of planning boards expressed reluctant support. Bill Doolittle wrote an editorial encouraging his readers to learn to live with the APA. At least there would be a few more high-paying state jobs in the area now, he added.

Nelson Rockefeller signed the Adirondack Park bill on May 22, at a formal ceremony in the State Capitol building. "Fifty or one hundred years from now, when most other issues of the current session may be long forgotten, the New York State Legislature of 1973 may well be remembered and judged for its action in preserving the Adirondack Park," he said. The legislature made 1885 a landmark year for the Adirondacks when it created the forest preserve, Rockefeller said, and what happened in 1973 would be remembered as equally important.

He also played to his inexhaustible urge to become a national leader. "Regional and statewide land use planning is a number one environmental priority facing our nation today," he said. "With the signing of this bill, the Adirondack Park becomes the largest area in the country to come under comprehensive land use control . . . the Adirondacks are preserved forever."

Back up in the North Country, a few people thought they had been ruined. On April 12, Bill Kissel wrote to Tony D'Elia with a long list of questions the agency needed answered before the next permit application for Loon Lake Estates could be considered. D'Elia claimed that it took him several months and tens of thousands of dollars to answer those questions. As he did that, D'Elia's neighbors were organizing against him. They hired Kafin & Needleman to stop him. D'Elia's dream started to fade.

In Sugarbush, Shirley Delano Ryan was inspired to write a piece that she called "An Adirondack Fable."

> Once upon a time, there lived a ruler who had obtained great power because of his riches. He looked upon the land and saw that a portion thereof was exceedingly fair and he said unto himself, "I will attain great fame among men, even as do my brothers, if the fairness of this place is attributed to me. . . ."

The Ruler said unto the people, "I will decide what is best for you, your land, and your children, so I have decreed. My disciples will make a map with colored marks. We will show you what will come to pass. . . ."

The people were angered and cried out in a loud voice: "An unjust law is made only to be broken. . . . So shall the wealthy sleep uneasily in their ill-gotten seclusion. We have spoken!"

"Never underestimate the survival potential of the Adirondack native," Ryan wrote. "We are not poor. We just don't have any money—never did, and probably never will. Like the mountains themselves, we will probably still be here when the APA is only a dusty file."

# CONCLUSION

## *Convinced against Their Will*

When Nelson Rockefeller signed the Adirondack Park Land Use and Development Plan into law on May 22, 1973, most of the major environmental laws of the United States were already in place. The Wilderness Act passed in 1964. The National Environmental Policy Act and the Clean Air Act passed in 1970, the same year the Environmental Protection Agency was formed. The Clean Water Act passed in 1972 after Congress overrode a presidential veto. And seven months after the revisions to the Adirondack Park Agency Act became law, Congress passed the Endangered Species Act.

All of these laws were propelled by overwhelming voter demands for environmental protection. In the summer of 1973, Congress was considering one more environmental bill. This was the one that would tie all the others together, and its passage seemed likely.

Senator Henry "Scoop" Jackson, a Democrat from Washington State, introduced the National Land Use Policy Act in 1970 and reintroduced it after reaching a compromise with Republican leaders in 1972. The act used incentives and sanctions to encourage states to develop land use plans for environmentally sensitive areas and large development sites. Its larger goal, Jackson said, was to encourage long-range thinking about the environment. "To a very great extent all environmental management decisions are ultimately related to land use decisions," he said. "All environmental problems are outgrowths of land use patterns."

Jackson's bill followed a wave of new state laws. In 1971, a study titled *The Quiet Revolution* profiled twenty-one regional land use planning programs, including the Adirondack Park Agency. In 1972, an expansive land use law passed in Florida. In 1973, an even more ambitious land use law passed in Oregon. The laws all encouraged cooperation between state and local governments. Their goal was to allow watersheds, ecosystems, and other geographies established by nature to sustain themselves as buildings, roads, and industries rose around them.

The Adirondack Park Land Use and Development Plan stood out from these efforts. Almost all of the designated wilderness areas in the United States were owned by the federal government and located in western states, but the APA's job was to protect the wilderness character of a state park that was much larger than any of the national parks that existed in 1973. The Adirondack plan was also the toughest in its class. Many regional land use plans of the era depended on local governments taking voluntary incentives, but the Adirondack law gave a state agency statutory authority to protect environmental quality by reviewing and modifying zoning regulations.

Scoop Jackson's bill easily passed the Senate in 1973, but it ran into trouble when Richard Nixon turned hard to the right. Nixon had spent decades tacking between the moderate and conservative wings of the Republican Party. In February 1974, the House of Representatives was considering articles of impeachment, and Nixon was desperately looking for a lifeline. The president's staunchest supporters were antigovernment conservatives. So Nixon withdrew his support for the House version of Jackson's bill and switched to a much weaker substitute bill sponsored by Arizona Congressman Sam Steiger, a man who once commented on his snakeskin cowboy boots by saying, "I wear nothing but endangered species."

The House scrapped the bill in June 1974, when a motion to consider land use legislation failed by just seven votes. Then Nixon resigned, a severe economic recession deepened, and the chance did not come again. The vision of regional land use planning survived in many parts of the country. The

APA survived, too. But the optimistic era that created the APA ended almost as soon as the agency was born.

Governor Rockefeller signed the 1973 APA Act five days after the Senate Watergate hearings began. Nixon's support eroded quickly during those hearings. It suffered a mortal blow on July 13, when an aide revealed that conversations in the Oval Office had been taped. Then on August 7, the *Wall Street Journal* broke the story that Vice President Spiro Agnew, Nixon's logical successor in the 1976 election, was under investigation for taking bribes. A few days after he learned about Agnew, Rockefeller began telling his staff that he would resign as governor in December 1973 to make his fourth run for the Republican nomination for president.

Nelson Rockefeller might have been the most powerful governor in New York's history. His power, combined with overwhelming public support for environmental protection, pushed the APA laws of 1971 and 1973 over the finish line. But less than a year after Rockefeller resigned, Democrats controlled the governor's office and the state assembly. The Rockefeller era of optimism, data collection, and faith in top-down government solutions ended abruptly.

Passing land use laws was the easy part. Making them work would be a lot harder.

An idea as audacious as the APA couldn't have become law at any other time. In fact, serious proposals were made to draft comprehensive plans for the park at least two other times, and both of them went nowhere.

In 1962, State Senator Eustis Paine (Ron Stafford's predecessor) proposed an Adirondack Park Commission "to assist in the planning, zoning, and development of state and private lands within the Blue Line." "Eustie" (as his cousin, Peter Paine Jr., called him) envisioned a system of state incentives that would encourage towns and villages to voluntarily draft zoning plans. In 1961, he wrote a letter to the chairman of the state Republican Party (and copied Richard Lawrence on it) suggesting a nine-member board, six of whom would be park residents. The board's purpose would be to protect water purity and natural beauty by preventing inappropriate development.

Environmental groups in 1962 had not yet coalesced into a force in New York State politics. They didn't say much as town officials, chambers of commerce, and others in the North Country howled that Eustis Paine's bill would take away their right to home rule. The bill never made it out of committee, despite the support of (future Temporary Study Commission member) Jim Loeb, who pleaded with locals in an editorial that zoning would mean "protection of their rights rather than the loss of them."

Another effort at a comprehensive plan happened in 1989, well after the environmental revolution of the 1970s. Environmentalists convinced Governor Mario Cuomo that the 16-year-old APA Act needed a tune-up. Cuomo appointed a study commission that had a lot of familiar faces. Peter Berle was its chair, Harold Jerry was a commissioner, and George Davis was executive director. In April 1990, the Commission on the Adirondacks in the Twenty-First Century released 245 recommendations that were at least as visionary as the Temporary Study Commission's had been. But this time the antiregulation forces were well funded, well organized, and a lot louder than the environmentalists. The governor decided to cut his losses rather than confront the opposition, and the report was shelved.

The Land Use and Development Plan of 1973 became law only through a rare combination of people and events. The result was a big step forward for sustainable development. But the 1973 law also changed the responsibilities of the APA. It was now required to enforce the rules, like a referee. And by 1977, Harold Jerry, George Davis, and other hard-core environmentalists were complaining about the agency almost as bitterly as developers did.

Nobody likes referees. Players and spectators are expected to criticize their calls. But they accept the ref's authority so they can continue to enjoy the game.

The APA is passing a milestone fiftieth anniversary in 2021, and it has a great deal to celebrate. The Adirondacks are one of the largest and least-fragmented temperate forest landscapes remaining on Earth, and the agency is the park's steward. But the research for this book showed that even as it approached its golden anniversary, the APA's critics were more vocal than its fans. Perhaps the reason is best stated by Calvin, the young hero in Bill Watterson's comic strip *Calvin and Hobbes*, who said that "a good compromise leaves everybody mad."

What difference has the APA made? You'll get one answer from a contractor relaxing after work at the Nick Stoner Inn, the bar-restaurant across the road from the Glenn H. Harris Municipal Park in the southern Adirondack hamlet of Caroga Lake. You'll get a different opinion from the tourists at the Big Slide Brewery, an upscale brewpub south of Lake Placid where folks relax after a day of hiking in the High Peaks.

Like a lot of bar questions, the one about the APA's impact is really several questions rolled into one. It is also a question with no easy answers. What can be said is that the APA had three main goals. It did really well with one of them, not so well on another, and on the third, its success created new problems.

The agency's first goal—and for Harold Jerry, the most important one— was to prevent building in the park's backcountry. That was a complete success. The zoning categories established in 1973 have held firm. In 2020, the law allows only one building for every 43 acres on 53 percent of the park's private land, and one per 8.5 acres on 33 percent of the land. Those are very strict controls on 2,662,619 acres of private land. The rest of the park's private land is zoned one building per 3.2 acres (9 percent) and one building per 1.3 acres (3 percent). The remaining 54,000 acres of towns and hamlets (2 percent) have no limits.

Jerry had to wait until the late 1990s to see his dream truly realized, however. That is when the state bought an easement on the 72,000-acre Santa Clara Tract at the northern edge of the park from the timber company Champion International. Today about 781,000 acres, or 23 percent of the park's private land, remains in timber production but is covered by conservation easements that permanently prevent subdivision and development. Most of the easement land also permits public access for hiking, canoeing, fishing, and hunting.

It is impossible to precisely identify the role the APA played in the permanent protection of the park's private forests. Forestry companies sold their land in the park starting in the 1980s because it was not as profitable as land in other regions. In 2021, many of the private forests in the Adirondacks are owned by firms that manage the lumber as investments for wealthy clients who want to diversify their portfolios. Yet there is also evidence that the Land Use and Development Plan did have an effect.

Over the last fifty years, an enormous amount of uncontrolled development has occurred in many US counties that contain protected land, just as Laurance Rockefeller feared it would. But that kind of development didn't happen in the Adirondacks.

In the 1970s, Americans started moving closer to wilderness. Population growth in rural western counties that contain federally designated wilderness areas increased 31 percent between 1970 and 1980, three times faster than the growth rate for metropolitan counties. Wilderness counties have been growing quickly ever since. Their population increased 11 percent between 2011 and 2017, more than twice as fast as that of metropolitan counties. Meanwhile, nonmetropolitan counties in the United States that do not contain wilderness areas are actually losing population.

When someone makes a long-distance move for noneconomic reasons, geographers call it "amenity migration." Most moves of this kind happen in towns that are close to beaches and ski areas. The moves also happen on a much smaller scale in cold, wet places like New York's North Country. Sales of lakefront homes in upstate New York have remained strong while other kinds of rural properties have gone vacant. But this trend doesn't bring in numbers big enough to reverse the long-term economic malaise that affects the entire rural Northeast, according to an exhaustive 2019 analysis by Peter Bauer and James Long of the advocacy group Protect the Adirondacks.

Bauer and Long found that the overall population of the sixty-one towns located entirely within the Adirondack Park increased just 10.6 percent between 1970 and 2010, from 91,000 to 100,600. The population of the thirty-one towns that are partially inside the Blue Line increased 35.8 percent, from 95,400 to 129,600. Overall growth inside the Blue Line was just slightly faster than the average for the rural Northeast, which increased 16.4 percent between 1970 and 2010. And another 45,200 people whose legal residence is outside the park own seasonal homes there, according to a 2008 analysis by the APA.

Why have the Adirondacks grown slower than other counties containing wilderness areas? There are many reasons, and exploring them would take another book's worth of research. The important point is that the land use plan prevented large-scale residential development from happening in the Adirondack backcountry. In other areas where public open space and private lands are intermixed, such as Michigan's Huron-Manistee National Forest, residential construction on private inholdings has created significant problems. To list just one example, the suppression of wildfires near homes on inholdings allows brush to accumulate, which reduces species diversity throughout the region. It also makes fires more dangerous when they inevitably occur.

The APA's second goal for the Adirondacks—the one George Davis drove his staff so hard to achieve—was to make sure that development happened in places where it would not hurt the park's wild character. And develop-ment did happen. About 1,000 new houses per year were built in the park between 1973 and 1992, according to an APA analysis, and 850 new houses a year went up in the 1990s, according to a separate study by the Residents Committee to Protect the Adirondacks.

Construction inside the Blue Line since 1973 has been largely concentrated in hamlets and moderate-intensity zones, which encompass about 5 percent of the park's acreage. So the APA also succeeded in its second goal, but this achievement in guiding development created a new problem—overcrowding. It's a six-million-acre park, and the vast majority of it is still almost empty. But high-season visitors to Lake Placid, Old Forge, and the most popular lakes, mountains, and snowmobile trails of the Adirondacks don't see those wide open places. They often see traffic jams and herd paths.

Another goal of the land use plan was protecting Adirondack shorelines. The APA didn't do as well here. Lakefront lots are the most valuable real estate in the Adirondack Park, and the last-minute compromise that in-creased the density limits on lakefronts had a huge impact. The compro-mises allowed the same kinds of "piano-key" lots and large, prominent homes that are found on lakes that are not protected by land use plans. The com-promises destroyed the park's "primeval character" in many of its most beau-tiful places.

Several threats to the ecological health of the Adirondacks have also emerged that are beyond the park agency's power to control. In the 1970s, emissions from coal-fired power plants in the Midwest increased the acidity of precipitation that fell in the park, causing severe damage to lakes and wet-lands that is still being felt. Invasive species from Europe and Asia, brought into the park by powerboats and four-wheel-drive vehicles, crowd out native vegetation while they attack stands of ash and hemlock. And a warming cli-mate means that Adirondack winters are shorter, rainstorms are heavier, and the woods are filling with ticks that carry Lyme disease. The environmental challenges to the park are much bigger now, and much more serious.

The APA's biggest failure was with local people. It faced determined op-position from Tony D'Elia, Frank Casier, and other developers who imme-diately organized efforts to abolish it. The activists intimidated and encouraged local officials who refused to cooperate with the agency. Activ-ists who organized around the slogan "Abolish the APA" managed to frame the agency in the minds of locals as an uncaring, inept enforcer from a corrupt big city. Some observers say that this negative reaction couldn't be helped. "An old Irish saying applies," said Bill Curran, who retired after a thirty-year career with the APA in 2002. "A man convinced against his will is of the same opinion still."

The antagonism of permanent park residents crippled the APA's original strategy, which was to gradually reduce its authority as local planning boards met state-approved zoning standards. The problem was that a lot of Adirondackers didn't want to do things the APA's way. They didn't trust governments to solve their problems. They ignored expert opinions on poverty, pollution, and other chronic Adirondack woes, preferring instead to put their faith in home rule and their own abilities.

Local opposition had become a serious threat to the park agency when a new board chairman, Robert Flacke, began making strategic compromises in 1976. By that time, many Americans had been converted to the Adirondackers' position. They rallied around the 1975–1976 presidential campaign of Ronald Reagan, who was generally opposed to government regulations and ambivalent about scientific research. The Adirondack story became a struggle between two visions of America. The bitter, occasionally violent conflicts that erupted in the Adirondacks in the 1970s, 80s, and 90s offered a preview to the rest of the country.

Given the obstacles the APA has faced over fifty years, it could be that its biggest accomplishments are simply sticking to its mission and surviving. The APA Act truly made the Adirondacks into a park, and its rules have mostly held. "That is an extraordinary achievement," said Henry Diamond. "In land use planning, the Adirondacks stand as a very tall tree."

# ACKNOWLEDGMENTS

This book emerged from long conversations with significant people. It began twenty years ago in Ithaca's Lincoln Street Diner, where Ted Hullar and I would meet for eggs, home fries, and talks that were liable to veer off in any direction. Ted witnessed several of the events described in this book when he was leading the Sierra Club's Atlantic chapter. In 2001 he was a senior program officer for Atlantic Philanthropies, and he had the foresight to ask me to capture the stories of Adirondack activists, staff, and politicians before they passed away. Atlantic's support made it possible for me to collect three dozen interviews between 2002 and 2007. Thank you, Ted.

I did most of the talking with my research team, which consisted of an archival partner, fact-checker, editor, and coach. We mixed it up countless times, and I was usually convinced. I could easily point to hundreds of places where this book was improved by the team's intelligence and dogged pursuit of facts. The team's name is Tania Werbizky. She is a team of one, as well as my beloved spouse, and my gratitude for her is unbounded. Thank you, Tania.

When I resurrected the project in 2018, the enthusiastic support of the Adirondack Experience (ADKX) allowed me to collect another two dozen interviews. I am grateful to Jerry Pepper, Laura Rice, David Kahn, Ivy Gocker, and others on the ADKX staff for their advice and encouragement. An additional grant from Furthermore allowed us to include color illustrations.

I knew little about the Adirondacks in 2002. My first interview, with Clarence Petty, yielded so many questions that it took four more sessions with him to answer them all. Over the next eighteen years, I noticed that people who love the Adirondacks are also likely to be good storytellers. I have wonderful memories of the people I interviewed, who are listed in the Sources section. Clarence and many others are gone now, and I remain grateful to all of them.

I was assisted by several archivists who went above and beyond to help me finish this manuscript, despite the challenges of a global pandemic. They are Margaret Amodeo and Matthew Golebiewski at Union College, Mary Ann Quinn at the Rockefeller Archives Center, Jodi Boyle and Brian Keough at State University of New York at Albany, Keith Swaney and Jim Folts at the New York State Archives, and Paul Doty and Paul Haggett at St. Lawrence University. Peg Olsen of the Adirondack chapter of the Nature Conservancy provided materials that allowed me to tell that group's story accurately. Melinda Hadley donated early records from groups that opposed the Adirondack Park Agency. And Cathy Moore, the longtime publisher of the *Adirondack Daily Enterprise*, generously granted access to the newspaper's clipping files.

Thanks are also due to Michael McGandy, my editor at Cornell University Press, for bringing the project in on a tight schedule without compromising its quality; Tracy Ormsbee, publisher of *Adirondack Explorer*, for loaning office space and suggesting the title; Peter Beck, a talented copy editor who straightened out many interview transcripts and then gave the text its final polish, all without complaint; Jon Crispin, for the author photo; David Gibson, Denise Oates, and Anita Davis, who shared personal photographs; Nancy Bernstein, for her hand-drawn maps; and Brian Balogh, Tim Barnett, Richard Booth, George Davis, Evelyn (Schaefer) Greene, Adam Hochschild, Peter S. Paine Jr., and Andrew Zepp, who read and corrected early drafts.

I am grateful to many friends for their hospitality and advice, including Rocci Aguirre and Emily Eisman, Steven Engelhart, the Kirchner family

(Betty, Bob, Jim, Peter, and Christie Kroll), Henry Tepper and Jane Henoch, and Anne Van Ingen and Wes Haynes.

This project got a huge boost when Phil Terrie decided to retire to Ithaca. Phil is the best and most knowledgeable historian of the Adirondacks, by far. Our conversations and his careful review of the text boosted my confidence, saved me from embarrassing errors, and made me appear smarter than I actually am. Thank you, Phil.

I first saw the Adirondacks in 1973, as a fourteen-year-old from a small town in Florida. My uncle Larry invited my brother Brian and me to go on a one-hundred-mile canoe trip that started at the Boy Scout camp at Floodwood Mountain, ran large sections of the Raquette River, and ended on the banks of the Saint Lawrence, at the Akwesasne Mohawk Reservation. That trip gave me a love of wild landscapes that has never gone away.

Forty-seven summers later, as I was finishing this book, Tania and I spent a week in the High Peaks with my children, Will and Emma; their spouses, Zoe and Ayyappan; and my five-month-old grandson, Charlie. Larry is gone now, but I remain grateful to him for introducing me to the Adirondacks, and it was a special joy to see the love of wilderness growing in my children and grandchild. This book is dedicated to them.

# A NOTE ON SOURCES

**Interviews**

I collected thirty-five oral history interviews between 2002 and 2007, and another twenty-eight in 2019 and 2020. The men and women whose recollections illuminated this story were almost always gracious and generous. Their anecdotes were touching and funny, and the details they shared helped me reconstitute the flavors of important events. But in many cases, the verbatim transcripts of our conversations were extremely difficult to read.

Taped interviews are challenging because conversations almost never spool out in complete sentences. I edited the interview transcripts for clarity with help from my friend Peter Beck, trying to stay as close as possible to what the speakers actually said. I took additional steps when choosing quotes for this book. This meant occasionally rearranging sentences and adding factual details to keep things moving along. While doing so, I tried to preserve the essential meaning of the words as much as possible.

The interviews also posed factual challenges because old memories, like old paper, tear easily and must be handled gently. A person's recollection of an event that happened decades ago is never entirely complete. For this reason, I sent the edited transcripts to the speakers for revision and approval, and I added their revisions to the final versions of the transcripts. I also did not treat a speaker's assertion as a fact unless it could be corroborated by a second interview or a documentary source. In a few cases, speakers provided interview statements off the record.

The audio and video files, original and edited transcripts, and supporting documents for these interviews are in the collection of the Adirondack Experience (ADKX) library in Blue Mountain Lake, New York. The 2002–2007 interviews were with the following people:

Harry Albright
George Canon
Frank Casier
Almy Coggeshall
John Collins
Arthur Crocker
Raymond Curran
George Davis
Henry Diamond
Robert Flacke Sr.
Robert Glennon
Andrew Halloran
Beverly Sawaya Harris
James Hotaling
Jocelyn Jerry
Howard Kimball
Marge Lamy
Barbara McMartin

David Newhouse
Peter S. Paine Jr.
Ronald W. Pedersen
Richard Persico
Archibald Petty
Clarence Petty
Chuck Pishko
Richard Purdue
Gary Randorf
Arthur V. Savage
David Sive
Neil Stout
Peter Van de Water
Norman Van Valkenburgh
Michael Whiteman
Richard Wiebe
Henry Williams

Additional interviews collected while writing this book in 2019 and 2020 were with the following subjects:

Tim Barnett
Richard Beamish

Jennifer Birckmayer
Holt Bodinson

Richard Booth
William Curran
Anita Davis
William Doolittle
Gary Duprey
Bob Glennon
Eileen Rockefeller Growald
Melinda Hadley
Sandy Hayes
Don Hickey
Neil Huber
Ted Hullar

Larry Hyde
Art Jubin
Robert Kafin
Bill Kissel
Oliver Koeppel
Peter Lanahan
Matt McCabe
Charlie Morrison
Barbara D'Elia O'Connell
George Pataki
Samuel Sage
Nancy Trautman

The book also draws from the following first-person documents, which are available in the ADKX library:

- George Davis, interviewed by William Verner in 1976
- Harold Jerry, interviewed by Richard Beamish in 1996
- Richard Lawrence, interviewed by William Kissel in 1998
- Peter S. Paine Jr., interviewed by Philip Terrie, Jerold Pepper, and Christine Campeau in 2013
- Peter S. Paine Jr., transcript of a 2018 presentation
- Harry Albright, chapter from an unpublished memoir

### Digital Resources

Once upon a time, books, journal articles, and primary sources were kept behind locked doors. Historians had to ask permission to borrow them, and they could only see the most valuable items in the library itself. But now, after several decades and billions of scanned pages, researchers can get almost anything they want online, any time they want it. Almost. These internet sites were valuable to my research.

- **Adirondack Experience, The Museum on Blue Mountain Lake** (theadkx.org): ADKX is located in a remote hamlet, so it has long emphasized online resources as a way to extend its outreach. The museum's online collection catalog includes more than sixty-five thousand records for photographs, maps, manuscripts, objects, books, and ephemera documenting the history of the Adirondack Park. Many of these items are available digitally, and the number is constantly growing.

- **Historic Saranac Lake Wiki** (localwiki.org/hsl): The local non-profit Historic Saranac Lake maintains a site where volunteers post images, articles, and clippings. The wiki has grown to more than seven thousand pages and covers the entire park, with an emphasis on the Saranac region.
- **The Kelly Adirondack Center, Union College** (muse.union.edu /adirondack): The Kelly Center is an expansion of Paul Schaefer's home, so it includes the "Adirondack Room" described at the beginning of chapter 3. The online catalog for its fine research library includes scanned photographs and documents. This site also maintains a comprehensive listing of online resources devoted to North Country history, including links to smaller museums and historical sites.
- **New York State Library Digital Collections** (nysl.nysed.gov /scandocs): The state library's collection of more than eighty thousand documents includes many relating to the Adirondack Park. The site is overwhelming and searching can be tricky, but the "help" page offers a guide.
- **Adirondack Almanack** (adirondackalmanack.com): The online news journal of the monthly magazine *Adirondack Explorer* is where Adirondack historians share research on the region's people and places.

Online newspaper sites are a quick, reliable way to establish the dates of events and find additional quotes. Commercial sites (such as newspapers.com) are the easiest to use and most comprehensive, but they require a monthly subscription fee and are rarely available at libraries. Free sites, like the Google News archive (news.google.com/newspapers) and Fulton History (best accessed through fultonsearch.org), offer millions of pages but are harder to use.

The two primary newspaper sources for this book are the *New York Times* and the *Adirondack Daily Enterprise*, the only daily newspaper published inside the Blue Line. Both of these sources are available online.

- **The New York Times** (nytimes.com): Every issue of the *Times* from Thursday, September 18, 1851, to the present is fully accessible to subscribers, or at no charge at most public libraries. Searching is easy and the scans are legible. This source is consistently amazing.
- **New York State Historic Newspapers** (nyshistoricnewspapers.org): This collaborative project, curated by the Northern New York Library Network, provides free access to more than 10.8 million pages from about 850 newspapers across all New York counties, including the *Adirondack Daily Enterprise* and other North Country newspapers. The site is reasonably easy to use, although some scans are copied from old microfilm that skips pages and is difficult to read.

### Archival Sources

It's often said that 80 percent of success is showing up, and archival research proves that the old saying is still true. Online sources do not cover everything, and online guides to archival collections usually do not describe everything that is actually inside the boxes. You have to go there.

The following are the main collections I used at the Adirondack Experience museum library:

- Association for the Protection of the Adirondacks records
- George Davis papers
- Richard Lawrence papers
- Richard Lawrence Adirondack Park Agency records
- Clarence Petty papers
- Harold Hochschild Adirondack Park Agency correspondence
- Temporary Study Commission on the Future of the Adirondacks records

I used the following at the Adirondack Research Library, part of the Kelly Adirondack Center of Union College:

- Citizens' Northway Committee papers
- Arthur Crocker papers

- George Davis papers
- Harold Jerry papers
- Erwin Miller papers
- Per Moberg papers
- Arthur Newkirk papers
- Gary Randorf papers

At State University of New York at Albany's M. E. Grenander Special Collections & Archives Department, I used the following:

- Leo O'Brien Papers, 1939–1966
- Frank Casier Papers, 1974–1994
- Perry B. Duryea Papers, 1961–1972
- Sierra Club Atlantic Chapter Records, 1964–1999
- Ronald B. Stafford Papers, 1956–2002

In addition, I consulted the following records:

- Adirondack Park Agency Collection, St. Lawrence University, Canton, New York
- Adirondack Daily Enterprise clipping files, Saranac Lake, New York
- Adirondack Park Agency Administrative Files on Establishment and Early Planning of the Adirondack Park Agency
- Adirondack Park Agency Planning Division Administrative Files of the Temporary Study Commission on the Future of the Adirondacks, New York State Archives, Albany, New York

Page-by-page notes listing sources cited in this book are available online with links to the many sources that are also available online. I invite readers to explore my website (bradedmondson.com) or the Adirondack Experience's digital collection (adirondack.pastperfectonline.com, search for "A Wild Idea"). A paper copy of the source citations is also filed with the original oral history collection documents at the Adirondack Experience museum.

# BIBLIOGRAPHY

Adirondack Park Agency. *Annual Report*, August 1, 1973–July 31, 1974. State of New York Executive Department, 1974.

Adirondack Park Agency. "Adirondack Park Land Use and Development Plan and Recommendations for Implementation," submitted to Governor Nelson A. Rockefeller and the Legislature of the State of New York Pursuant to Section 805 of Article 27 of the Executive Law on March 6, 1973.

Adirondack Park Agency. "Adirondack Park State Land Master Plan," prepared by the Adirondack Park Agency in consultation with the Dept. of Environmental Conservation, submitted to Governor Nelson A. Rockefeller, June 1, 1972.

Angus, Christopher. *The Extraordinary Adirondack Journey of Clarence Petty: Wilderness Guide, Pilot, and Conservationist*. 1st ed. Syracuse, NY: Syracuse University Press, 2002.

Anzalone, Jonathan D. *Battles of the North Country: Wilderness Politics and Recreational Development in the Adirondack State Park, 1920–1980*. Environmental History of the Northeast. Amherst: University of Massachusetts Press, 2018.

Barnett, Lincoln. *The Ancient Adirondacks*. New York, NY: Time Life Books, 1974.

Benjamin, Gerald, and T. Norman Hurd, eds. *Making Experience Count: Managing Modern New York in the Carey Era*. Albany, NY: Nelson A. Rockefeller Institute of Government, 1985.

Bloom, Nicholas Dagen. *How States Shaped Postwar America: State Government and Urban Power*. Chicago: University of Chicago Press, 2019.

Callies, David L., Bosselman, Fred P. *The Quiet Revolution in Land Use Control.* United States: U.S. Government Printing Office, 1972.

Caro, Robert. *The Power Broker: Robert Moses and the Fall of New York.* New York: Alfred A. Knopf, 1974.

Citizens Committee for the Outdoor Recreation Resources Review Commission. *Action for Outdoor Recreation for America: A Digest of the Report of the Outdoor Recreation Resources Review Commission, with Suggestions for Citizen Action.* United States: The Committee, 1964.

Colvin, Verplanck. "Report on the Adirondack and State Land Surveys To the Year 1884." Albany, NY: Weed, Parsons and Company, 1884.

Commission on the Adirondacks in the Twenty-First Century. "The Adirondack Park in the Twenty-First Century." State of New York: The Commission, April 1990.

Connery, Robert Howe, and Gerald Benjamin. *Rockefeller of New York: Executive Power in the Statehouse.* Ithaca, NY: Cornell University Press, 1979.

Crompton, John L. *Twentieth Century Champions of Parks and Conservation: The Pugsley Medal Recipients 1965–2007.* Laurance Rockefeller entry. United States: Sagamore Publishing, L.L.C., 2007.

Daly, Jayne. "A Glimpse of the Past—A Vision for the Future: Senator Henry M. Jackson and National Land Use Legislation." *The Urban Lawyer* 28, no. 1 (Winter 1996): 7–39.

Davis, George. *Man and the Adirondack Environment.* Blue Mountain Lake, NY: Adirondack Museum, 1977.

D'Elia, Anthony N. *The Adirondack Rebellion.* 1st ed. Onchiota, NY: Onchiota Books, 1979.

Desrochers, Pierre, and Christine Hoffbauer. "The Post War Intellectual Roots of the Population Bomb: Fairfield Osborn's 'Our Plundered Planet' and William Vogt's 'Road to Survival' in Retrospect." *Electronic Journal of Sustainable Development*, 2009, 1.

Dilsaver, Lary M., ed. *America's National Park System: The Critical Documents.* Lanham, MD: Rowman & Littlefield, 1997.

Ehrlich, Paul R. *The Population Bomb.* San Francisco, CA: Sierra Club Books, 1968.

Engel, Robert, Howard Kirschenbaum, and Paul Malo. *Santanoni: From Japanese Temple to Life at an Adirondack Great Camp.* Keeseville, NY: Adirondack Architectural Heritage, 2000.

Folwell, Betsy. "Present at the Creation: The APA's Job Left Undone." *Adirondack Life*, August 1989, 56–61.

Freeman, John P. "The Adirondack Mountain Club: Its Programs and History." *Adirondack Journal of Environmental Studies* 12, art. 5, no. 1 (2005).

Gooley, Lawrence P. *Oliver's War: An Adirondack Rebel Battles the Rockefeller Fortune.* Peru, NY: Bloated Toe Publishing, 2007.

Graham, Frank, and Ada Graham. *The Adirondack Park: A Political History.* 1st ed. New York: Knopf, 1978. Distributed by Random House.

Harvey, Mark W. T. *Wilderness Forever: Howard Zahniser and the Path to the Wilderness Act.* Weyerhaeuser Environmental Books. Seattle: University of Washington Press, 2005.

Hochschild, Adam. *Half the Way Home: A Memoir of Father and Son.* 1st ed. Boston: Houghton Mifflin, 2005.

Hochschild, Adam, ed. *Harold K. Hochschild 1892–1981.* Self-published, 1982.

Hopsicker, Peter. "'No Hebrews Allowed': How the 1932 Lake Placid Winter Olympic Games Survived the 'Restricted' Adirondack Culture, 1877–1932." *Journal of Sport History* 36, no. 2 (2009): 205–222.

Jacoby, Karl. *Crimes against Nature: Squatters, Poachers, Thieves, and the Hidden History of American Conservation.* Berkeley: University of California Press, 2001.

Jamieson, Paul F., ed. *The Adirondack Reader.* 2nd ed. Glens Falls, NY: Adirondack Mountain Club, 1982.

Jones, Courtney. "Challenge in the Adirondacks." *Living Wilderness* (Winter 1972–1974): 25.

Ketchledge, Edwin H. *Forests and Trees of the Adirondack High Peaks Region: A Hiker's Guide.* Lake George, NY: Adirondack Mountain Club, 1996.

Knott, Catherine Henshaw. *Living with the Adirondack Forest: Local Perspectives on Land Use Conflicts.* Ithaca, NY: Cornell University Press, 1998.

Kramer, Michael S., and Sam Roberts. *"I Never Wanted to Be Vice-President of Anything!": An Investigative Biography of Nelson Rockefeller.* New York: Basic Books, 1976.

Leopold, Aldo. *A Sand County Almanac: And Sketches Here And There.* New York: Oxford University Press, 1949.

Liroff, Richard A., G. Gordon Davis, and F. Frank Lyman. *Protecting Open Space: Land Use Control in the Adirondack Park.* Cambridge, MA: Ballinger, 1981.

Long, James McMartin, and Peter Bauer. "The Adirondack Park and Rural America: Economic and Population Trends 1970–2010." North Creek, NY: Protect! The Adirondacks, 2019.

McHarg, Ian. *Design With Nature.* Garden City, NY: Natural History Press, 1969.

McHarg, Ian. *A Quest for Life: An Autobiography.* United Kingdom: Wiley, 1996.

McMartin, Barbara. *The Adirondack Park: A Wildlands Quilt.* 1st ed. Syracuse, NY: Syracuse University Press, 1999.

McMartin, Barbara. *The Great Forest of the Adirondacks.* Utica, NY: North Country Books, 1994.

McMartin, Barbara. *Perspectives on the Adirondacks: A Thirty-Year Struggle by People Protecting Their Treasure.* 1st ed. Syracuse, NY: Syracuse University Press, 2002.

McMartin, Barbara. *The Privately Owned Adirondacks: Sporting and Family Clubs, Private Parks and Preserves, Timberlands and Easements.* Caroga, NY: Lake View Press, 2004. Distributed by North Country Books.

Miller, Char. *Gifford Pinchot and the Making of Modern Environmentalism.* United Kingdom: Island Press, 2001.

Nash, Roderick, and Char Miller. *Wilderness and the American Mind.* 5th ed. New Haven, CT: Yale University Press, 2014.

*The New York Red Book.* Albany, NY: Williams Press, 1964–1974. Published annually.

New York State Department of Conservation. *The Adirondacks: New York's Forest Preserve and a Proposed National Park.* Harold Jerry and Clarence Petty, unsigned, 1967.

New York State Department of Conservation. *The Conservationist* 6, no. 3 (December/January 1951–1952): 2.

New York State Department of Conservation. *The Conservationist* 6, no. 4 (February/March 1952): 2.

New York State Department of Conservation. *The Conservationist* 6, no. 5 (April/May 1952): 2.

New York State Department of Conservation. *The Conservationist* 6, no. 6 (June/ July 1952): 28.

New York State Department of Conservation. *Reports, 1950–1970.*

New York State Division of the Budget, Office of Statistical Coordination. *New York State Statistical Yearbook.* Albany, NY: Nelson A. Rockefeller Institute of Government, 1973.

New York (State) Office for Regional Development. *Change, Challenge, Response: A Development Policy for New York State.* Albany, NY: State Office of Planning Coordination, 1964.

New York State Joint Legislative Committee on Natural Resources. *Reports, 1952–63.*

Outdoor Recreational Resources Review Commission. *Outdoor Recreation for America.* US Government Printing Office, 1962.

Outdoor Recreational Resources Review Commission. *Wilderness and Recreation—A Report on Resources, Values, and Problems.* US Government Printing Office, 1962.

Pearson, Byron E. *Saving Grand Canyon: Dams, Deals, and a Noble Myth.* Reno: University of Nevada Press, 2019.

Pinchot, Gifford. *Breaking New Ground.* New York: Harcourt Brace, and Co., 1947.

Porter, William F., Jon D. Erickson, and Ross S. Whaley, eds. *The Great Experiment in Conservation: Voices from the Adirondack Park.* 1st ed. Syracuse, NY: Syracuse University Press, 2009.

Reich, Charles A. *The Greening of America: How the Youth Revolution is Trying to Make America Livable.* United Kingdom: Random House, 1970.

Richardson, Jesse J., and Amanda C. Bernard. "Zoning for Conservation Easements." *Law and Contemporary Problems* 74, no. 83 (2011).

Rienow, Robert, and Leona Train. "Why Spoil The Adirondacks?" *Harper's Magazine,* October 1959.

Rockefeller, Laurance. "The Adirondacks and the Future." Address before the Adirondack Mountain Club. Warrensburg, NY, October 28, 1967.

Rockefeller, Nelson. *Our Environment Can Be Saved.* New York: Doubleday, 1970.

Schaefer, Paul. *Adirondack Cabin Country.* Syracuse, NY: Syracuse University Press, 1993.

Schaefer, Paul. *Defending the Wilderness: The Adirondack Writings of Paul Schaefer.* Syracuse, NY: Syracuse University Press, 1989.

Silverman, Michael Robert. *The Impact of Competing Pressure Groups on the Passage of the New York State Adirondack Park Land Use Bill of 1973.* New York University, PhD thesis, 1976.

Siskind, Peter. "'Enlightened System' or 'Regulatory Nightmare'?: New York's Adirondack Mountains and the Conflicted Politics of Environmental Land-Use Reform during the 1970s." *Journal of Policy History* 31, no. 3 (July 2019): 406–430.

Smith, Richard Norton. *On His Own Terms: A Life of Nelson Rockefeller.* 1st ed. New York: Random House, 2014.

Temporary Study Commission on the Future of the Adirondacks. *The Future of the Adirondack Park.* Albany, NY: Temporary Study Commission, 1970.

Temporary Study Commission on the Future of the Adirondacks. *Technical Reports 1–7.* Albany, NY: Temporary Study Commission, 1970.

Terrie, Philip G. *Contested Terrain: A New History of Nature and People in the Adirondacks.* Syracuse, NY: Syracuse University Press, 1999.

Terrie, Philip G. *Forever Wild: A Cultural History of Wilderness in the Adirondacks*. 1st ed. Syracuse, NY: Syracuse University Press, 1994.

Thompson, R. C. *The Doctrine of Wilderness: A Study of the Policy and Politics of the Adirondack Preserve-Park*. Syracuse University, PhD thesis, 1962.

United States Department of the Interior Geological Survey Inter-Agency Steering Committee on Land Use Information and Classification. "Land Use Classification Scheme For Use With Remote Sensor." Including proceedings of the Conference on Land Use Information and Classification, June 28–30, 1971.

Van Valkenburgh, Norman J. *The Forest Preserve of New York State in the Adirondack and Catskill Mountains: A Short History*. Schenectady, NY: Adirondack Research Center, 1983.

Whitaker, John C. *Striking a Balance: Environment and Natural Resources Policy in the Nixon-Ford Years*. Washington, DC: American Enterprise Institute for Public Policy Research, 1976.

White, William Chapman. *Adirondack Country*. York State Books. Syracuse, NY: Syracuse University Press, 1985.

Winks, Robin W. *Laurance S. Rockefeller: Catalyst for Conservation*. Washington, DC: Island Press, 1997.

Wirth, Conrad Louis. "A Report on a Proposed Adirondack Mountains National Park." 1967.

Yonavjak, Logan, and Todd Gartner. "Gaining Ground: Increasing Conservation Easements in the U.S. South." *World Resources Institute Issue Brief* #7, August 2011.

Zahniser, Howard, Ed Zahniser, George D. Davis, Paul Schaefer, and Doug Scott. *Where Wilderness Preservation Began: Adirondack Writings of Howard Zahniser*. Utica, NY: North Country Books, 1992.

# INDEX

National Environmental Policy Act (1970),
120, 172, 194–195, 261
National Land Use Policy Act, 250, 261
National Parks Service, U.S., 54, 56, 68–69,
71, 74
National Wilderness System, 56
Natural Resources Defense Council, 193
Nature Conservancy, The, 53, 55, 141;
Adirondack Chapter, 204–210, 232
Nelson, Sid, 198, 200
Newhouse, David, 5, 14, 35, 49, 57, 95, 105,
164, 191, 216–217
Newkirk, Arthur, 48, 49, 54
New York Central Railroad, 12
New York City, 10, 16, 27, 74, 85, 103, 104, 115,
124, 125, 134, 151, 154, 174, 208, 217, 237,
240, 244; drinking water, 94, 104, 110–111;
environmental activism, 192–193
New York State: population, 10, 63, 75
New York State Assembly, 57, 253, 256
New York State Advisory Council on the
Forest Preserve, 33
New York State Agricultural College, 22, 96
New York State Board of Equalization and
Assessment, 103, 158
New York State Conservation Council, 33,
44–45; interests, 54, 121; reaction to national
park proposal, 79; Northway Committee, 50
New York State Conservation Department,
14, 16, 22, 24–26, 29–32, 35, 67, 73, 84, 88,
93–113, 128, 183, 217–219; compared to
U.S. Forest Service, 108; control over
vehicular traffic, 39; enforcement policies,
30–31, 87; organization, 121. *See also* New
York State Department of Environmental
Conservation
New York State Constitution, 11
New York State Constitutional Convention
(1967), 57–58
New York State Council of Parks, 68, 74–77,
121, 125, 128, 150, 121, 125; response to
national park proposal, 80–82
New York State Department of Civil Service,
170
New York State Department of Environmental Conservation: announced, 114, 121, 130;
Health Department, 121, 200–201;
involvement in control of park, 131–132,
140, 149–150, 151, 162, 169, 189, 212, 214,

216, 218–222, 225; represented on APA, 175.
*See also* New York State Conservation
Department
New York State Department of Health, 121,
200–201, 225
New York State Department of Public Works,
49–50, 54
New York State Department of Transportation,
222
New York State Forest Practices Board, 155
New York State Hudson River Valley
Commission, 75, 97
New York State Joint Committee on Natural
Resources, 33, 35–36, 80
*New York State Land Master Plan* (1972), 181
New York State Land Use and Natural
Resources Inventory, 98–99
New York State Legislature, 2, 214; passage of
APA Act, 157–167
New York State Joint Legislative Committee
on Environmental Management and
Resources, 151, 162, 216
New York State Office of Planning
Coordination, 97, 100
New York State Office of Planning Services,
65, 92, 175, 184, 189, 215, 252
New York State Office for Regional
Development, 65–68
New York State Office of Parks and
Recreation: involvement in park manage-
ment, 123, 126–130, 215. *See also* Lau-
rence S. Rockefeller
New York State Parks Division, 5
New York State Public Land Review
Commission, 74
New York State Public Service Commission,
167
New York State Route 3, 26
New York State Route 8, 13, 16
New York State Route 9, 16, 49–50
New York State Water Power Commission, 94
*New York Times*, 54, 63, 64, 81, 93, 115, 129,
138, 162, 178, 193, 195, 199, 243, 249
New York Zoological Society, 47
Nixon, Richard M., 101, 120, 182, 243, 248,
262–263
Noonan, Patrick F., 206
North American Wildlife Conference
(1946), 45